Night of
Tragedy

Dawning
of Light

Da

with Kevin Shriy,
and Chip Gillette

SHAW

NIGHT OF TRAGEDY, DAWNING OF LIGHT
A SHAW BOOK PUBLISHED BY WATERBROOK PRESS
5446 North Academy Blvd., Suite 200
Colorado Springs, CO 80918
A division of Random House, Inc.

Unless otherwise noted, all Scripture quotations are taken from the New King James Version of the Bible, (c) 1979, 1980, 1982 by Thomas Nelson Inc., Publishers.

Scripture quotations marked NIV are taken from the HOLY BIBLE, NEW INTERNATIONAL VERSION®. NIV®. Copyright (c) 1973, 1978, 1984 International Bible Society. Used by permission of Zondervan Publishing House. All rights reserved.

The "NIV" and "New International Version" trademarks are registered in the United States Patent and Trademark Office by International Bible Society. Use of either trademark requires permission of International Bible Society.

For all other acknowledgments, please see last page.

ISBN 0-87788-585-0

Shaw Books and its circle of books logo are trademarks of WaterBrook Press, a division of Random House, Inc.

Cover design by Chris Patchel
Cover photo © 1999 Fort Worth Star Telegram. Taken by Ron T. Ennis. Used by permission.
Interior design and typesetting by Carol Barnstable/Carol Graphics

Library of Congress Cataloging-in-Publication Data
Crawford, Dan R., 1941-
   Night of tragedy, dawning of light : the Wedgwood Baptist shootings / Dan R. Crawford with Kevin Galey and Chip Gillette.
     p. cm.
   ISBN 0-87788-585-0
   1. Wedgwood Baptist Church (Fort Worth, Tex.) 2. Mass murder—Texas—Fort Worth.   3. Grief—Religious aspects—Christianity.
4. Consolation. I. Galey, Kevin. II. Gillette, Chip. III. Title.
BX6480.F6649 C73 2000
286'.17645315—dc21

                                      00-026551

Printed in the United States of America.
04 03 02 01 00
10 9 8 7 6 5 4 3 2

Dedication

This book is dedicated to the memory of:
Kristi Beckel
Shawn Brown
Sydney Browning
Joey Ennis
Cassie Griffin
Kim Jones
Justin "Steggy" Ray

"Blessed are the dead who die in the Lord"
(Rev.14:13)

and in honor of:
Jaynanne Brown
Robert DeBord
Kevin Galey
Justin Laird
Jeff Laster
Nicholas Skinner
Mary Beth Talley

"That I may know Him . . . and the fellowship of His sufferings" (Phil. 3:10)

and in respect to the hundreds of people who were present at Wedgwood Baptist Church on the night of Wednesday, September 15, 1999.

Contents

Foreword

When a lone gunman entered our church on the night of September 15, 1999, bent on destruction and death, he was increasingly frustrated and angered that so few people took him seriously. The youth who were assembled for a rally to celebrate the See-You-at-the-Pole gatherings that day were convinced that it was a skit, written in light of the Columbine High School shootings, to see who was really "sold out" to the Lord.

Thinking it was an act with blanks or paintballs, there was giggling mixed with the sound of gunfire. Some kids even popped up saying, "Shoot me!" then popped back down again.

In fury the shooter screamed, "This is real!"

We ask, *What is real?* The average American believes reality to be a matter of squeezing out a living, paying the bills, passing a test or performance review. Reality consists of a nine to five job on a track to nowhere, trying to breathe life into a dead marriage, dealing with ungrateful children or the neighbor's dog or the IRS.

But this is not genuine reality; it is only the thin veneer of our existence. We are spiritual beings, and reality must, therefore, be spiritual in nature. Our problems are not that disinterested spouse or that grumpy boss or that curmudgeon of a teacher. As the apostle Paul reminds us, "For our struggle is not against flesh and blood, but against the rulers, against the authorities, against the powers of this dark world, and against the spiritual forces of evil in the heavenly realms" (Ephesians 6:12, NIV).

This spiritual perspective is our primary view of the tragic shootings that took place in our church buildings that Wednesday evening. Gun control is a serious issue and must be addressed by knowledgeable and responsible people. But gun control was not the real issue that evening. Our mental health system is in dire need of reconstruction on many levels. But that was not the essential concern that night. The heat of the issue that night was warfare: darkness vs. light, evil vs. good, Satan vs. God. One deranged man, in the grip of the evil one, sought to wreak havoc upon the people of God. When confronted by the Truth, the spirit of death and destruction fled. The shooter, confronted by his terrible actions, took his own life.

What would the outcome of this havoc be? Would the church be shocked into paralysis? Would they cancel services? Would they cave in to bitterness and hostility? Would depression and grief cause them to lose hope? Would the tragic death of seven of their brightest and best young believers cause them to lose faith and hope? The answer to all these questions is a resounding NO!

Read the story of how the grace of the One who is

the Light turned tragedy into triumph and brought great good out of terrible evil. The darkness shall not overcome the kingdom of Light!

Dr. Al Meredith, Senior Pastor
Wedgwood Baptist Church
Fort Worth, Texas

Publisher's Preface

Why a book about a gruesome crime spree in a church? This is not a book for violence voyeurs to read about the bloody details. This is not a book for people who are looking for a tear-jerking story. So what is it?

This is first a story about individuals—the individuals who were killed that night. This book is a memorial to seven young people, seven believers, whose lives ended on September 15, 1999.

This is, second, the story of a church and how it responded to the violation of its sanctuary and its congregation.

Third, it is the story of how a theological seminary would react to a crisis involving many of its students and faculty.

And, finally, it is the tale of how Christians and churches all over—from down the street to halfway around the world—have responded to the news of the violation of a church.

We believe these stories are worth reading. They will show you how God has worked through believers to assert His sovereignty over all things, especially His people in His sanctuary.

The Editors
Shaw Books

Author's Preface

My personal pilgrimage to the authoring of this book is a vital part of God's work before, in the midst of, and following the events of September 15, 1999. In the early days of September, I was feeling guilty of poor stewardship. My name appears on the cover of nine books, either as author or editor. My ninth, and most recent book, *The Prayer-Shaped Disciple* recently had been released. But in September of 1999, I was writing nothing and feeling guilty. I had to admit to the Lord that I had no passion for any subject, and if I was to write God needed to tell me what it was.

On September 18, 1999, three days following the shooting at my church, I was flying to Houston. I was thinking that someone ought to write a book on the Wedgwood shooting. Every time I thought this, it was as if God was responding, "Well? You wanted to write, so here's a subject for you." The problem was I did not yet believe that God was definitely saying, "You write this book."

With this certain uncertainty, I made a deal with God. I know, I know! One should not make deals with God, but I did, nevertheless. I told God that if I was to write this book, then someone else would have to ask me without my bringing it up. I also told God that if I wrote the book neither I nor anyone else associated with it would accept royalty for our work.

On Monday morning when I downloaded my e-mail, I had a message from a colleague at Southwestern Baptist Seminary, fellow Wedgwood member and good friend, Bob Garrett. Bob wrote, "I believe that someone should write a book about the Wedgwood tragedy. I prayed about this last night and asked God if I could do it. I don't have any peace about distracting my attention from other things right now. For some reason I felt impressed to mention the possibility to you."

I'm not non-spiritual, just hardheaded. So, I made a second deal with God. "Okay, God," I said. "I'll write the book but only if my pastor approves of my writing it." Although I was present most of the night on September 15 and in the early morning hours of September 16, I am often absent from Wedgwood because of my frequent speaking engagements. I wanted to be sure I would not get involved in something that would be contrary to what God was doing in our church. In a meeting with my pastor, I was told not only that I was the one to write the book but that the church wanted to commission me as the writer of a church-endorsed book on the shooting. This was recommended in a church business meeting and approved by unanimous vote.

I still had one more deal for God. I told God my calendar was full, as if God didn't know that I always overbook myself. I said, "God, you need to help me clear some time on my calendar so I can devote some days to the writing of this book." Within twenty-four hours, I received a call from the Southern Baptist International Mission Board canceling an eight-day trip to Turkey scheduled for late October. I had already secured substitutes for my seminary classes and a supply preacher for my interim pastorate. My week was absolutely clear. It was as if God said, "Could you use eight free days?"

I have played enough baseball in my life to know that three strikes and you're out. Only this time, three strikes and I was in. What I did not know was the enormous task that was before me. The next weeks would be filled with hours of personal interviews; endless reading of e-mails, letters, cards, posters, and banners; long periods of agonizing prayer; intense conversations with publishers; late nights and early mornings pecking away on my laptop; and the emotional trauma of reliving the story each day and dreaming about it each night. But with the help of God and a lot of friends, the task was accomplished. From the time the first words were typed onto the computer screen until the manuscript was mailed to the publisher was less than eight weeks. As the Wedgwood teen-agers would say, "It was a God thing!" Indeed it was.

But then there was the next phase of writing. A first-draft manuscript receives the "red ink" of the editor and then undergoes a rewrite. I feared that my emotional involvement in the story had diminished my journalistic skills. The editor agreed. But when would I have time for a massive rewrite? On December 29, a visit to my doctor's office revealed that I had an upper respiratory infection that had affected my voice. I was told to "go home, take medicine, drink hot liquids, and don't speak for three or four days." On the way home, I checked my mail. There was a letter from the editor with suggestions for the rewrite. Now I had four days at my laptop with no voice to be interrupted by the telephone, and doctor's orders to stay home. Many cups of coffee later, we had our rewritten manuscript. God does indeed move in mysterious ways.

Acknowledgments

I want to express my special thanks to all of the following:

- ✦ The families of the victims, who painfully shared many details with me related to their loved ones, then graciously read and approved the manuscript before it was sent to the publisher. More than anything I wanted them to be proud of the book.

- ✦ My writing assistants: Kevin Galey, minister of counseling and community at Wedgwood Baptist Church; and Chip Gillette, Wedgwood deacon, Sunday school teacher, and the first Fort Worth police officer on the scene of the shooting.

- ✦ My research helpers: Debbie Gillette, Anne McEowen, Dale Shively, and Jim Morris.

- ✦ Fellow "Wedgies"—what members of Wedgwood Baptist Church lovingly call each other—who trusted me enough to vote in favor of commissioning me to write the church-endorsed book of the tragedy and its aftermath.

- ✦ Youth ministers and pastors who had groups present at Wedgwood on September 15 and were willing to share their stories with me.

- The best pastor a victimized church could ever have, Dr. Al Meredith.

- The best church staff a victimized church could ever have—Wedgwood ministerial and support staff.

- God's greatest gift to any writer—a great secretary, Beth Cochran.

- Southwestern Baptist Seminary secretaries who transcribed cassette tape programs onto computer disks of information—Beth Cochran, Cristina Herrington, LeAnn Linton, Kim McIlrath, Laverne Smith, and Karen Strange.

- My family—Joanne, Danna, James, Carrie, and especially Whitney, who saw too much violence for a seven-year-old but learned to "walk before God in the light of the living" (Ps. 56:13).

- My prayer partners, "always laboring fervently . . . in prayers" (Col. 4:12).

- My non-Baptist friends who, realizing I needed to be touched, laid hands on me when they prayed for me.

- Special faculty colleagues at Southwestern Baptist Seminary who advised me through some of the more difficult parts of this story and counseled me when I needed personal help.

✦ My seminary students who listened to endless stories about Wedgwood and either
learned from them or acted as if they did.

Now let me speak on behalf of my fellow
church members. Members of Wedgwood Baptist
Church owe a debt of gratitude to Christians from
around the world for their outpouring of support in
our days of tragedy. Due to the effectiveness of
modern communications, word of the shooting at
Wedgwood spread rapidly around the world. With
the spreading of the word, came the spreading of
the concern. In the days immediately following the
shooting, Wedgwood Baptist Church received over
85,000 hits on its computer web page, more than
14,000 e-mail messages, thousands of cards, letters,
faxes, and phone calls. In addition to this, individual church members who sent reports and prayer
requests to their friends and prayer partners found
their messages forwarded to thousands, placed on
Christian web sites, and shared from pulpits and
talk shows. Some Wedgwood members received
hundreds of e-mails and cards.

Among the responses was a message from the
grandmother of Cassie Bernall of Columbine High
School:

Dear family and friends of those slain at Wedgwood Baptist Church, our brothers and sisters
in Christ. We have always been bonded with

you because of our mutual love for Christ, but now more so since your tragedy. I weep for you, having experienced your pain, especially you grandmothers and grandfathers. Please hold closely and dwell upon the fact that your beloved ones are in Heaven's Hall of Martyrs with our beloved Cassie. I will pray every day until I know your pain is subsiding (and it will get better in a few months) that Jesus will grant you the peace he has promised and that you will be comforted. My love and prayers are with you.

A message from the father of one of the victims of the shooting in Paducah, Kentucky, read: "My daughter was one of those that were killed at the prayer service before school at Heath High School on December 1, 1997. My heart goes out to you friends."

This message came from Melody Green, wife of the late musician Keith Green:

My heart goes out to you and the families who have suffered such a great loss. My late husband, Keith Green, and two of my little children are in heaven. It will be a wonderful homecoming when I arrive there, but it was a very difficult thing not to have them with me here on earth. My deepest sympathy and prayers are with you all.

Representative of the worldwide support was this message from Malaysia: "I, Olabisi, cannot really feel the way you are feeling now because I am writing from Kuala Lumpur in Malaysia. [But] God knows that the little I can feel in fact has brought tears out of my eyes and made my heart sorrowful."

And representative of the outpouring of support from across denominational lines was this message from the Archbishop of Canterbury: "Together with representatives of many Anglican Churches gathered here in Dundee, Scotland, we encourage you in our Lord. He is still Lord and King when our hearts are weak and the questions are accusing."

The light that enabled us to see our way in the darkness was reflected off the concerns of people around the globe. So, on behalf of a lot of Wedgies, thanks for helping us make it through our night of tragedy.

This book is a record of the tragedies and victories of Wednesday, September 15, 1999, and the days following. It is a story of ordinary people with an extraordinary God, of a church that was found faithful. It is, above all, a story of the Wedgwood shooting and its aftermath—a night of tragedy, a dawning of light.

After an initial gift designated for the victims' fund, all book royalties will be paid to the International Mission Board, Southern Baptist Convention, and Tarrant Baptist Association, Fort Worth. These funds will be designated for use by current and former members of Wedgwood Baptist Church under appointment of the International Mission Board for mission projects in World A—among unreached people groups of the 10-40 window— where the majority of the population has never heard of Jesus Christ.

Prelude

The Powers of Darkness and the Power of Light

"Even the Darkness Will Not Be Dark to You" (Ps. 139:12, NIV)

In the early morning press conference of September 16, 1999, Wedgwood pastor Dr. Al Meredith would quote these lines from the apostle Paul to describe the broken, yet hopeful members of Wedgwood Baptist Church:

> We have this treasure in earthen vessels, that the excellence of the power may be of God and not of us. We are hard pressed on every side, but not crushed; perplexed, but not in despair; persecuted, but not forsaken; struck down, but not destroyed—always carrying about in the body the dying of the Lord Jesus, that the life of Jesus also may be manifested in our body. (2 Cor. 4:7-10)

While we did not have answers to many of the why questions, we did have the answer to some of them.

+ Why was the Wedgwood faith so strong?

+ Why was Satan defeated on Wednesday evening?

+ Why do Wedgies testify in times of tragedy?

+ Why forgive the gunman?

. . . because even though "the light is darkened by the clouds" (Isa. 5:30), we know what the Old Testament prophet Micah knew: "When I sit in darkness, the Lord will be a light to me" (Micah 7:8). We testify with John, "The light shines in the darkness, and the darkness did not comprehend it" (John 1:5). We say to those who walk in darkness, if you knew Who we know, you'd understand why we do what we do. While we are only earthen vessels—fragile clay pots—we are filled with the manifest presence of the light of the world, Jesus Christ. We are people of the light.

Yet still there is darkness and how strongly we feel it. While the purpose of this book is not to glorify the darkness, this story cannot be told without acknowledging its influence. What happened at Wedgwood Baptist Church on September 15, 1999, may well have begun as something else, but it quickly escalated into full-blown spiritual warfare. The powers of darkness and the power of light collided in the buildings at the corner of Walton and Whitman avenues in southwest Fort Worth.

As Satan journeyed through the suburbs of Fort

Worth, he came upon Wedgwood, a mostly quiet subdivision of approximately 12,000 people developed from a 1200-acre cattle ranch in the 1950s. Three generations of families have lived in what has been described as one of the safest and nicest areas of Fort Worth. The average length of residence is twelve years. The surrounding subdivisions, from which Wedgwood Baptist Church also draws members, are strikingly similar. Many of the teen-agers present at the rally on September 15 were students at nearby Southwest High School and Wedgwood Middle School. Others were from schools in surrounding communities.

When Satan took a look that day at Wedgwood Baptist Church, he saw a growing suburban church of more than 2400 members. Before Dr. Al Meredith became pastor twelve years ago, the church had been without a pastor for seventeen months and had declined in membership. Today the church sprawls over half a city block, and a new community life center is under construction. Located approximately four miles from Southwestern Baptist Theological Seminary, Wedgwood is the church for many students and several faculty and staff members.

Having observed the Wedgwood community and one of its churches, the enemy ventured to the east a few miles and found one whom he could use, a troubled man filled with anger and disappointment—one who in his earlier days as a member of the Junior High Preacher Boys' Class at the Glen

Garden Church of Christ in Fort Worth would not likely have been a candidate for Satan's schemes. Now, however, in his confusion he was vulnerable to the temptations of the evil one. A disturbed man was available to disturb men.

We believe the gunman, in his emotional state, did what under better circumstances he would not have done. Out of respect for his family and the families of the victims, his name will be mentioned only once in this book for the purpose of historical record. Hereafter, he will be referred to as the gunman or the shooter.

Larry Gene Ashbrook spent his final day, the day before his forty-eighth birthday, in destructive activity in the family home. While it is uncertain how much of the destruction took place on the final day, it was obvious that some, if not most, did. Pictures were slashed and defaced. Concrete was poured into the toilet fixtures. Motor oil filled showerheads. The family Bible was ripped apart page by page. Walls were destroyed. Furniture was turned upside down. Then, strangely, he meticulously tended to the well-maintained yard, pruning the pear trees in the backyard and watering the potted plants. Yet, in perhaps a farewell act of defiance, neighbors say he apparently poisoned the trees in his front yard.

The death of his eighty-five-year-old father in July had intensified the anxiety level of an already troubled son. Described by neighbors as a recluse, he had written two letters to a local newspaper, one letter in July and the other in August. These letters contained bizarre accounts of encounters with the CIA, psychological warfare, being assaulted by co-workers, and drugged by police. He expressed fear that some people mistakenly thought he was a child abductor or a serial killer. While nothing in the letters appeared to be threatening, they were written in a rambling style and difficult to follow. In numerous conversations with the Fort Worth chief of police stretching over the past eight years, this lonely man had described his paranoid belief that the police were following him. Now, distraught over not having a job and fearful that his father's house was going to be sold out from under him, he was about to become violent.

Neighbors indicated that the shooter left the house that Wednesday at approximately 6:30 P.M., politely pulling over to let a neighbor pass. The nine-and-a-half-mile drive would have taken him twelve to fifteen minutes before he exited south into the Wedgwood subdivision. If the gunman traveled on I-20, he would have passed ten churches clearly visible from the highway before arriving at Wedgwood. Four of those churches were located in the gunman's own subdivision. One of the churches passed was another Baptist church. Some reported that he stopped to watch children practicing soccer at the park adjacent to an elementary school before driving the final block and parking in a handicapped parking space in front of Wedgwood Baptist Church.

While there is no indication that the gunman had ever been to Wedgwood Baptist Church before this night and while the church is difficult to find, there is a large map in the yellow pages of the local telephone book. In that ad there is a listing of the church's activities with times, as well as its Internet web site. On the web site there is an even better map along with directions and a section entitled "Visiting Wedgwood for the First Time," which includes a picture of the south entrance and a description of what one would encounter upon entering the south doors.

The prince of darkness had his plan in place. He would unleash a full attack at Wedgwood Baptist Church. But Pastor Meredith would respond, "We will not let the powers of darkness overcome the power of light." And a teen-ager would later write on the concrete floor bared when the bloody rug was removed, "Satan, you picked on the wrong church!"

Prayer around the flagpole at Bruce Shulkey Elementary School.

Photo by James Morris.

1

Countdown to Tragedy

"Work . . . While It Is Day; the Night Is Coming" (John 9:4)

On September 15, 1999, while Satan was doing his work in the darkness preparing a man with a weapon, some of God's finest people were working in the light of their last day on earth.

The Exciting Beginning to a Tragic Day

See-You-at-the-Pole was attended by at least five of the seven who were killed. Hundreds more of those present at Wedgwood that Wednesday night had been involved in some way with Pole activities earlier that day.

See-You-at-the-Pole is an annual student-led prayer meeting held around school flagpoles on the third Wednesday in September. What began in 1990 with a small group of students in Burleson, Texas, has increased to an estimated three million students worldwide. According to the SYATP web site, a small group of teen-agers in Burleson, Texas, came together for a DiscipleNow weekend in early 1990. On Saturday night God penetrated their hearts as never before. The students were humbled before God and burdened by love for their friends. Compelled to pray, they drove to three different schools that night. Not knowing exactly what to do, they went to the school flagpoles and prayed for their friends, schools, and leaders. Those students had no idea how God would use their obedience.

God used those teen-agers and others to bring forth a plan among youth leaders across Texas. The plan was that students throughout Texas would meet at their school flagpoles to pray simultaneously. The challenge was named See-You-at-the-Pole at an early brainstorming session. The vision was shared with 20,000 students in June 1990, at a convention in Dallas, Texas. That following September 12 at 7:00 A.M., more than 45,000 teen-agers met at school flagpoles in four states to pray before the start of school.

A few months later, a group of youth ministers from all over the country gathered for a national conference in Colorado. Many of them reported that their students had heard about the prayer movement in Texas and were equally burdened for their schools. It was clear that students across the country would be creating their own national day of student prayer. There was no stopping them.

Now each year millions from across our nation

and around the world pray at school flagpoles on the third Wednesday of September. A more recent development has been the Wednesday evening rallies, concerts or prayer gatherings, sometimes called Post-Pole Rallies. Members from several churches had joined the youth from Wedgwood in one such rally on Wednesday, September 15, 1999.

A Day in the Lives of Seven Who Died

Kristi Beckel began the day as a student at Bethesda Christian School, where she was a member of the National Honor Society and the junior varsity volleyball team. Kristi and her mother, a second-grade teacher there, arrived at their school early for See-You-at-the-Pole activities. Leaving her books in her mom's classroom, Kristi went to the flagpole to be with her friends. Vivian Underwood remembered that Kristi prayed for unity at their school and thanked God for letting her attend there. Debbie, Kristi's mom, said, "One of my fondest memories of Kristi was right after the Pole prayer time at school when I saw her linked arm in arm with a group of her friends, walking and laughing and going back into the building—so happy and so loved."

Kristi was a normal teenager with curly brown hair who loved to laugh with her friends and talk about typical "girl stuff" like makeup. Since there was no volleyball practice that day, Kristi rushed home for a quick meal before the evening activities. She had been excited about the concert by the Forty Days musical group for weeks and couldn't wait to get to church. Seated in the Wedgwood worship center with her friends Jennifer and Cassie as the youth rally began, Kristi was ready to praise God. Jennifer Hart wrote, "Cassie and I had this thing that on any song we would find each other, no matter where we were, and we would try to make the song more exciting by doing extra noises or motions or singing different parts. That is what we were doing—jumping up and down and doing the motions—when the shooter came in. Cassie and I were trying to get Kristi into it, but she was laughing too hard."

Shawn Brown began the day as usual as a student at Southwestern Baptist Seminary in Fort Worth pursuing his master of arts in Christian education, preparing for future youth ministry. On Tuesday evening, Shawn's wife, Kathy Jo, went to a PTA meeting while Shawn worked out. They finally arrived home together about 8:30 P.M. Shawn then shared with Kathy Jo his strong sense that he should pray for her and for his friend John Roland. Then he described what he had learned in class that day. She remembered, "He paced back and forth telling me what he had been learning. He had a big interest in spiritual warfare, the reality of demonic control, and Satan's desire to destroy people."

On Wednesday, Shawn met his wife where she taught elementary school for the See-You-at-the-

Pole service. "That very morning," Kathy Jo Brown said, "he came to my school and prayed with my students at the pole. I am so thankful that he was there with me that day and prayed for us. In his prayer, he voiced a strong desire that hearts would be changed in our country."

After leading in prayer at the school, Shawn went to work. He was back on the seminary campus in time for his classes and was at home when Kathy Jo arrived from school at 4:45 P.M. A friend had called to ask them to baby-sit that evening, but they had been planning to go to the Wedgwood concert. They determined that Shawn would go to the concert and Kathy Jo would pick up the friend's children at baseball practice and take them to Wedgwood for the concert, too. After supper together Kathy Jo got up to leave to get the children but stopped at the door and went back, sat down in Shawn's lap and said, "We haven't kissed enough today." After several kisses and "I love you's" Kathy Jo left and Shawn drove to the church and prepared to serve.

Sydney Browning began her day as usual also. A member of the adult choir at Wedgwood and director of the children's choir, she was a teacher at Success High School, a night school for troubled youth. Tom August, a close friend of Sydney's shared these insights:

After the incident at Columbine High School,

> one of Sydney's students asked her, "Miss Browning, if a gunman came in our schoolroom, would you try to protect us?" Sydney answered, "He'd have to get through me to get to you. If someone came in here tomorrow with a gun, I pray I'd be the only one to get shot."

Sydney's parents added to the story by saying that when the students persisted to know why, Sydney's reply was, "Because I'm the only person I know for sure would go to heaven, and secondly, I'm probably the only one in here with any health insurance."

On September 5, just ten days before the shooting, some of the Wedgwood single adults went to get coffee after an all-church barbecue. After most had finished their coffee and left, Tom and Sydney remained. It was during this conversation that Sydney shared with Tom a nightmare she had recently had of being shot. She thought this would likely be at her school in the inner city of Fort Worth or in her apartment complex, which had a high crime rate. Never did she think it might happen at church, the place where she felt the safest.

On Wednesday, Sydney visited some of her students in their work places as a part of her teaching job, then was back at school about 2:00 P.M. According to her principal, "we had the blessing of an ordinary day." Sydney met with her classes from 4:00 until 6:00 P.M. On Wednesdays she would normally leave school, grab a quick meal, and head for the church, where she could customarily be seen sitting on the couch near the south entrance, talking to friends and waiting for choir practice. On this night Sydney would be the last of the group to arrive, approximately five minutes before the gunman entered the south doors and began shooting.

Joseph "Joey" Ennis began the day as a student at Brewer High School, where he was a point guard on the ninth-grade basketball team. He was also a participant in the youth group of the First Baptist Church of White Settlement and had recently discussed being baptized.

Joey especially enjoyed "family nights" with his mother. They would play board games or watch one of approximately six hundred videos in their collection. Joey was such an avid basketball fan that last Fourth of July weekend his mom had joined him in painting his bedroom red and black, the colors of his favorite team, the Chicago Bulls. No wonder that a few days before his death, Joey told his mom, "I'm so lucky to have you."

On Wednesday, Joey and his mom had a discussion about his promise to go to the concert that night with his cousin. Joey had decided to cancel the concert engagement and go somewhere else with another friend. His mom, in an attempt to teach him to keep his commitments, insisted that either he go to the concert with his cousin or stay at home. On the way to his church to catch the van to Wedgwood, Joey told his mom again how much he loved her.

Joey and his cousin, Chris, arrived at their church thirty minutes early and apologized for being so early. They asked and received permission to play basketball until time to get on the van for the concert. Once on the van with his ever-present basketball, Joey bobbed his head with the radio, did choreographed hand movements, and sang along all the way to Wedgwood. The last song on the radio was, "I'll Fly Away." According to Allison, one of the teen-agers with the group, they arrived late because they had difficulty finding the church but quickly took seats and began to worship.

Cassandra "Cassie" Griffin began the day as a student at North Crowley High School in Crowley, Texas, where she played clarinet in the band. She was a member of Wedgwood Baptist Church and active in the youth group.

On Wednesday Cassie awoke excited about the See-You-at-the-Pole Rally at her school. For two weeks she had been handing out invitations and inviting her friends. On most mornings Cassie would have been in band practice, but because so many band members wanted to attend the pole rally the band director had cancelled practice that morning. So Cassie's mother picked up several of Cassie's friends and got them to school in time for the rally.

When one of Cassie's friends did not make it to the rally after promising to be there, Cassie wrote her a note: "I was crying this morning for you and every other non-Christian in our school. It's just that I love you so much I don't want you to go to hell. I've been praying for you a lot. I love you sooooo much." Kristen Dickens remembered that "Cassie showed God's love to everyone, especially that day."

Following school that Wednesday, Cassie invited four friends over to her house for dinner before going together to the concert. Kristen joined them after volleyball practice and another was picked up on the way. According to Cassie's father, "The last time I saw Cassie alive she introduced me to two new friends I'd never met before." That's the way she was.

The trip to Wedgwood was filled with discussing uplifting movies and playing with a fast-food meal toy. Kristen Dickens said, "Everyone in the car was really excited. You could just tell by the conversations going on." The seven girls arrived early at the concert to get seats in the second row. There, they waited in anticipation.

Kim Jones began her day as a student at Southwestern Baptist Seminary, where she was pursuing a master of divinity degree. She was also a member of the adult choir of Wedgwood Baptist Church.

On Tuesday night Kim had spent much of the evening leading a Bible study with a sorority at Texas Christian University, her alma mater. One of the girls there that evening reported, "The message Kim shared that night, from Psalm 139:16, will always be remembered. She wanted to make sure we knew God was in control of everything in our lives."

On Wednesday, Jenni Burris recalled, "I ran into Kim before chapel. She was telling me how much she loved seminary. She said she was having the time of her life. Kim looked so beautiful on that day. She was definitely beautiful inside and out."

After her Baptist history class, Kim met with her professor to discuss an assigned paper. Over the front entrance to the seminary there is a frieze of twenty-one prominent Baptist leaders. The class assignment was to recommend Baptists to add to this sculpture. According to Professor Stookey, Kim was requesting permission to recommend a female missionary.

In the afternoon, Kim went to her new job at a childcare center in Fort Worth, and then as was her custom, she went to Wedgwood for the Wednesday prayer service. However, on the way to the prayer service, she was invited to attend the youth concert, so she took a seat near the back of the worship center. According to friends seated with her, she was singing loudly and praising God when they heard shots. Knowing it was real, they immediately dropped to the floor for protection. Kim continued praising God in prayer as the gunman entered the worship center.

Justin "Steggy" Ray began the day as a student at Cassata High School looking forward to a December graduation. He was actively involved with the youth group at Wedgwood. On Wednesday Justin attended classes at Cassata in the morning and arrived at Southwest High School in time to assist Tim Hood, a media production teacher and "sound man" at Wedgwood, with some projects. Because he had planned to have lunch with his mother, Steggy ran by his house to ask permission to eat lunch with a friend who had come into town.

Receiving permission, Steggy and his friend hurried off to meet other friends for lunch, returning to the school soon afterwards to continue their work. At 3:30 P.M. Steggy went to Wedgwood to meet the band and assist them in setting up their sound equipment. When the band's sound man arrived, Hood told Steggy that he was not needed to run the sound so he could go on to his regular job if he wanted. Steggy declined, indicating a desire to remain for the concert and assist in any way he could. For the next couple of hours, Steggy assisted Hood in patching some videotape. He then left to get something to eat and to stop at home before the concert. His mom, Judy, remembered, "He was so excited about working with the band and was hoping to do some future work with them. On his way out he told me he loved me."

Before dinner Steggy called his grandmother. He had arranged to take her out on a dinner "date" that night and was asking to change the date so he could attend the concert. After they set a new date, he told his grandmother he loved her and was looking forward to seeing her soon. Arriving back at the church, he brought food for Hood and others.

Hood assigned Steggy a video camera and sent him to the balcony to cover the concert. With video camera in hand, Steggy Ray was busy doing the job assigned to him as the concert began.

And Four Who Were Wounded . . .

Kevin Galey began that Wednesday by taking his oldest son to school, then going to teach a class at Southwestern Baptist Seminary. That day the seminary students submitted papers on their family systems, papers which would become difficult to grade later on since each carried the date of September 15 on the cover sheet. At Wedgwood later in the day, Galey met with several counseling clients. Due to a cancellation of an early evening appointment, Galey was in his office sorting through some conference materials when the concert started. It was as he delivered a set of these materials to a secretary that he became involved in the tragedy.

Justin Laird awoke a little earlier than usual that Wednesday morning to get to school for the See-You-at-the-Pole event. He was especially excited as it was his sixteenth birthday. His mother drove him to school and then picked him up to go get his driver's license before returning home. Lori, Justin's mother, recalled, "I watched from the front door as Justin walked to the truck for his first ever 'solo' drive. I remember his confident walk, his jingling of the keys, his trendy sunglasses, and the big grin on his face as he turned to go to the driver's side door. He was on top of the world. As he drove away I called John at work to describe the scene, and we laughed about our 'baby' passing this new milestone in life." Later that same day Justin would confront another milestone in life.

Jeff Laster experienced a routine Wednesday. Since he had no classes to attend that day at Southwestern Baptist Seminary, he had gone early to his custodial job at Wedgwood. The normal Wednesday routine was to make sure everything was clean and ready for the evening's activities. In addition, Jeff was available to the band for their set-up needs and enjoyed listening to them practice. Late in the afternoon Jeff visited briefly with Shawn Brown when Shawn arrived early to assist with the program. As the concert began, Jeff was seated next to Sydney Browning, visiting with friends in the south foyer of the church, just a few feet from the door where the gunman was about to enter.

Mary Beth Talley, by her own admission, lives a very routine life. On Wednesday she was at Southwest High School in the early morning for band practice and so missed the See-You-at-the-Pole events. But one special event occurred that day when she went home for lunch and found a message from her mom reminding her that she was loved. After school, Mary Beth went to the church early to practice for the skit that was to be part of the evening program. After skit rehearsal she remained at the church, handing out programs at a door to the worship center. That's where she was serving when the gunman entered the building.

As the light of day began to yield to the early hours of darkness, the lives of these people and many others including one gunman intersected at the Wedgwood Baptist Church.

Emergency vehicles surround Wedgwood Baptist Church.

2

The Dark Night of Wedgwood's Soul

"By His Light I Walked through Darkness" (Job 29:3)

Inside the worship center of the Wedgwood Baptist Church, four to five hundred teen-agers and sponsors had gathered for the post See-You-at-the-Pole Rally. They were about to walk through their darkest night, but they would not walk without the Light of the world. In the midst of Job's long period of testing, he reflected on earlier days when he walked through such dark valleys surrounded by God's light: "By His light I walked through darkness" (Job 29:3). In the same way would those gathered at Wedgwood endure the darkness.

Excitement and anticipation was the order of the early evening. Prior to the concert by Forty Days, an announcement was made about the agenda for the evening, which was to include a skit. Among those gathered for the concert were Kristi Beckel, Joey Ennis, Cassie Griffin, Kim Jones, Shawn Brown, and Steggy Ray. As the music played in the worship center, several people, including Sydney Browning, were seated on the couch near the front door waiting for choir rehearsal to begin. Having yielded the worship center to the youth on this night, the adults were meeting in the fellowship hall just a few feet down a hallway from the front entrance of the church. In the choir room behind the choir loft, the church orchestra was practicing. Activities for younger children were being held in their customary places throughout the church, and the nursery was filled with its usual Wednesday night crowd of youngsters.

Tragedy Begins

Just outside the front door of the church's main entrance, a lone figure dressed in a dark green jacket, jeans, tennis shoes, a white hat, and sunglasses arrived in a 1982 Chevy that had belonged to his father, parking in a handicapped parking space. The man had armed himself with a 9 mm semiautomatic pistol, a .380-caliber semiautomatic pistol, a pipe bomb, and approximately two hundred rounds of ammunition. Calmly lighting a cigarette, he proceeded to enter the building.

Arriving late for the concert, De'an Simpson recalled, "As I was walking to the sanctuary I noticed a man that looked out of place. I almost asked him if I could help but decided to go on in because the concert had already started."

Church custodian and seminary student Jeff

Laster approached the gunman intending to see if he needed help and to ask him to extinguish the cigarette. Before Laster could speak, the gunman fired two shots, asking, "Is this where that religious meeting is going on?" and punctuating his question with profanities. One gunshot did extensive damage to Laster's abdomen and the other to his arm. Later, he said, "I remember hearing voices, but from that point on it was as if everything else was on TV and I was in another world. I walked out of the south doors and around the building towards the playground. I thought briefly about going back in the door near the fellowship hall but decided against it." With assistance, Laster made it past the playground and inside the building where the children were meeting. He remembers thinking, "I've been shot in the abdomen and I could die." Then came the assurance of the Holy Spirit saying, "You're not going to die."

Having shot Laster, the gunman turned to the couch and chairs on his right. He fired several shots, hitting Sydney Browning twice. Another shot hit elementary schoolteacher Jaynanne Brown, grazing the back of her neck. Still other shots missed those nearby including Larry Clark, the church organist, and his wife Glynda. Sharon Thompson was sitting in the group with her back to the south doors. She turned to look, and the gunman's determined walk reminded her of a disgruntled parent who had come to pick up a child. She thought that maybe he was a father who had not given permission for his

Map of Wedgwood Sanctuary and Surrounding Building

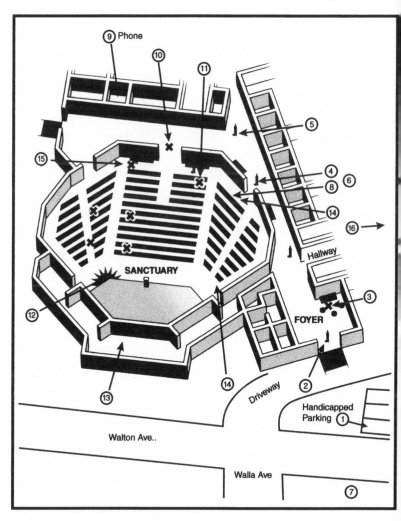

Adapted from World magazine ©1999.

Time and Map Code for Shooting:

The rally began at approximately 6:40 P.M.

1. Gunman parked car in handicapped parking space off Walton Avenue.
2. Gunman entered Wedgwood through south doors at approximately 6:50 P.M. and immediately shot and wounded Jeff Laster.
3. Having turned to the couch and chairs on his right, the gunman shot and killed Sydney Browning and wounded Jaynanne Brown.
4. Standing in the hallway at the Forty Days CD sale table, Kevin Galey turned and approached the gunman, was shot twice and wounded.
5. Entering the hallway from the north, Mike Holton was shot at twice, then ran back to the library and placed the first 911 call at 6:55:37 P.M.
6. Adults in the fellowship hall prayer meeting heard shooting and dismissed the meeting, only to walk into the hallway and see Kevin Galey laying on the floor, wounded.
    ✦ Nursery worker Laurie Cox made the second 911 call at 6:55:42 P.M. The call was answered by an operator who had attended Wedgwood Baptist Church and was familiar enough with the facilities to direct emergency vehicles to the proper locations.
7. Having been informed of the shooting, Fort Worth police officer Chip Gillette made a call on his police radio from his home across Walton Avenue from the church. The time was 6:56:23.
8. Gunman shot out glass in worship center door and entered the doors, moving across the back of the worship center, cursing and shooting.
    ✦ Laying under a pew in the front of the worship center, Kay Bynum made a frantic 911 call on her cell phone. It was the only call made from within the auditorium. Shots and screams were heard in the background. The time was 6:57 P.M.
9. Jay Fannin began a twenty-two-minute cell phone call to 911 operators. The time was 6:57:06. The line remained open as Fannin went from the church office to the worship center and then outside among the wounded.
10. Seeing a figure through the glass, the gunman opened the worship center door, shot and killed Shawn Brown outside the doors, and left the worship center.
11. Re-entering the worship center, the gunman shot and killed Kim Jones, Cassie Griffin, Kristi Beckel, Joey Ennis, and Steggy Ray while wounding Robert DeBord, Justin Laird, Nicholas Skinner, and Mary Beth Talley. X marks the approximate locations of the deceased.
    ✦ Children were evacuated from church buildings.
    ✦ In the midst of the shooting, Jason Ferguson's cell phone rang. It was a call from his pastor that went unanswered. The time registered on the phone was 6:59 P.M.
12. The pipe bomb exploded.
13. Bullets went through the walls of the choir loft into the choir rehearsal room where the orchestra was playing. Orchestra members evacuated.
    ✦ Jeremiah Neitz confronted the gunman at approximately 7:00 P.M.
14. Fort Worth police officers Chip Gillette and Charles Gonzalez entered the worship center through side doors just before 7:02 P.M.
15. The gunman killed himself at approximately 7:02 P.M.
    ✦ Officer Gillette made a call on his police radio at 7:02:28 P.M. saying that the gunman was dead. Shortly thereafter, emergency medical personnel entered the worship center.
    ✦ According to Southwestern Baptist Seminary student Scott McIntosh, who checked his watch, the first emergency vehicles arrived at 7:03 P.M.
    ✦ Jason Ferguson returned the call to his pastor from inside the worship center at 7:07 P.M. to inform him that Joey Ennis had been killed and Justin Laird wounded.
    ✦ By 7:24 P.M. the last of the wounded arrived at the hospital, twenty-eight minutes after the first 911 call was received. At about the same time, the possibility of a bomb on the gunman was reported and the worship center was evacuated for several hours.
16. Survivors, friends, and families gathered at Bruce Shulkey Elementary School across the street from the church.
    ✦ At approximately 4:00 A.M., families were allowed to identify the bodies of the victims.

child to attend the rally. Seconds later she was crouched behind a chair, praying for her life.

At this point, Kevin Galey, the minister of counseling and community at Wedgwood, came down the hallway toward the gunman, all the while thinking this was a part of the planned skit. The gunman fired one shot over Galey's left shoulder. Then a second bullet hit him in the upper right chest and lodged under his arm. Even after seeing the blood, Galey thought the shooter was using a paintball gun because he was expecting a skit.

Galey turned and cautioned five people who were standing behind him at the CD sales table so that they would not get hit by paintballs. As a third bullet hit Galey in the left hip and lodged in his right hip joint, three of the women ran into the worship center while the other two exited the hallway through the north doors. Observing the gunman change clips in his revolver, Galey was finally convinced this was not a skit. Seeking help, Galey turned to go to the fellowship hall where the adults were having prayer meeting. He would make it about forty-five feet down a hallway to the door before he collapsed. Galey was assisted to the outside of the building, where he would later be transported by helicopter to a hospital.

One of the women who observed this scene was Laurie Jackson. She later wrote:

I was standing in the corridor near the CD display table, talking with the wives of two of the ministers. Their husbands as well as my two children were inside the worship center. I was facing the south lobby doors when the gunman came in. I wasn't really paying any attention to him until he started shooting. I saw him shoot four or five times into the area where I knew friends of mine were sitting. My daughter was to be in the skit later in the program so I knew this was not the skit. I ran around the corner of the L-shaped hallway and into the darkened and noisy worship center, yelling, "Get down, he's shooting. He's coming, get down!"

Knowing I could not warn all the others, I ran outside to look for a way to call 911, but I fell in the parking lot. I looked back into the church hallway and saw the youth minister, Jay Fannin, crouching down in the corridor and looking in through the sanctuary doors. I lay there praying.

The gunman had turned back to the area near the front door and shot again at those hiding there behind furniture, hitting Sydney Browning. "We could still see his face. I begged him not to kill us, but he turned and shot Sydney," recalled Larry Clark.

Sharon Thompson recalled looking up from behind her chair when she heard Jaynanne Brown say, "I've been hit! My head! I'm bleeding!"

"I realized," said Thompson, "that we couldn't

do anything for Sydney but we could help Jaynanne, so we got her out of the building and to the nursery where we used diapers to wrap her wound."

Inside the worship center, as the band finished leading the singing of "Alle," Jay Fannin, Wedgwood's minister of youth and organizer of the rally, remembered he had forgotten to project the lyrics of the song on the screen. He had just gone to the balcony to attend to this task for the next song when the shooting started. On the lower floor Daniel Cox and Shawn Brown heard the shots being fired in the hallway. Having been seated in the back row near the east door, they got up, opened the door, and stepped out to look.

About this time, Mike Holton, minister of education and administration, heard shots and came down another hallway only to face the gunman. Asking if he could be of some help, Mike was shot at twice, with a bullet going to his right and another going above his head to the left. He turned and ran to the church library to call 911, the first of twenty-three such calls from people inside and outside the church building. Walking out of the library, Holton saw Jeff Laster wounded and lying nearby. Meanwhile, Cox and Brown had re-entered the worship center.

Already Praying

In the fellowship hall, prayer meeting participants

had mistaken the shots a few feet away for someone hammering on the wall and had sent a representative to find out what the noise was. Having been warned of a gunman in the building, they left the room. Some stopped to assist Kevin Galey. Others ran to get the children safely out of the church to the elementary school across the street. Still others with family members in the worship center ran to look in through the glass doors.

A Wedgwood couple who are missionaries in a country torn by civil war recalled:

> Where we serve there is constant shooting in the marketplaces and on the streets. We attend two security meetings each week, carry walkie-talkies everywhere we go, stay away from large crowds, get home before curfew, and have an evacuation plan. We arrived back in Fort Worth just a few days before the shooting. On September 15 we were at our home church without an evacuation plan. Even though our ears are accustomed to hearing gunfire, we thought the Wedgwood shots were from someone hammering in an adjacent room. When we realized the noise was gunfire, we ran from the fellowship hall into the hallway to see if we could help.

In the church office, the pastor's secretary, Debbie Gillette, called her husband, Fort Worth Police Officer Chip Gillette, at their home across the street from the church. Prior to Debbie's call, Gillette had been alerted by his four-year-old Labrador, Jake. "Every hair from the tip of his nose down his back was sticking straight up like a razorback hog," said Gillette. He continued, "When I saw that, I went outside and was met by Paul Glenn who said there was shooting in the church. I went back inside and made a call on my police radio for back-up support." Gillette quickly put on his bulletproof vest and got his revolver.

With the Children

Kim Herron, Wedgwood's minister to children, was overseeing staff responsible for approximately 130 children on this night. When the shooting began, Herron was at the cold drink machine near the hallway of the worship center. She heard pops, and three women ran past her saying there was shooting in the hallway. Herron ran quickly to the children's rooms with instructions to lock the doors. "I thought there might be gunmen everywhere, so I wanted the children locked up," stated Herron. "Then I heard there was a bomb threat," she continued, "so I said, 'get the kids out of the building.'" As various ones arrived in the children's rooms to warn of the danger and assist with the evacuation, Herron thought of her own seventeen-year-old daughter, Haley, who was in the worship center. "I knew our

God was in control but at the same time, I'm a mom and it was so, so scary," Herron said.

One of those who arrived to help evacuate the children was Wedgwood Sunday school director Bruce Coleman. Daughters Katie, a third grader, and Amanda, a first grader, were in their Girls' Auxiliary missions classes. Mike Holton ran into the library and told Coleman that there was a gunman in the worship center. Coleman reflected:

> I first ran toward the fellowship hall in disbelief. After hearing four shots, reality sank in, and I ran for the second floor where the girls and their leaders were. A second dose of reality faced me as I started to go up the stairs. There lay Jeff Laster, with a bullet wound to the abdomen but still alive. Not knowing they had already been warned, I opened the first classroom door and saw a look on the teachers' faces that did not belong—a look of anxiety and fear. I motioned to them calmly and quickly to move the girls across the street to the elementary school. The girls moved down the stairs, past Jeff, and outside to the street and the school among the noise and movement of several emergency vehicles. As we arrived at the back of the school, the leaders quickly involved the girls in times of prayer and singing.

Another attendee who was instrumental in removing the children was Tom Clemmons, a staff member at Southwestern Baptist Seminary who had been leading a Bible study for adults in the fellowship hall when the first shots rang out in the foyer. Clemmons recalled:

> I stopped in mid-sentence and asked, "What *is* that?" Someone said, "It sounds like hammering." We heard a few more shots and shortly thereafter, Kevin Galey fell at our door yelling, "I've been shot! I've been shot! I'm not kidding!" I saw blood on his arm and side and immediately told everyone to evacuate the room. I *knew* I wasn't leaving the church with my two boys still in the building. They were with other kids in the Mission Friends classes, so I ran back to their part of the building to evacuate them. Someone had already been there and told the teachers to close the doors, turn off the lights, and get the kids down on the ground behind the tables.
>
> When I ran into the hallway near the children's classrooms, I saw the emergency exit at the end, so I kicked it open. It led to a new parking lot that had a construction fence around it, and it wasn't near the sanctuary. Believing that to be a safe exit, I started yelling, "This is Tom Clemmons. Everything's okay! Teachers! Open your doors. This is Tom Clemmons, and we're leaving the building."

The teachers began to peek out, and I encouraged them to get the kids lined up and lead them through the hallway into the parking lot. The construction fence was a big problem, however. Some adults jumped a concrete fence in the rear into a neighbor's yard, and we began to lift kids over the fence into the waiting arms of other teachers. Then the teachers led their classes out of the yard and across the street to the elementary school, as far from danger as we could get them.

After seeing my sons in the parking lot and handing them over the fence, I was quite relieved. Things had happened so quickly. One of the teachers told me what Zachary, my five-year-old, said when he heard me yelling in the hallway, "This is Tom Clemmons and everything is okay." Zachary jumped up and said, "That's my dad, let's go!" It was reassuring to him that his dad was there to save him. It was ultimately reassuring to know that our heavenly Father was there to save us!

Laurie Cox, a paid nursery worker for the church, had gone into the church office to pick up the checks for the other workers and remembers, "I had an *eerie* feeling that I needed to hurry and get out of the office." The same word, *eerie,* was used by Jo-anne Crawford, who had just been in the church office to deliver a sympathy card to the pastor on the death of his mother. With her checks in hand, Cox continued:

> I walked by the cold drink machine where two nursery workers, Molly and Kim, were talking. I handed Molly her check but had to go back to the office to get Kim's. There I felt the same spooky feeling. When I got back to the nursery building the lights were off. As I left the building to get custodian Jeff Laster, I saw Kim Herron yelling that there was a man with a gun inside our church. I went back in the nursery and called 911 and stayed on the phone with a 911 operator who had once attended Wedgwood. Then we vacated the building and took the children to the elementary school.

In the background of this call, Jaynanne Brown could be heard being brought into the nursery with a bullet wound to the head.

Lorinda Bodiford was among several women who were working with the children and had teenagers of their own in the worship center. "What does a mother do," she asked, "when her children are in danger and she can't protect them?" She was helping with Girls' Auxiliary and the next thing she knew they were being rushed out of the building. *But I can't leave!* she thought. *My babies are still in there under a stranger's gun. Oh, God, help me!* She saw the SWAT team and heard the click of their guns. She saw blue uniforms running in the opposite direction than she was running. Helicopters were close and loud. *Oh, God, help my daughters!* She was behind the elementary school and still couldn't find her daughters. Were they being held hostage? "My heart was pounding. I could not breathe," she reported. "I felt sick and then started singing, 'Jesus loves me.'"

Praising God, she saw one daughter, but the other was still missing in the chaos. *Please be alive,* she pleaded. Finally, someone said they'd seen her. Thirty minutes later, she was brought in. She had blood on her backside and on her shoes—not hers but someone else's. Lorinda's daughter had been too close to death. Her mother could not protect her, but her mother had protected other mothers' daughters.

Tragedy Moves in and out of the Worship Center

At various times the gunman asked where the prayer service was being held. The question was offered to no one in particular but in the hearing of those who were in the hallway. Looking to his left and making eye contact with seventeen-year-old Glen Bucy, who was inside the worship center, the gunman fired a shot through the glass window of the side door. "I was standing in the back of the church, and the next thing I knew bullets started coming through the window," said Bucy. "I looked at him, and he looked at me. We made eye contact. Then he started shooting right at me through the glass. Glass flew all over." Hours later Bucy would still have glass shards on his T-shirt and in his hair.

As the shots came through the door, Daniel Cox and Shawn Brown were standing on either side. They then ran along the back wall to the center doors, which would lead them to a telephone. As they exited the center doors, Cox ran ahead, hearing Brown call his name and assuming he was following. Cox exited the building, jumped a fence, and ran to the nursery area where his wife, Laurie, was working.

At this point Youth Minister Jay Fannin was coming down the stairs from the balcony. Seeing Brown near the water fountain, Fannin yelled at him to go to the office and call 911. Since the office doors were locked, Brown had to wait until Fannin arrived. "One minute Shawn was standing next to me as I opened the door, and then he wasn't there," recalled Fannin. "I went in and called 911 several times, getting a busy signal," Fannin continued. "It was then I heard two loud shots and went out to see Shawn lying on the floor."

Fannin's 911 call was finally completed on his cell phone, and the line remained open for approximately twenty-two minutes. The tape of the call included sounds of people running out of the worship center, shots being fired, descriptions of the injuries, prayers being offered in the background, and sirens.

For some reason Brown had walked back over to the center doors of the worship center. While Brown was looking in, the gunman opened the doors and fired. As Brown turned away, he was hit twice, dying instantly. According to Amy Galloway, a fellow Southwestern Baptist Seminary student who had been seated in the back row, the gunman left the worship center for the explicit purpose of shooting Brown. "I thought, 'he's leaving,' but then he came back in and resumed shooting. He went down three aisles shooting at people. I thought it was strange that the band's bass player kept playing through all this." The bass player could not hear the gunshots because the music was so loud.

With the gunman turning his focus toward the worship center, the activity intensified. Word had spread throughout the church buildings. News media had already interrupted regular programming to share the "breaking story." Telephone lines were busy. Prayer force was increasing. The spiritual battle was raging.

Tragedy Focuses on the Auditorium

Having re-entered the auditorium after shooting Shawn Brown, the gunman crouched down by the rear pew and shot and killed Kim Jones, who had been seated there. During the next few minutes, the gunman shot and killed Cassie Griffin and shot Kristi Beckel, who would die later at the hospital. The gunman also shot and killed Joey Ennis and Justin "Steggy" Ray.

Teen-ager De'Leasha Simpson described the scene: "We were sitting on the third row saving some seats for friends. The concert started, and when we were on about the third song we heard gunshots. We thought it was a skit and stood up, looking straight at the gunman. We knew it was real when he pointed the gun at us. We went straight under the pew. When he shot again, he hit Cassie. Then we were sure it was real."

From where she was handing out programs, Mary Beth Talley saw the gunman come into the building. She dropped the programs and ran into the worship center. She knew it was not a skit because she had a part in the skit. In the darkness of the worship center, Talley saw her lifelong friend, Heather MacDonald, who suffers from Down syndrome, and Heather's mother. Unable to be heard above the music, Talley went right to Heather's mother and explained about the gunman and then assisted her in getting eighteen-year-old Heather to bend down on the pew. Mary Beth lay on top of her to keep her calm. "My full body was in view of the gunman. I heard a shot and then I felt it," Talley remembered. "I thought, 'don't freak out' or Heather would start freaking out and he would notice her, too." The bullet had penetrated between her shoulder blades and traveled to her lower back. Weeks later surgery would be required to remove the bullet where it was embedded in muscle tissue.

Heather's mom, Laura MacDonald, remembers, "Mary Beth told me she thought she had been shot. She told me several times that she was beginning to feel faint. Every time she said that I remember feeling panicky." MacDonald continued, "I was concentrating so hard on keeping Heather down and was so concerned about Mary Beth's wound that I just shut out everything that was going on around me."

Elsewhere in the worship center, two-hundred-pound junior varsity offensive lineman Justin Laird was having a great sixteenth birthday. He had acquired his driver's license, and a surprise birthday party awaited him after the rally. Sitting near his parents when the shooting started, Justin was hit twice by bullets, and one of them paralyzed him.

Somewhere in the melee, Robert Debord, another high school student, was hit with a bullet above his chest and suffered a collapsed lung. Nicholas Skinner, a high school band member, sustained a bullet wound to the upper arm.

In the semi-darkness of the worship center, many of the worshipers thought the gunman and the shots to be a part of the promised skit. Even as the music group led the teens in singing "I Will Call Upon the Lord," some paused to applaud the gunman while others yelled at him. "We thought it was a joke," said Kristen Dickens, who was sitting in the second pew when the shots began. Some teen-agers were standing up and yelling to the gunman, "Shoot me! Shoot me!"

On the first row of the center section, Rebekah Gillette was lying on the floor when she saw a pool of blood flowing from the row behind her. Two teens had been shot there. Even though she saw a man smoking a cigarette, she still wasn't sure if it was a skit because the band kept playing as shots were being fired. Even after the rest of the band ran off the stage, the bass player continued to play.

De'an Simpson heard what she thought were firecrackers. When she saw glass breaking in the door and a man with a gun start shooting, she fell to the floor. She could feel bullets going over the top of her head and started to pray for her daughter. She learned later that as she was praying her daughter made eye contact with the gunman and ducked down just as he pointed the gun at her and fired a bullet into the pew above her head.

Teen-ager Bethany Bynum continued to look at the gunman as bullets whizzed by her. She was convinced, as were some of her friends, that the man firing the shots was the same man that had been seen at the Wedgwood Middle School that morning, though this was never corroborated.

As shots continued to be fired, people slowly realized that it was not a skit. The gunman kept yelling, "This is real!" Some people ran outside through side doors while others dived under pews for cover. Stalking to and fro at the back of the worship center, the gunman would aim at various persons, sometimes shooting and sometimes not.

Wedgwood member Stacey Grey recalled hearing shots, very loud, seemingly amplified. Some of the youth were giggling. One boy was crawling on the floor. She plugged her ears and peeked over the pew. The man was standing at the back of the church with a gun in his hand. More shots were fired, a pause, and then something exploded near the front. The gunman had thrown a homemade pipe bomb toward the front pulpit area. The bomb exploded, sending shrapnel into the balcony area. It was at this point that Tim Hood, who was running the lights, remembers thinking, "This is real" and began to bring up the lights slowly. According to Hood, "the lights were at one or one and a half on a scale of ten." As the lights began to brighten, it got extremely quiet in the worship center, according to some. Then the shooting began again. "By the time the lights were up to ten," said Hood, "the shooting had stopped."

In her seat near Hood in the balcony, Wedgwood member Jody Thuett thought it was great being above all the kids and watching them worship and praise the Lord. About halfway through "Alle" she heard a pop, then again pop. "My first thought was that it was a teenager who had brought firecrackers and how awful it was to do that after the

Columbine shootings," she said. "I continued to hear the pop, pop, pop sounds. I was watching Jay Fannin to see if his reaction would tell me if this was a skit or not." Jay left the nearby sound booth, really angry. On the way out of the doors he said, "This is not funny anymore." The band kept playing. Some of the kids were laughing. All of a sudden, kids dropped to the floor between the pews. "I guess I was in shock," said Thuett, "because I couldn't do anything. I just kept seeing these terrified faces looking up at me from between the pews. I could see some of the kids bleeding. About that time there was a big explosion that shot debris up into the right side of the balcony."

Tragedy Moves Outside

In the choir room, the orchestra was practicing when the first shots were heard. Minister of music Jonathan Gardner assured those who were present that a skit was planned for the youth and that the noise was probably a starter pistol. When the bomb exploded in the adjacent sanctuary, John Baker responded that it sounded as if the band blew one of its speakers. The orchestra had begun to play again when Baker, a detective for a nearby police department, saw a hole appear in the wall above their heads. Realizing it was a bullet hole, he led members of the orchestra out of the choir room to safety, while one orchestra member stayed hidden in a closet until police arrived.

As Baker and his teen-age son headed toward the exit, they stopped to pull Gardner back from entering the worship center. Gardner had walked up the steps to the auditorium and smelled smoke but heard no screaming, so he was about to enter when Baker grabbed him. Together, they exited through the southeast fire doors while several bullets hit the door frame and walls as the gunman shot from the back of the worship center into the passageway between the sanctuary and the choir room. As they exited, orchestra member Russ Miller saw Chip Gillette running across the street yelling into his police radio, "Roll every unit you have!" The first unit would arrive less than a minute later coming from the east, and the officer would leave his siren on as he and Gillette went into the building.

Art DeForde, a paramedic, had been standing by the east door of the worship center when the glass was shot out. He ran down the aisle out of the sanctuary and through the southeast fire door to the outside. There he found Jeff Laster wounded and leaving the building. Looking at Laster's wounds, DeForde saw no exit hole and knew there could be much internal bleeding. He did not know if the gunman was alone or if he was still in the worship center. DeForde determined the best action was to get Laster into a safe area, the children's building. Later, having checked on his family,

DeForde would go back to offer medical assistance to Jaynanne Brown, who already had a bandage on her head, and to Mary Beth Talley until she was loaded into an ambulance.

The Tragedy Culminates in the Worship Center

Back in the worship center, the gunman continued to shoot until he had fired between sixty-five and one hundred rounds of ammunition. But his time was running out.

In the back of the worship center, a nineteen-year-old guest of one of the youth groups allowed God to use him. Jeremiah Neitz, who admits to a troubled past before getting right with God three months prior, stood up and confronted the killer. "Sir, you don't have to be doing this." The gunman yelled at Neitz to shut up, punctuating his statement with profanity. "Sir, what you need is Jesus Christ." The killer pointed the gun at Neitz and cursed him. As Neitz relates the story, "I held my hands out to my side and said, 'Sir, you can shoot me if you want. But I know where I'm going. I'm going to heaven. What about you?'" The gunman would shout one last expletive, put the gun to the side of his head, and fire. Having watched this from her position under the back pew, Amy Gallaway would yell, "He shot himself. Let's go!"

According to Lana Bull, a Southwestern Baptist Seminary student who was lying on the floor next to Kim Jones and within a few feet of the gunman, the last statement of the gunman was, "I'm not interested in y'all. I wanted adults."

Adam Hammond, the youth minister at Southwayside Baptist Church, had brought Jeremiah Neitz to the rally. When he heard the conversation, he looked to see that it was, in fact, Neitz speaking to the gunman. "I grabbed at his pants to try to force him to get down," Hammond said. When Hammond heard one more shot, he thought Neitz had been hit. But the gunman had ended his own life. Neitz thinks he might have influenced the gunman to end the killing. "I think I got to him. I don't know how, but I think that's why he ended it. After that, I just got out of there as fast as I could," said Neitz.

David Peyton, a youth minister and former police officer, had been thinking, *I've got to get that gun.* After hearing a muffled shot, Peyton saw the gunman slumped over with blood trickling from the side of his head, the gun still clinched in his hand. "I guess I've seen too many movies where the bad guy keeps coming to life," Peyton said. So, crawling on his hands and knees, Peyton was the first person to reach the gunman, prying the 9 mm handgun from his fist. Walking out into the foyer area, Peyton laid the gun down on the floor before leading his youth group out of the building.

Meanwhile, Chip Gillette had been joined by another Fort Worth police officer, Charles Gonzalez, and together they entered the chaos that the gunman had created inside the worship center. Having circled the auditorium with weapons drawn, the two officers worked their way from opposite directions slowly past blood and bodies toward the gunman, now seated on the back pew. "There was a heavy, heavy gunpowder smell, and shell casings were everywhere," Gillette said. "When I reached the gunman, he was sitting straight up with his eyes open. I pointed my revolver at his face and waited for him to move. Then he slowly slumped over, and I saw the bullet wound. I made a call on my police radio that the gunman was dead." That call was made approximately twelve minutes after the gunman entered the church building. Shortly after that, police officers would swarm into the worship center and begin the evacuation process.

Tragedy Spills into the Streets and Beyond

Several blocks away, Debbie Beckel parked and ran through the maze of red lights to pick up her daughter Kristi. Frantically asking if anyone had seen her, she got no positive response. Because of an apparent bomb threat, officers told Beckel to remain inside the elementary school. As she waited, friends called area hospitals to no avail. An identification mistake had been made and thus Kristi was not identified until 11:15 P.M. Beckel had waited for four hours at the school before a police officer took her to the hospital. Meanwhile, Kristi's father was waiting in a Phoenix, Arizona, hotel room. A phone call from his wife would confirm his worst fears: Kristi was brain dead, killed instantly, yet still medically alive.

Running late, Kathy Jo Brown had arrived at Wedgwood, parked, and entered through a back door. As she and the children she was baby-sitting passed the cold drink machine, they spoke to the children's minister, Kim Herron. Suddenly the door opened and three ladies ran past them just as gunshots were heard. "It's a gun!" one of the ladies said. Kathy Jo left, taking the children back to the car. She took them to a friend's house before returning to the church and being diverted to the elementary school to wait.

Kelly Ferguson and Lori Laird had run out of the worship center and across the street when instructed to do so. John Laird realized Justin wasn't filing out with the rest of the kids and went down two rows to tell him to leave. Justin replied, "I can't move. I can't feel my legs, Dad." Lori had just realized that Justin hadn't followed them out of the church. "I looked back at the church and saw John dragging Justin into the foyer. I ran back, and Justin was lying on the floor being attended to by a Fort

Worth police officer. Justin was lying face down and there were three holes in the back of his shirt." The officer cut off his shirt to discover that there were two entrance wounds and one exit wound. He said he needed to check his front side to see if there were any wounds there. There was not another exit wound, which meant the bullet was still inside.

Across town, at the Laird's church, First Baptist Church of White Settlement, the congregation had just completed a business meeting during which they had voted to join a program called Lighthouses of Prayer, when word came of the shooting at Wedgwood. Not knowing the extent of the situation, Pastor Jim Gatliff reconvened the congregation for prayer. Then the pastor's cell phone rang. It was the church's youth minister, Jason Ferguson, calling to say, "I lost a kid—Joey." Ferguson went on to share the news that one of their teen-agers had been killed and another was paralyzed. The congregation would go back to prayer as many parents scurried out of the building to try to find their teenagers.

Scenes similar to this would be repeated in churches all over the Dallas-Fort Worth area as word of the shooting spread. Churches of many denominations interrupted their activities and began to pray. As their intercessions went out to the Father of Lights, the lights in the worship center at Wedgwood had come up to full power, dispelling the semi-darkness through which so many had walked.

Still in the Worship Center

After the shooting stopped, Tess Price, a mother herself, was dramatically used by God to comfort someone else's daughter. She tells her story:

> All week long, my oldest daughter, Cherise, had been talking about the concert on Wednesday night. I had wanted to attend a youth function as a support person for some time. I really sensed strongly that the Lord wanted me to go and be a part of this. So, in spite of some last-minute struggles within, I eagerly surrendered to the prompting and went to church. I was full of anticipation of the blessing that lay ahead. My daughter scurried off to find her friends, leaving me to find myself a seat.
>
> I heard some popping noises out in the lobby and thought the skit was beginning. Something hit my left thigh and stung, and I remember thinking that it was a powerful blank. As the shooting continued, I noticed how loud the shots were. He kept firing over and over. I thought it might be wiser for me to get on the floor, so I did.
>
> I watched the shooter from under the pew. He was about fifteen feet away from me. I could see the light-colored soles of his shoes as he paced back and forth. I caught a glimpse of his

profile. He had a large nose and wore dark clothing with a cap. His face was scruffy-looking as if he had neglected to shave for a while. After more shots, I heard Jay Fannin rush in and tell everyone to get out quickly. There was a look of horror on his face. I picked up my purse and started to go out. As I passed the back, I noticed a young woman with her head lying on the pew. A girl stood up beside her. The girl's back was covered with blood. Instinctively, I reached over to the woman lying against the pew and felt her neck for a pulse. There was none. She felt slightly cool.

Something inside me clicked. All I could think of was, *What if someone is in here and needs help? What if they couldn't get out by themselves?* I set my purse down and started going around and checking bodies for a pulse.

The fourth body I came to was Kristi Beckel, leaning against a pew in a sitting position. She was breathing. There was a bulge above her right ear where she had been shot. I looked up and saw a man in white come in the back. I yelled at him, "This one is still alive. She's breathing." He came over and helped me lay her back in my arms. She needed to have her head slightly elevated to prevent her from drowning in her own blood. As I held her, I prayed for her, "Please, Jesus, help her." Then I felt very impressed that this girl's mother would want to be holding her. She moaned and her left arm and leg moved. I started to talk to her. I said, "Your mama can't be here with you right now. But I am here. And we're going to do this together. Lord, please be our strength." About that time, she moaned and moved again. I looked up to see a man come in along with some police officers. I told him, "She's still breathing." He helped to straighten her legs out a little more. I started to stroke the girl's forehead. I wanted to sing to her but I couldn't think of a song.

The paramedics finally arrived. They pulled her up off my lap. I backed out and they carried her out into the aisle. As a police officer guided me out, I kept noticing bodies.

It took me two days to find out that Kristi died that night. I have struggled with what purpose I served. "Why was I there when she was dying anyway?" Someone said that I was there for her. As time goes by, I realize that she was there for me as well.

Debbie Beckel, Kristi's mom, knows that Tess was there for Kristi. Had Tess not been there to inform the medical personnel that Kristi was still alive, she would possibly have been left in the worship center rather than transported to the hospital. Because she died at the hospital rather than in the worship center, Kristi could be an organ donor. Others were given a new chance at life through Kristi's organs.

There remained several hours of frightful darkness before the morning would come. Even in this, God's presence would be felt in powerful ways. After the wounded had been removed from the worship center and before the police department had declared the area a crime scene, two men re-entered the sanctuary. Tim Hood had been running the lights for the concert and needed to know if one of the young girls whose body was still in the pew was his daughter. Chip Gillette accompanied Hood. "I don't know how else to describe it, but when we entered the room there was a sweet aroma, not like the smoky gunpowder smell of earlier in the evening," said Hood. "The blood stains running down toward the altar were like some scene out of the Old Testament, yet even with the bodies still lying around, it was so peaceful. You just felt God's peace." God's light had begun to overcome the darkness.

And by God's light, God's people would walk toward the dawn.

Pastor Al Meredith and police hold a news conference at dawn.

Photo by James Morris.

3

The Darkest Hour Is Just before Dawn

"He Turns the Shadow of Death into Morning" (Amos 5:8)

It is true that the darkest hours are just before the dawn. While parents and teen-agers searched for each other and dozens headed for hospital vigils, the early evening twilight turned to darkness. Facts were sketchy. Rumors were rampant. Satan's man had taken his own life, but Satan himself was enjoying the havoc he had created in the darkness. While the deeds of this darkness would be devastating, they would be short-lived. The darkness would soon begin to turn into the light of dawn.

Even though many had walked through "the valley of the shadow of death" (Ps. 23:4), they would now begin to understand the song of Amos. As the Old Testament prophet called God's people to understand the injustice around them, he exclaimed of God, "He turns the shadow of death into morning" (Amos 5:8).

In the Darkness

In the darkness, Kristi Beckel, who had been kept alive on life support systems, slipped from life to death to eternal life. Because she had always been such a giving person, her parents made a decision to donate her organs so that others might live. Her heart, liver, a lung, and other tissues were used to add life to others, and authorities speculate that as many as seventy people were helped by her donations.

In the darkness, other parents learned that it was their child who was killed or wounded as ministers, friends, and counselors hovered around them.

In the darkness, teen-agers and adults faced the reality of lost friends as front yards became triage centers and the elementary school became a waiting area for frantic parents, other relatives, and friends.

In the darkness, Adam Hammond found his group except for James Gomez. After much searching and prayer, Gomez appeared. At the first sounds of gunfire, he had run out of the worship center, across the parking lot, through a yard, over a fence, and across another yard without stopping. Finally feeling he had run far enough to be safe, Gomez ran through a back door without knocking and into a stranger's den, shouting for the residents to call 911. As the wife was calling, Gomez was answering the husband's questions, which included why God would allow such a thing in a church. This opened a door for witness. Gomez later would receive a letter from the wife thanking him for sharing a positive witness with her non-Christian husband who now was showing interest in going to "that church." In the months that followed, the couple would become regular attenders at Wedgwood.

In the darkness, pages of names circulated through the crowds. These were sign-on sheets, lists of names penned by those who had survived the massacre. "She's here," a mother would scream, bursting into tears of relief as she read the list of names.

In the darkness, David and Tralissa Griffin were sent to John Peter Smith Hospital to look for their daughter, Cassie. Not finding her there, they checked at Harris Methodist Hospital to no avail. Finally at 2:00 A.M. they returned to the elementary school to wait still longer before being told what they already suspected, that Cassie was among those whose bodies were still in the worship center. Finally, around 4:00 A.M., nine hours after the shooting, they were allowed to make an identification of the body.

In the darkness stunned teen-agers and parents arrived at their homes without remembering driving there, while others stared across police tape at their vehicles, now inside the crime scene area and not to be released until Friday.

In the darkness, dozens of trained grief counselors arrived at the elementary school to begin the long healing process for those whose feelings were still numb. They listened for hours to traumatized people talk and reassured them that their fears were normal.

In the darkness, little-used phrases like Post-Traumatic Stress Disorder were used frequently, and names little mentioned before this night were suddenly on everyone's tongue and in everyone's prayers.

In the darkness, Lori and John Laird would learn from doctors that the bullet that entered Justin's body and did not exit was lodged between two vertebrae, causing what the doctors said would be permanent paralysis.

In the darkness, bomb squad members carefully searched the gunman's body for suspected explosives, finding another ninety rounds of unused ammunition, while families waited patiently for the bodies of their loved ones still inside the church building.

In the darkness, people wept uncontrollably and unashamedly as police and media helicopters flew overhead, mixing their spotlights with the brilliant television lights and throwing eerie shadows in the grass and on the walls.

In the darkness, police officers searching the church building would find an envelope on the round table in the foyer near Shawn Brown's body. The envelope was addressed simply to "Detective" and contained fourteen copies of the directions for the board game, "Anatomy of a Murder." After some interesting theories, it was discovered that the Single Adult Sunday School Department had recently played a game in the church building and this envelope was left over from their game.

In the darkness, Walter Norvell, like many parents, found his sixteen-year-old son who had been in the front row of the worship center. "I was so elated to see my son, I inspected his arms and legs as if he were a newborn," said Norvell.

In the darkness, questions were raised that could not be fully answered in the light, much less in the dark. Children, like seven-year-old Whitney Heiliger, who had been rushed through the chaos and past the wounded, asked, "Why were those people shot?" and "Do I ever have to come to church here again?" Another child would agree to attend church again on Sunday only if she were allowed to wear tennis shoes in order to run if she had to.

In the darkness, Amy Galloway, who had gone to choir practice and decided to sit in on the concert, remembered a suspicious person standing in the aisle near her before the shooting began. Seeing him again outside, she informed a nearby police officer. Rumors and early news reports would speak of a second person who had been detained. The reports were untrue.

In the darkness, Jeff Laster was undergoing

major surgery, clinging to life, having lost five units of blood due to internal bleeding. The doctors would later explain to Laster how close he came to death.

In the darkness, Glynda Clark made a telephone call to the First Southern Baptist Church in Phoenix, Arizona, where the pastor took members of Sydney Browning's family into his office and told them of the call. The Brownings called Glynda Clark and were told that they needed to get to Fort Worth as soon as possible because Sydney had been shot.

In the darkness, Wedgwood custodian Robert McDonald got a telephone call from his daughter, a volunteer police officer for the City of Fort Worth. She told him of a mass shooting in progress at the Wedgwood Baptist Church. He immediately went to the church because his other daughter worked with the babies there. Upon arriving, he saw many police cars, ambulances, fire trucks, and at least two helicopters. He remembered, "There was mass confusion all around. The youth at this event were all crying and hugging one another. Police started moving everyone back due to a bomb scare. After what seemed like hours, I finally found my daughter."

In the darkness, Mike Holton walked Kathy Jo Brown into a side room of the elementary school and told her that her husband, Shawn, was still in the worship center among those fatally wounded.

In the darkness, he whose deeds are evil walked among the crowds. While he was suffering a temporary setback at the hands of hope, he was not finished. The chaos and the trauma continued.

In the darkness, Southwestern Baptist Seminary student and Wedgwood member Scott McIntosh wrote:

> It has been six hours and I'm still in a state of shock. We evacuated the church. I waited and watched the sun set behind the cross on the steeple. What a surreal reminder that God was still in control. It looked so unnatural having such beauty next to such tragedy. But that is what life is, is it not? Some beauty, some tragedy? I saw life. I saw death. I watched as they took my friends away. I sat and waited when there was nothing to do but cry. But a new day is dawning with hope, the day with a sunrise but no sunset. A day where death dies and life lives again. A day of rebirth. A seventh hour is coming.

In the darkness, Wedgwood teen-agers began to implement their youth choir theme, so clearly displayed on one of their T-shirts, "We're putting a wedge between the darkness and the light," from 1 John 1:6-7.

The Dawning of a New Day

As it always does, darkness began to give way to the dawn. In an early morning press conference, Wedgwood pastor Al Meredith set the pace for a new day when he said, "We will not let the powers of darkness overcome the power of light." Somewhere, in the early morning light, a thousand Amens! were heard. They reverberated around breakfast tables where bleary-eyed people needed a spiritual boost. Amens echoed down hospital corridors where sleepless friends maintained silent, prayerful vigils. Their sound could be heard across the street in the elementary school where grief counselors had worked the night away. And as the refrain resounded across the land and around the world, Satan must have shuddered. This is not how he had planned it. This was to be the darkest night of the soul. This was to be a demonic victory. Yet, the power of light was prevailing.

Misty Wilson, a staff writer for the Southwest High School newspaper *Raiders' Review*, wrote:

> The tragedy of what had happened did not begin to sink in until some time Thursday morning at school. Seeing halls crowded with people crying and reliving the nightmare of the night before shook students.
>
> The most obvious sign of hope, healing, and grief was the meeting at the flagpole Thursday during first period. Thursday's gathering brought an estimated four hundred of Southwest's grieving students. Standing, holding

hands, with tear streaked faces, they sang, prayed, and comforted each other.

Similar gatherings were held at Crowley High School and North Crowley High School, and that evening a candlelight vigil was held at North Crowley High School to honor the fourteen killed and injured.

Likewise that Thursday grieving students, faculty, and staff filled Truett Auditorium at Southwestern Baptist Seminary during chapel time to hear guest speaker Dr. Rex Horne, pastor of the Immanuel Baptist Church in Little Rock, Arkansas, say:

> Peter Marshall, chaplain of the U.S. Senate, died as a young man himself. He made this statement that I often think about and I think about it today with you. "Life is best measured," he said, "not by its duration but by its donation."
>
> There is so much in your hearts already today. I thought about this as I came to this high honor of speaking before you today, particularly in light of what occurred yesterday. I thought about those young people and I thought about your friends and colleagues. I thought about how the day started: "You gonna be at See-You-at-the-Pole?" and "I'll see you at the pole!" Perhaps as they were breaking up from there, they said to one another, "I'll see

you tonight at church at the concert." In my mind's eye, as they looked around the auditorium last night, singing and praising the Lord, they looked upon each other, not knowing that in just a moment they would move from "see you at the pole," and "see you at church," to "see you in heaven." That's a full and good day isn't it?

So many people came to the church on Thursday that the yellow crime scene tape had to be adjusted to allow gifts to be placed on the corner of Walton and Whitman avenues by the church sign. Hundreds of flower arrangements, posters, cards, bears, and balloons covered the sign.

The ministerial staff of Altamesa Church of Christ, located just three minutes from Wedgwood Baptist Church, received word of the shooting while on a staff retreat in east Texas. They packed and drove back to Fort Worth, knowing only that they needed to be at home. In the early hours of Thursday morning, they planned a community memorial service for Thursday night. Exactly twenty-four hours after the shooting, eight hundred people gathered a few blocks from Wedgwood Baptist Church to weep and pray together. "Because the gunman grew up in a Church of Christ and because many of our members knew him and his family, we needed to do something," said senior minister Danny Sims. "We felt privileged to help."

On Thursday Ginger Robinson wrote a letter to her friend Sydney Browning:

Dear Sydney, Just had to tell you what I did at 4:00 P.M. September 16. I visited with your students at Success High School. What an awesome group of young people! You must have been so proud of them. How they grieved over losing you. And once there was composure, they wanted to share what you meant to them. So through the tears and the laughter, they talked about you—their mentor, teacher, confidante, and friend. You stood at the door to greet each student each day and before they could come in they had to smile. Just a day or two before you left us, the students said, you took a running leap and slid across the front of the room in front of the chalkboard. Your comment was, "That's the reason I wore these shoes." Some students shared the nicknames you had given them. I noticed that life had not been easy for some of these students. They shared what their grades had been in other high school attempts, and they delighted in telling what their average was at the present.

P.S. Tan, Jim, and Mike were late again. Could you send them a tardy slip?

Don and Diana Browning went to Wedgwood to pick up Sydney's red truck. They recalled, "We saw it with a sign saying 'We Love You Sydney,' and with other notes and flowers. We were overcome and realized we needed to leave it there a little longer. That was a defining moment of grief for us."

Thursday night at the Delta Gamma sorority house at Texas Christian University was described by Wedgwood member Kristie Harrick, a close friend of Kim Jones:

Approximately three years ago, Kim Jones gave her life 100 percent to Jesus. A few months after this life-changing event, she asked if I would help her start a Bible study in the sorority house. So, in 1997 we began with three Christians, one non-Christian, and two leaders. Following one of the Bible studies, Kim asked that I remain longer with her because she wanted to pray that every sorority member would have the opportunity to hear about the Good News of Jesus Christ. We prayed that night and continued to pray that prayer for the next five semesters. Our group grew to ten. This fall Kim returned as a leader instead of a student, continuing her same prayer.

On Tuesday, September 14, Kim shared from Psalm 139. She talked about how God knew the number of our days on earth and how we are to live each day for Him. The next day, Kim went to be with the Lord.

The following Thursday night, September

16, sorority sisters gathered to talk about the loss of Kim. One by one, new and old members stood and shared about Kim and her Lord. Jesus was being proclaimed in that room of the sorority house. Between this meeting and Kim's funeral, the members heard the gospel presented several times. The prayer that was offered several semesters ago was answered. We now average twenty young women attending the Bible study. We, too, will be lights on the campus and especially in the sorority house.

In the Light of Friday and Saturday

Police investigators let Pastor Meredith and Mike Holton back into the church building about 8:00 A.M. Friday. By noon the secretaries and most of the staff were there, and by 2:00 P.M. they let church members in to clean and start repairs as well as reclaim items left behind in the rush to vacate the building.

During Thursday's chapel service at the Christian school where Kristi Beckel had been a student, David Barnett, an Assemblies of God evangelist, sat at the piano improvising a melody. Said Barnett, "The Lord had been using spontaneous worship as a source of creative inspiration for us lately. As we sat in the choir room later that day with the students, I began to play the same melody on the piano. I took a piece of paper and began writing and finished the lyric later in the evening." At Kristi Beckel's funeral on Monday morning and again at Cassie Griffin's funeral on Monday afternoon, the following lyrics were sung by Barnett and his wife, Juliana, a ninth-grade English teacher at Bethesda:

Only heaven knows the reasons
For the changing of the seasons
Why the bitter cold of winter brings new life
   in spring.

Only heaven has the answers
To the questions that command us
And the mysteries that escape our
   understanding.

And sometimes, tears fall like rain
From situations we can't explain
And sometimes, lost in our sorrow,
All we can hold to is "only heaven knows."

Only heaven feels the hurting
In the hearts of heaven's children
And the pain of love and loss that knows
   no soothing.

Only heaven knows the courses
Of the roads that lie before us
And the beauty of the prize that is awaiting.

And sometimes, our lives are changed
By situations we can't explain
And our seed of faith is left to grow
In the life-giving truth that "only
　　heaven knows."

Inside the crime scene tape, church members worked to get their church ready for Sunday services. Blood stained, bullet-ridden pews were removed and replaced with chairs. Shot-out lights were replaced. Bullet holes were patched. Blood-stained carpet was removed.

When the music had finally stopped on Wednesday evening and those present had begun to leave the worship center, the song that had just been sung was, "I Will Call Upon the Lord." It was the last song to be projected on the overhead screen. In the haste to get out of the worship center, no one turned off the overhead projector. With these words as their inspiration, police officers, firefighters, emergency workers, and members of the bomb squad had performed their jobs. Crime scene investigators likewise had worked under the glow of the words on the overhead screen, as did the police crew assigned to finish up the task before returning the church to the members. On Friday, when church staff members were allowed to re-enter the worship center, there in bold view, still shining, were the words to, "I Will Call Upon the Lord." What was found on closer examination? A bullet hole was found in the screen—through the line of the song that proclaims, "So shall I be saved from my enemies."

Many people involved in the tragedy were making statements—some verbal and some not—about the events that had occurred. Outside the church, a Fort Worth police officer, by his own choice, was planting flowers that he had purchased to replace those that had been trampled in the chaos of Wednesday night. He had been on duty there since the tragedy, and this was his special gift to the church and his way to deal with his grief. When people began noticing what he was doing and praising him for it, he stopped and waited until dark when the crowds left so that he could do his good deed in secret. When he called his wife and told her how they were making a donation to the church, she cried.

The shocked family of the gunman, who later would donate the body to medical research and hold a private memorial service, issued a public statement:

> As a God-loving family, we grieve for the families affected by this tragedy and for the people whose lives will be forever changed by the actions of our brother. Our thoughts and our prayers are with the congregation of the Wedgwood Baptist Church, their families and friends, and all of the people who were in the building at the time of

the tragedy. We know that there can never be a satisfactory explanation for this action. We only know that we are heartsick along with everyone in Fort Worth and the nation. This will be the only statement that the family will make on this situation. We hope to convey our heartfelt grief and that, through God, we can all begin the healing process.

The family of Kim Jones also issued a statement:

We are not angry, and we have peace that God is in control. Kim would not want us to be sad. She would want us to rejoice because she is now with her heavenly Father and her best friend, Jesus, her Lord and Savior. However, she will be missed by those of us left here. She was a joy and a delight. She was fervent in her desire to tell others about Jesus and to live a life that would be an example to others. If she were here today, she would want to ask you if you had ever met Jesus. Then she would challenge those who already know Him to spend time in His Word and in prayer.

And later that same day, Pastor Meredith would appear on *Larry King Live* and affirm about those killed,

We know exactly where they are. Jesus Christ

himself said that He was the resurrection and the life, and whoever lives and believes in Jesus Christ would never die. Though our bodies pass away, our souls and our spirits are forever with him. And so we grieve, but not as those who are without hope. Our hope is in Jesus Christ, and that is a confidence that in the midst of a tragedy like this grows stronger as we band together. It's not whistling in the dark. It is a confidence born out of a personal relationship with Jesus Christ.

On Friday morning at Brewer High School, the school of Joey Ennis and Justin Laird, a memorial service would be attended by 1200 students and school personnel. Hundreds of students would sign a "Pledge of Reconciliation" written by Brewer High School principal Dale Brock. In this pledge, they agreed to "be a part of the solution, and not a part of the problem." Volunteer counselors would lead many teen-agers to faith in Jesus Christ. Other students made decisions at a community memorial service in White Settlement, a nearby suburb.

Wedgwood secretary Laura MacDonald returned to the worship center where Mary Beth Talley had shielded Laura's Down syndrome daughter, Heather. She recalled:

When I went back into the sanctuary on Friday after the shooting, I stood at the back pew where I had been and realized how close we had been to the gunman. I noticed that the hymnal in the pew rack in front of me had a bullet hole in it. I know that angels had been there protecting us. My praise is that Mary Beth never, ever let up on Heather even after she was shot. I'm thoroughly convinced that had Heather been able to sit up, the gunman would have taken a shot at her.

Donna Ennis would receive son Joey's belongings from the coroner's office. In his wallet, she would find a receipt from the restaurant where she had treated him to dinner on his birthday almost a year ago. He'd saved it!

Messages of support began to arrive early. In the next few days Wedgwood would receive more than 14,000 e-mail messages; 20,000 cards, letters, and notes; hundreds of posters and banners and 85,000 "hits" on the church web page. Texas Governor George W. Bush would drop by Pastor Meredith's house and join in a staff prayer meeting.

Interviews with ministers and church members would circle the globe. Millions would hear the personal accounts of the shooting almost always accompanied by a testimony of God's grace. The world would literally stand amazed at the testimonies of God's people at Wedgwood, especially the godly teen-agers.

As tragic as the events of these early days were,

they were not without irony. At the Saturday funeral of Sydney Browning, a mysterious bagpipe player arrived and led the casket and family procession into Truett Auditorium, returning to lead them out at the conclusion of the service. No one seemed to know from whence he came, who invited him, who he was, or where he went afterwards. This mystery was finally solved after much speculation, including the possibility of "an angel playing a bagpipe." Sydney's mother, Diana Browning, shared the following explanation:

> Kate Ross, the funeral director, was responsible for the bagpipes. It seems she uses them occasionally and has an expert player she calls upon when she needs him. When she decided this would be a good touch for Sydney's service, she called the guy and he said he was unable to do it because of a contest his students were in that day. But he suddenly remembered that one of his best players was not going to be able to go because of bad grades at school. His mother had grounded him. He called the mother to see if she would consider letting the boy play for the service. When she heard about it, she said, "He will be glad to play and, furthermore, he will do it without a fee!" So, the mystery bagpipe player was a sixteen-year-old high school student who was having to "pay the piper" for bad grades by "playing the pipes."

Not content to just host a community prayer service on Thursday night, thirty members of nearby Altamesa Church of Christ arrived on Saturday to help get the Wedgwood worship center ready for Sunday morning. Their spirit of support became characteristic of those first days following the tragedy.

Those who responded in professional roles played a critical part.

Photo by James Morris.

4

A Vulnerable Protector and a Wounded Healer

"Sons of Light" *(1 Thess. 5:5)*

Some lives shone especially bright throughout the tragedy of Wedgwood. The apostle Paul wrote, "You, brethren are not in darkness . . . you are all sons of light and sons of the day" (1 Thess. 5:4-5). Two of the sons of light who shone brightly were Chip Gillette, Wedgwood deacon, Sunday school teacher, and the first Fort Worth police officer on the scene, and Kevin Galey, minister of counseling and community at Wedgwood.

Chip Gillette, a Vulnerable Protector

The first Fort Worth police officer on the scene of the shooting was Chip Gillette. Even though he came to fulfill his role as protector of the people, he came very vulnerable. Here, in his own words, is the testimony of Chip Gillette:

My given name is Sherwood Merrill Gillette, Jr., but I have been called Chip for as long as I can remember. As a member of Wedgwood Baptist Church, I serve as a deacon and a Sunday school teacher. The class that I teach are the parents of the teens that were in the worship center the night of the shooting. Debbie, my wife, is secretary for our pastor and our minister of music. We have four children. Rebekah, our youngest, was on the front row during the shooting.

As I think back on the events of September 15, it becomes very hard to separate my thoughts from my feelings and emotions. The physical facts that answer the questions of who, what, when, where, why, and how (the standard questions that the cop in me wants answered) are not easily removed from the overpowering reality of God's great presence in all that took place that night and in the following days. The physical things and the spiritual realities are not far apart and are bound to each other.

For thirteen years I have been a police officer in the City of Fort Worth, working the midnight shift in the patrol division for the city's east side. For the past several years, I have settled into a routine of going to work at 9:00 P.M., coming home to be in bed and hopefully to sleep by 8:00 A.M., then awakening around

11:30 A.M. By 6:30 P.M. it's time to be on my way back to sleep for a quick nap before repeating the whole process again.

All the early events of September 15 had fallen neatly into the daily plan. Our family had assembled around 5:30 for the usual quick dinner before darting off to church activities. My wife, Debbie, had to get back to the church office to try and rescue lost files on her computer that had crashed earlier that day. Rebekah, fifteen, was eager to get to the church to see her favorite group, Forty Days. I thought about going to the concert to take pictures but remembered the film was in the freezer. I went into the living room and settled into the usual place on the couch along with Jake, our Labrador retriever.

As I was being lulled to sleep by the low volume on the television, Jake suddenly got up and ran to the front room, barking wildly. I thought that someone must be at the door and I had just missed hearing the knock. When I got to the front room, Jake was not at the door but was standing on top of a padded hope chest and was looking out of the large front window, still barking. All the hair along his back was standing in a ridge from the tip of his nose to the tip of his tail. I looked out of the glass thinking I would see someone teasing Jake, but I saw nothing.

As I drew away from the window, I saw two

men walking from the west side of the church building. They were looking up at the wall and then out to the adjacent street in both directions. Thinking that something had happened, I walked out in bare feet, short pants, and a T-shirt to see what was going on. I was thinking that someone must have driven by and thrown a rock at the windows or maybe even shot at them. As I got to the curb of my front yard, I saw Wedgwood member Paul Glenn running toward me. He was out of breath and stopped about thirty feet from me and began to yell, "Go call your SWAT buddies. You're going to need them."

My reply was, "Okay, Paul. Why do I need SWAT?" He took another breath and told me that there was shooting in the church and that Kevin Galey was down on the ground with a gunshot in his chest.

Something came over me in that instant. I guess it was a hard slap in the face with the heavy hand of reality. It took what seemed like a long time for his words to sink in. I then saw Kevin down on the ground. Turning to run toward the house, my heart began to pound. I thought of Debbie and Rebekah and then of what could be going on over there. Was it a botched robbery, some kind of stupid gang stunt, or a mad church member gone off the deep end?

I ran through the door and into the bedroom. Grabbing my police radio, I quickly turned the channel selector and tried to break onto the air. I could hear the dispatcher asking for units to clear to handle a "shots fired in the area" call and possibly a related "man with a gun" call. At the same time I was trying to slip on a pair of shoes and had grabbed my (bulletproof) vest and draped it over me. I was able to get air time and said "close the channel!" I then gave the address and name of the church. I said that there was shooting in the church and that people were hit and down. I asked for all available units to respond and for Medstar (our local ambulance service) and the fire department to be sent. I then grabbed my uniform shirt and duty pistol and ran out of the house.

While I had been in the house, I had heard the phone ringing, then my cell phone started ringing. I later found out that it was Debbie calling me from the church office telling me to get my vest and come over.

As I ran to the church my mind was going a thousand miles an hour. I thought again of the kids in the worship center and shouted into the radio that there was shooting in the church and that young people were in there. I felt myself losing it.

Then God took control. A calmness hit me like a wave from the ocean. Thoughts ran in and out of my mind. As quickly as I had a negative thought, God would take it away or answer it as if it were a prayer. As I ran toward the church, I thought, *I only have the rounds in my pistol and no extra magazines.* I was going to go back to the house and get my pistol belt with the extra magazines. But that thought left me and I continued. Hearing sirens and looking down the street, I saw a patrol car speeding toward me. I waved like a madman, wanting him to come to me and not to go to the location that the street numbers would have taken him to. He came right to me. It was Officer Charles Gonzalez. He jumped out of the car, and we both entered the south doors of the church.

Upon entering the doors, I saw Sydney Browning lying across the end of a couch. The smell of spent gunpowder was almost overpowering. There were empty shell casings all over the carpet. Charles and I looked at each other for a quick moment and then the pounding sound of gunshots rang out. I think it took us both by surprise. Charles keyed his radio and said, "Secure the perimeter. We have shots being fired in the building." Just then someone stuck their head out and said, "He's a white guy at the back of the church wearing a dark coat." I keyed my radio and gave this description over the air. The thought then came over me that people were being killed in the worship center.

Almost as one, Charles and I both then ran toward the closest set of doors that led into the worship center.

As we traveled up the hallway, two young men came out of the access hall that runs from a set of worship center exit doors. One of them had blood all over his shirt. Charles and I both yelled at the top of our voices for them to get out of the building. They saw us and shouted back that there was a man shooting in the church. I responded, "I know. Just get out NOW!"

I motioned to Charles and said that there were doors just down the hallway ahead of him, and I moved to the other set of doors that the two men had just exited. These doors seemed closer to me, and I was thinking that we needed to get the shooter in a crossfire. As we ran toward the doors, the shots continued. I reached for the door handle and was opening the door to enter when one more shot went off. Then there was a pause and I thought that the shooter must be reloading. At this same time I saw someone stand up. I was pointing my weapon at him when I recognized him as one of our youth. He shouted out, "He shot himself. Get out."

In that very same instant, hundreds of people came up from off the floor and out from under the pews and began running toward the doors. I was running from the front of the auditorium to the back where I saw a subject seated there dressed in dark clothes. As I got to him, I had my weapon about five feet from his face. He was sitting up and seemed to have a blank look on his face. Then he started a slow slump over to his left. That is when I saw the wound to the right side of his head and knew that he was no longer a threat.

I looked around and saw police coming into the worship center from every possible entry point. The whole room looked like a battleground. There were injured and dead everywhere. I looked over to see someone I thought was my daughter lying on the floor. An officer came over toward me. Officer Gonzalez and I had met in the face of the shooter. I asked him to guard the dying shooter and a handgun that was close to his feet. Keying up the radio, I said that we were secure in the building and that the shooter was down. I said to send in the Medstar and fire department. I told the dispatcher that we needed five to ten ambulances and for him to alert Care Flight (the air ambulance service).

I was doing that as I moved toward the lifeless form under the rear pew. It was not my daughter. I couldn't look into another face on the floor. As I walked out of the back door, I saw Shawn Brown, down just outside the doorway. I was losing it. A friend of mine, Officer Pat

Blauser, came over and took me with him as he searched the church office for other victims or shooters. I was selfishly looking for my wife. No one was there.

When we came back out to the foyer from the office suite, we saw more officers, fire department personnel, and Medstar attendants coming into the building. I walked back into the worship center to see lifesaving work being done all over the place. Others were moving through the room checking and rechecking for signs of life in those that were dead, as if they couldn't really believe what they were seeing. It was an unbelievable scene. I looked back over at the shooter and heard a medical attendant say he was still alive. Moments later he died.

There was a swarm of activity going on just outside of the doors of the church. When I finally walked down the hallway toward the south doors, I could see hundreds of people all over my front yard. I walked toward them intent on finding my wife and daughter and praying that my daughter was not one of those still in the worship center. Pushing open the church doors, I could see ambulances were parked all along Walton Avenue. The sky was full of helicopters. Cameras and reporters were everywhere beyond the church property. Police were moving the media out of the way of the fire department and medical personnel. Injured persons were lying in my front yard and being treated. I ran over to my house and found Debbie, Rebekah, and the rest of my family all huddled together. We hugged for what seemed forever. I looked around and saw the same scene being repeated by families everywhere. I saw some wandering around yelling for their loved ones and in a panic going from huddled group to huddled group asking, "Have you seen . . . "

Then the word came from the police officers, now flooding into the area, that there was the possibility of a bomb in a car in the parking lot and a bomb inside the church. I was called back into the building to assist the crime scene officers and all those standing around the church were herded over to the elementary school across the street. The fire department was able to determine that there were no bombs. A bulge in the shooter's clothing was found to be six pistol magazines loaded with fifteen rounds each of 9 mm ammunition. A car in the parking lot that was used by the shooter was searched and no bombs were found.

The rest of the night was filled with events all seemingly happening at the same time. The police were hard at work investigating the crime. Parents, families, friends, media, and onlookers were gathering in the streets and at the elementary school. Counselors were arriving from the school district and Southwestern Baptist Seminary. Witnesses were transported to police headquarters to be interviewed. Mobile command centers were established for the police and fire department. SWAT was assembled and entered the church to make a full room-by-room search of all the buildings. Homicide detectives arrived and took control of the investigation and the crime scene.

The day never really ended, but just seemed to slowly flow into the next. Our recovery from the tragic night was beginning as the dawn arrived.

Chip Gillette's shift was over.

Kevin Galey, a Wounded Healer

Kevin Galey is the one to whom the Wedgwood family looks in times of tragedy. He is the professional healer of the congregation. This time, in Wedgwood's greatest corporate crisis, the healer was wounded. What follows is the first-person account of Kevin Galey, Wedgwood's wounded healer:

It was approximately 6:45 P.M. on the night of September 15, and I was in my office dividing up some literature that I had just received. I had decided to give a copy to Karren McDaniel, one of our church secretaries who is also a counselor. After dividing the material, I went to the office only to find that she was not there, so I left the material on her desk and proceeded into the north hallway across from the sanctuary. Hearing the loud music, I went toward the east hallway.

I had walked down the hallway to the CD and tape table where five women were standing and had picked up a CD to look at when I heard a loud pop-pop-pop-pop-pop sound coming from the south foyer at the end of the hallway. There I saw a man dressed in jeans, a green jacket, and a ball cap firing a gun at someone or something along the wall that separates the foyer from the hallway. One of the women at the table said, "He's part of a skit for the youth rally."

To that I responded, "Well that's kind of dumb!"

At that moment the gunman looked up and began walking toward me. By this time I had put down the CD and was walking toward him believing him to be part of the skit. The gunman pointed his gun at me and fired a round that went over my left shoulder. Not seeing the muzzle fire or smoke, I believed he was firing blanks. I was thinking to myself, "Ok, this guy is going to get into his role as the bad guy out here with the adults and then he is going to go in and scare the youth for some reason." Still thinking this, I continued to go towards him. The gunman fired another round that hit me in the upper right chest. As a reflex action, I turned to see where the women were in relation to me, and I saw one of them running out through the construction hallway. The gunman fired another round that hit me in the hip, and I immediately went down.

After being hit and falling to the floor, I rolled under the table to get out of the way of the gunman. I reached back to check my hip and saw a red milky substance on my hand. Still thinking this was a skit, I believed it was paintball paint and that this guy had just ruined a nice shirt and pants. I looked up and could see the gunman standing with his back to me at the east door of the sanctuary with the right door opened and his right foot holding it. I could see the darkened sanctuary, hear the loud music, and see the backs of some of the youth as they stood singing a rock version of "Alleluia." I saw the gunman lift his right hand up holding the gun, press a button on the side, and an empty gun clip fell to the floor beside him. With his left hand he reached into what appeared to be an army utility belt where he took out another clip and reloaded the gun.

I finally realized that this was no skit and this madman was no hired actor and the red substance was no paintball paint. After trying to get up off the floor unsuccessfully, I realized that this man was going to murder youth and youth workers unless I did something about it. I could feel the pain setting into my legs, but didn't think I was seriously hurt. I thought about my three boys, all of whom were at the church that night. I thought about the unsuspecting youth about to die by the gun of a madman. I thought about my wife who, if I were to get up and try to take the gunman down by myself and fail, would have to raise my three boys without a father. I have often wondered what would have happened if I had been able to take the gunman down while his back was to me and he was reloading. Perhaps six people would still be alive today and the tragedy that has surrounded Wedgwood would have quickly become yesterday's news. However, my best solution at the time was to go to the area on the other side of the wall where the adults were meeting for prayer and Bible study. I slowly got up and made my way about thirty feet to the doorway. Behind me, I could hear the gunman firing a succession of rounds into the darkened auditorium. I feared the worst.

Not knowing whether he was the only gunman, my hope was to warn the adults of the attack and to get help to go back into the sanctuary to aid the kids. I opened the door and, holding my side, yelled, "I've been shot. This is not a skit. There is a gunman in the sanctuary. Someone call 911. This is for real!" The initial response was shock and silence. I then looked up and saw Carol Glenn coming out of the prayer meeting to see what was going on. I said to Carol, who is a nurse, "Carol, please help me; I've been shot."

At that time I fell to the ground, feeling the pain in both of my hips and unable to move. The prayer meeting dismissed and adults scattered to find their children and get to safety. Not knowing whether the gunman was going to come through that hallway, nor the extent of my injuries, the decision was made to move me outside. Several men helped move me to the grassy area just outside of the east doorway leading into the building.

Once outside, I could see a flurry of activity. I saw one police officer coming towards the church, then a fire truck, then another officer, and then many emergency personnel. I could see and hear youth and adults being evacuated from the building with panic and fear on their faces. I was later to learn that my six-year-old son was brought down and led through the door near where I lay. When he saw me he stopped and became very upset that his daddy was going to die.

My wife later told him that "Daddy was shot

in the bottom, and he has a lot of padding back there." This explanation seemed to calm him down for the meanwhile!

The people attending to me removed my shirt and could see the entry and what appeared to be an exit wound further to the right of my chest. I told them that I had also been shot in the bottom, but they could not see the wound. Now the pain could be felt in my chest area as well, and I remember thinking that with all these emergency people here I would soon be attended to and be on my way to a hospital. But the EMTs didn't stop for me except to see if I was breathing and still conscious.

A detective stopped to ask me for a description of the gunman and asked me if I wanted them to contact my wife. I told them she was in the nursery.

About that time I remember Al Meredith coming onto the scene and asking the people around me about my condition. They told him that I had an entry and exit wound and should be okay. Al then prayed a quick prayer and left. I finally convinced the people around me that I had another wound after another EMT had asked about my injuries. They helped me roll over to my other side where they could see the bullet hole. Someone told the people to remove my shoes and take my pants off halfway to get a better look at the hole. At this point I was laying there with my shirt opened, my pants halfway down my legs and my underwear half off my left buttocks. I had been on oxygen for a while, but was starting to feel a little drowsy. Two nurses, also church members, were working on me. The instruction was given by the EMT to start an IV into my right arm. I was still wondering why I continued to be attended to by church members and not the emergency personnel. I began to think, "Well perhaps I am not as injured as I feel. I am going to be okay." My next thought was "or it must be very bad in there."

Larry Clark came out of the nearby door and told me that Sydney had been shot and killed. I began to pray for the kids still inside, hoping that somehow they had escaped but knowing that many might be seriously injured or dead. Soon after that an EMT came and told me that I was going to be transported by Care Flight Helicopter to Harris Hospital. A backboard was brought to lay me on and prepare me for my flight across Fort Worth. The straps were tightened, and several men surrounded me to carry me to the waiting helicopter about eighty yards away. As they began to carry me, I could sense that they were straining under my bulky weight. As one man let go of his side, my head tilted so I could see a camera man with his camera pointed right at my face. For what seemed an eternity, the men walked until they stopped at the chopper. Having already loaded one victim, the chopper medics had a more difficult time loading me to the point of almost standing me on my head on the backboard to move me around inside.

Finally settled down and with the medics' apologies for the rough handling, I could hear the all-clear sign to lift off and the engines began to roar. But no liftoff. *What if I am too heavy for the chopper to get me off the ground?* I thought. *They will have to stand me back on my head to get me out of here and load me in an ambulance!* About that time the chopper began to lift, and my anxiety abated. I was finally off to get help, still not knowing the extent of what had just happened at the church. I would not find out for two more days. I found out on Friday after I got out of ICU, and I wept.

Five weeks later, on October 21, 1999, Kevin Galey would stand in chapel at Southwestern Baptist Seminary and continue his testimony to a packed auditorium of staff members, faculty, fellow students, and friends.

Fifteen years ago I came to this seminary as a twenty-three-year-old, single adult. One of my classes was Dr. MacGorman's New Testament class. That semester, Dr. MacGorman, his wife, and family were going through a particularly difficult time with the illness and eventual death of their son. Many days he would come to class right after seeing his son through chemotherapy treatments. He would take out his notes, but before he would get into his lesson that great man would begin to weep openly in front of us. We're learning from this guy, so we didn't know what to say except, "Dr. MacGorman, would it be okay if we prayed for you?" And Dr. MacGorman would say, "I'd appreciate that." When we finished our prayer, the class would be taught by a man who had demonstrated courage and strength in a time of great grief.

During this tragedy I have often thought about that period of my life. I am married now. I have children. But I've thought about the strength of a man, great as he was, crushed by the loss of a child and yet open and bold enough to demonstrate Christ for us. I would love to stand here and tell you all of the miracles God has done in my life to protect me from harm. I was hit twice, once in the chest and once in the hip, and I've had surgery. But all of the great miracles would pale in comparison to the miracle of salvation that God worked in my life as a ten-year-old boy on a bus ministry. Jesus Christ is the answer for the world today. It's not gun control. It's not greater limitations by the government. It's Jesus Christ.

About this time last year, my wife and I discovered through a sonogram that our unborn son had a crippling birth defect called spina bifida, in which the spine doesn't close completely over the spinal cord, and the spinal cord becomes damaged, resulting in permanent paralysis. It can cause problems with walking, bowel and bladder control, balance, and breathing. We were faced with a long-term battle with this, the second most costly birth defect of children. We prayed two prayers. We prayed a prayer for a miracle. I said, "God, do one of two miracles in our lives. Either heal our child of this crippling defect or give us the grace and peace to deal with this as his parents. Heal our child or do a healing work in our lives." And the word went out. All over the country people prayed for us. Many of you in this auditorium prayed for us.

Last year, almost to this day, God showed us a miracle. There is a medical center at Vanderbilt University in Nashville that does experimental procedures on children with spinal column defects. We were to be the twenty-first patient of theirs, and only two or three of the kids had been born. It was very experimental. We said, "God, if this is your miracle, then work it all out." God did miracles to work it all out. We had the surgery—performed through the uterine wall.

The baby was born, and just recently we went to a follow-up session with the surgeon and heard the greatest news imaginable. The doctors in Nashville said, "Your son is going to have great leg strength. He's going to walk. Your son is never going to have a problem with his bowel or bladder. Your son has got perfect ventricles in his brain. He's not going to have brain damage. For all intents and purposes, your child is going to be normal."

We returned from Nashville on September 11. We were still celebrating the victory that God had brought into our lives when we went to church on September 15.

There are only two reasons why I stand before you this morning. It is not because I am great or accomplished. One is that I wasn't fast enough to dodge the bullets. The other is that seven people were murdered at my church, not because they were special, not because they were extraordinary people, not because they were known for their great faith, not because they were known for their great testimony. They were gunned down because they were at the place where they always were. They were at church on a Wednesday night.

Throughout the past year with our son's condition, people kept quoting a verse to me. You know in the Bible it says, "God doesn't give you more than you can handle." I've looked for that verse. It has been a tough year and I have looked for that verse. I didn't find it in the New Testament. It wasn't in the Old Testament. I said, "Well, maybe it is implied in the Hebrew or the Greek." But it's not implied there. I have come to believe that it is not even true. God does give you more than you can handle. It's been more than my family could handle this year. And without the prayers of people, without your prayers and my church's prayers, prayers of people literally around the world, I wouldn't be standing here. Folks, we need each other.

Indeed we do.

Young men grieve the deaths of their friends.

5

The Martyrs of Wedgwood's Tragic Night

"The Blood of the Martyrs of Jesus"
(Rev. 17:6)

In its broader definition, the word "martyr" is used for one who is put to death for adhering to some belief, especially Christianity. While these seven did not stand up to the gunman and profess their faith in the face of death, as many martyrs have done, they were unashamedly adhering to their faith by being there for the express purpose of worshiping Jesus Christ. Add to the list of Christian martyrs the following seven believers:

Kristi Beckel

Kristi Beckel was born in Little Rock, Arkansas, in 1985. Having become a Christian at the age of nine, Kristi was baptized on Easter Sunday, 1994. All of those who knew her described her as a happy person with a servant's heart. Her parents described Kristi as a giving person, tenderhearted, easy to discipline, who enjoyed playing "slug-bug" and "shotgun" with the family and shouting goodnight to each family member after going to bed. She loved her friends, her family, dogs, laughing, singing, watching "I Love Lucy" reruns, volleyball, talking on the phone, having friends come over to her house, going on family trips to Colorado, and attending church with her friends. Kristi disliked doing the dishes and "rug burns" from volleyball falls. Her favorite Bible verse was, "Now may the God of patience and comfort grant you to be like-minded toward one another, according to Christ Jesus, that you may with one mind and one mouth glorify the God and Father of our Lord Jesus Christ. Therefore receive one another, just as Christ also received us, to the glory of God" (Romans 15:5-7).

Kristi was a giving child so it was well within her character for her organs to be donated to others. Her name means Christlike and in her death she gave a part of herself that others might continue to live.

With her parents, Kristi had been visiting Wedgwood Baptist Church for four to five months and had been participating in the church's youth activities. According to her father, they had been looking for a Sunday when they could join Wedgwood as a family, but every Sunday, at least one family member had a conflict. The remaining family members joined Wedgwood on the Sunday after the shooting.

Shawn Brown

Shawn Brown was born in Dallas, Texas, in 1975 and raised in San Angelo. He had previously served as youth minister at the First Baptist Church in Bronte, Texas, and in seminary was preparing for future youth ministry. Shawn was a graduate of Howard Payne University, where he was a star baseball player. As a leader in the Baptist Student Ministry, he met Kathy Jo and the two were married on December 20, 1997. In addition to being a student at Southwestern, Shawn was employed by New Horizons of Fort Worth, a service for senior adults, where he was a mental health program assistant.

Shawn's parents were divorced when he was thirteen, and he lived with his mom until the age of sixteen when his mother contracted terminal cancer. She became a Christian on her deathbed six months after Shawn was led to faith in Jesus Christ. Shawn later joined the Hillcrest Baptist Church in San Angelo and moved in with his youth minister, Emmett Corker and family.

As partners, Shawn and Kathy Jo enjoyed cleaning houses, baby-sitting, house sitting, exercising, and attending Wedgwood softball games when Shawn was playing. Their favorite part of the day was when they returned home each afternoon after work. Before beginning supper or other activities, they always shared a time of laughter and fellowship about what happened to each other during the day. On their first vacation together, Shawn had learned to fly fish in Colorado, and both were excited about his new hobby.

In the week preceding September 15, Shawn wrote an essay for a seminary class and prepared a sermon. In the essay he said, "I think that as a minister, I will be sensitive to youth all around. I want them to know that they are valuable and loved." He was living out this philosophy of ministry as he and Kathy Jo taught a sixth-grade Sunday school class at Wedgwood. According to Kathy Jo, who pulled up Shawn's sermon on the computer,

> in that sermon from Hebrews 12:1-3 he had written about how we must run with perseverance the race marked out for us and fix our eyes on Jesus. He spoke of Columbine and of the ways that youth today are swayed in so many wrong ways. He wanted to help them see that they needed to throw off everything that hinders them so they wouldn't be tied down to sin in any way.

Sydney Browning

Sydney Browning was born in Bisbee, Arizona, in 1963. She was a graduate of Grand Canyon University and a 1991 graduate with a master of arts in Christian Education from Southwestern Baptist Theological Seminary. She loved her job as a teacher of troubled youth, and in her four years teaching she had been voted Teacher of the Year twice.

The principal under whom Sydney worked said,

> Sydney was a really wonderful, loving, happy upbeat person who never seemed to have a down day. Every memory I have of her is a good one. Sydney had been told by her doctor that she was four pounds overweight. Since she was so thin we joked about it, and she was determined to keep those extra four pounds. My last memory of her that Wednesday night was of her sticking her hand in my plate and taking a french fry as I ate. I knew if Sydney was given a task, it would be done right and it would be done ahead of time.

Even though Sydney did not see herself as very computer literate, she tackled the job of learning a computer program for the recording of grades. Often threatening to give up on learning, she nevertheless mastered it just a few weeks before her death. Coworkers remembered that Sydney was very proud of this accomplishment.

Quick-witted, with a great sense of humor, Sydney was known throughout the church family. Often on Friday nights she would attend high school football games where her married friends had teen-agers playing. On other Friday nights she would join the senior adults in playing table games. And she loved to be with the children.

Wedgwood members and missionaries Kathy and Ken Woods knew her well. Kathy wrote:

> It has been hard for Ken to go through Sydney's death. He knew her from the first day he went to seminary. I got to know her later on, and we roomed together for a year before Ken and I got married. She also sang at our wedding. She had just sent us a letter in May and a Prayer-gram in August saying she missed us. It is very hard to think about going back to Wedgwood without Sydney being there. I was so looking forward to her playing with our kids and getting to know them.

Joey Ennis

Joseph "Joey" Ennis was born in Fort Worth in 1984 and was a student at Brewer High School and a member of the youth group of First Baptist Church of White Settlement. More than anything, he enjoyed making people laugh, playing with his pet cats, and watching his pet ferrets fight with each other. Earlier in the school year, Joey had written a "mission statement" for a class assignment. He said, "My mission in life is to be kind and trustworthy with humor, always keeping promises especially as a friend, a son, and a pet owner." It was this outgoing, winsome personality that got Joey chosen a few years ago to be one of "Scott's Kids" on a local television station.

In spite of his short stature, Joey wanted to play professional basketball someday in the NBA. One of his coaches said that although Joey did not have an abundance of ability, he made up for it with a great attitude, hard work, and a big heart. In addition to basketball, Joey excelled in academics, making high grades in all of his subjects. According to the journal found in his school locker, Joey had set a goal of making all As during his freshman year in high school.

Late in the summer of 1999, Jason Ferguson, minister of youth, and Jim Gatliff, pastor at First Baptist, stood in a member's back yard where a church gathering had just finished. They were sharing the plan of salvation with a teen-age boy as Joey Ennis looked on and listened. Joey had just begun to participate in the church's youth activities at the beginning of the summer. At the conclusion of the presentation, Jason turned to Joey and asked, "How about you, Joey, have you accepted Jesus as your Lord and Savior?" To which Joey replied, "Yes." Two weeks before the shooting, Joey was discussing baptism with his mom and explaining to her that he needed to be baptized because he had accepted Christ. He was a young but obedient Christian.

When it came to Bible studies, Joey was at first a typical teen-ager, squirmy and giggly. But as time went by, he became more interested in the studies and how they could apply to his life. Then he just wanted to learn more and more.

Cassie Griffin

Cassandra "Cassie" Griffin was born in Lockney, Texas, in 1985 and was a student at North Crowley High School and a member of Wedgwood Baptist Church. Cassie had been raised in church, making a profession of her faith at the age of seven after Vacation Bible School. She had played the piano and had always been actively involved in church activities.

Cassie was faithful in reading her Bible and in January of 1999 had circled a verse with a cloud formation: "Whoever listens to me will live in safety and be at ease, without fear of harm" (Prov. 1:33, NIV). She had drawn a bold box around the word fear. Cassie's father was looking through his daughter's Bible and concluded, "The more I looked at that verse the more I realized that it does not say you will live without harm, but without the fear of harm."

During the week before September 15, Cassie had made a speech in speech class entitled, "My Three Wishes." They were these:

My first wish is to become a famous singer or

musician. I like to sing and I love to listen to music. If I was a famous singer I could share my faith with non-Christians. I could contribute lots of money to charities that work with solving world hunger in third world countries. . . . Everyone has goals and I'm sure you have yours, so hold on to them and never let go.

Cassie's love for frogs took on new meaning when someone shared with her the phrase, "Fully Rely On God." She often adorned her school assignments and letters with pictures and drawings of frogs.

Kristen Dickens described Cassie as "a kind, caring person who wanted everyone to come to Christ. She loved to make people laugh and always found a way to cheer them up if they had a problem. She was always there for you. She loved life and everyone in it. She was my role model and my best friend."

Kim Jones

Kim Jones was born in Dhahran, Saudi Arabia, in 1976 and thought of it as home even though she grew up in Alaska and Houston, returning to Saudi Arabia when not in school. Kim was a 1998 graduate of Texas Christian University and an alumnus of Delta Gamma Sorority. An outstanding student, Kim spent a semester of her senior year in a study abroad program in Australia. She was chosen by the faculty as the most outstanding student in the speech and communications department her senior year.

At Southwestern Baptist Seminary she was pursuing a master of divinity degree. Always outgoing, Kim had sung Christian songs all her life, loved Bible stories when she was young, and participated in many church plays and musicals. When Kim was in the sixth grade, she was baptized along with her brother, Tim, and her mother, Stephanie. Later, a very close friend was accidentally shot and killed by his own brother. Although Kim was not aware of it at the time, she realized years later that this event hardened her heart against God. As a university student Kim wrote, "I was raised in and out of church; however I really met Jesus when I was twenty years old. One night I went to a little church, got down on my knees, and cried out to the Lord. At that moment, I met Jesus, and he changed everything about me."

According to her mother, "Kim reached a point where she could no longer handle it alone and she turned it all over to Jesus. Kim believed you could not be a Christian unless you were 100 percent committed to Jesus." As evidence of this total commitment to her Lord, the last entry in Kim's journal was, "I don't want to ever lose the passion of being TOTALLY in love with You & You alone! God, please continue to stir my heart, make me passionate for you now and always."

Kim loved her family. She and her brother were

especially close and so often hugged that strangers would ask if they were dating. From January to April 1999, Kim served as youth director for a Baptist church in Hoensbroek, The Netherlands, through the Southern Baptist International Mission Board. After serving as a youth minister in the Middle East in the summer of 1999, Kim enrolled in Southwestern Seminary so she would be better prepared to serve the Lord wherever He wanted her and through whatever means He made available.

On her dorm room door were the following words from Romans 12:9-10: "Love must be sincere. Hate what is evil. Cling to what is good. Be devoted to one another in brotherly love."

Steggy Ray

Justin "Steggy" Ray was born in Amarillo, Texas, in 1982 and was a student at Cassata High School and Learning Center. A devoted member of Boy Scout Troop 613, Steggy was elected into the Order of the Arrow, a group for those deemed the most trustworthy, helpful, and courteous. Steggy was also a Cub Scout counselor who had only recently begun to get his life's direction in focus after struggling for two years. In the self-paced environment of Cassata, Steggy had blossomed, according to his teachers.

A member of Westcliff United Methodist Church, Steggy had been baptized there as a first grader and confirmed as a sixth grader. More recently, Steggy had been actively involved with the youth group at Wedgwood and, according to his mother, "would probably have joined there by Christmas."

After a minor run-in with the law, Justin had been assigned to community service and because he had been doing volunteer work since his elementary school days, he loved every minute of it. Partly due to his grandfather's recent bout with cancer, Justin had begun to pray more and was growing spiritually. As to his life's purpose, his mother commented, "The first day Justin walked into media tech class, he knew what he wanted to do the rest of his life." According to Laurie Gayle in Southwest High School's *Raiders' Review:*

> At Southwest Steggy found an outlet for his interests and talents through SHS productions. He loved it so much that he eventually set up a production company with a close friend and had hoped to become a media technology teacher later on in life. Even after he transferred to Cassata Learning Center, he came back to Southwest to help with various production shoots and visit old friends. He planned to graduate in December and was excited about where his life was headed. The eleven hundred people that came to mourn him did so because

at some point in their lives he had made a difference.

Known for his honesty, Steggy was once asked during a job interview at Office Max why he wanted the job. His answer was, "So I can get a car."

Two weeks before his death, Steggy had written for a school assignment, "Maturity is being able to handle adult matters without being childish. It's being able to ignore people who disrupt class and other gatherings with stupid remarks just to get a laugh out of someone. Maturity is being responsible and able to have a goal and work hard."

A Result of Martyrdom

What will be the result of these deaths? Tertullian, a prominent Latin writer in the second century, wrote in his *Apologeticus,* "The blood of the martyrs is the seed of the church." Reports have indicated that already hundreds, perhaps thousands, of people have placed their faith in Jesus Christ because of the martyrdom of these seven believers. As measured by the kingdom of God, their deaths have not been in vain.

Funeral services were characterized by warm, personal touches.

Photo by James Morris.

6

Saying Goodbye on a Saturday Afternoon

"Joy Comes in the Morning" (Psalm 30:5)

Prior to Saturday, September 18, 1999, most of those affected by the Wedgwood shootings had never attended the funeral of a martyr, one killed as he or she worshiped or prepared to worship in God's house. Before the weekend was over, there would be seven such funerals, four on Saturday afternoon.

While Christians and non-Christians go through the same valley of the shadow of death, there is a marked difference in their funerals. Christians live and die with the blessed hope of an eternity with God in heaven. No matter how dark the night, the believer can express with the psalmist, "Weeping may endure for a night, but joy comes in the morning." The following excerpts from the funerals of four Christians give testimony to the hope and joy of the eternal morning.

The Funeral for Shawn Brown

Shawn's funeral was at noon Saturday at Truett Auditorium of Southwestern Baptist Theological Seminary.

Ken Hemphill: Father, we pray that all honor and glory would go to You even as it has in Shawn's life and as it will in his death. Father, we seek Your comfort today. We grieve. We sense a tremendous loss to this family, to this seminary family, to the work of ministry around the globe that could have been a part of the future of Shawn's life. We thank you, Lord, for the assurance of God's Word that to be absent from the body is to be present with the Lord, and we rejoice in Shawn's home going. We pray that as he led many to Christ in his life, so there would be many more through his death. In Jesus' name, amen.

Kathy Jo Brown: Thank you so much for being here today. I need to tell you a little bit about Shawn. I loved being Shawn Brown's wife. We had a marriage based on God, and we often said we felt as if we were living a dream. We were a team. He was my best friend, and I am so thankful for good memories and no regrets.

Shawn loved Jesus and he loved people. Shawn's heart's desire was to know Christ and to make him known. He loved youth and our precious sixth grade Sunday school class. He also loved children like my first graders. And he loved adults—the senior adults at New Horizons where he worked downtown. We had reflected in the past couple of days about one particular experience he had leading an elderly woman to Christ. We are confident that Shawn and that woman are together today. She died two days after he led her to the Lord.

He also wanted to share that Jesus never changes. The last month, Shawn had been impressed with the idea that no matter how many horrible things are happening in this world Jesus is constant. If you don't know Christ, Shawn prayed for you. And his passion was that you know Him.

John Roland: Shawn was my partner for accountability and someone I dreamed of being on staff with. He and Kathy live next door to us, and Kathy is one of Becky's closest friends. Shawn told me numerous times about his favorite quote, which is from the movie, "Braveheart." The quote says, "All men die; but few really will live." Shawn Brown really lived. He lived a life of purpose, of passion, of meaning. He had such a passion and love of all people. He changed my life in the two years I have known him.

Dan Baiz: One of the many things that I loved about Shawn was his enduring, childlike qualities; for example, his almost mischievous rapid-fire giggle that made you realize he was totally and completely delighted. Shawn had such a fervor for life, soaking up and enjoying it all. Shawn was also energetic and a hard worker. He had a teachable spirit. I remember we got to go to the symphony one time. I was expecting to find that he would not have any interest in the music and would become quickly bored. Shortly after the music began, I looked over at him, seeing him enthralled with all the sounds, almost captivated, with a big smile on his face as he intently listened.

He also learned early on not to seek after greatness. Last night in a television interview, Kathy Jo said that the quote that he loved which I will paraphrase from Dietrich Bonhoeffer was that greatness is like a shadow. If you run toward it, you'll never catch it. If you walk away from it, it will always follow you.

Emmett Corker: I was Shawn's youth minister during his senior high year at Hillcrest Baptist Church, San Angelo. I've thought about Shawn Brown and some of the things he loved. He loved burritos. When he was serving as an intern at Hillcrest, we would go eat at Taco Bell and he would always order the seven-layer burrito, and I would ask him, "Shawn, is that all you ever eat?" He'd say, "It's all I ever need."

Shawn loved baseball. I got to watch him play in high school and college. Shawn loved his brothers in Christ. I suspect if I were to ask you to raise your hands, many of you would raise your hands and say he was a brother of yours. Shawn loved his baby, Kathy Jo. I had the privilege of doing their wedding, and I don't think I've ever in my life seen a young couple as much in love as those two were. Shawn also loved his Bible. I had a chance to see him grow in his faith.

Al Meredith: Today we stand and overlook the casket of a young man whose life held so much potential, so much hope, so much promise. His wife is left without the love of her life. Death is obscene. Death is awful. As I walked back into that church, saw the havoc that the Prince of Darkness, the Destroyer had wrought, I thought how obscene! I want to take you to a place today where death was never more obscene. Two thousand years ago a man was cruelly nailed to a cross while His tormentors howled. He was beaten to where you couldn't recognize Him; stripped naked and lifted up on that cross for a laughing, mocking world, not to mention all the powers of the darkness and the scum from the walls of hell taunting him. And He died in agony, crying for something to quench His thirst. No wonder the sun refused to shine. Obscene. Hopeless.

But I am here to tell you our God is a God of all hope and all comfort. And he proved that by taking the death of His own Son and turning it into the triumph that has brought hope to every one of us. Through this we have hope for this life, meaning and purpose, and a hope that cannot be shaken by death because of the promise that one who lives and believes in Jesus Christ shall never die.

Don't expect and expend too much energy trying to understand what went on at Wedgwood Baptist Church the other night. I can't explain it. Don't try to second-guess God. Focus on Him. Please understand this: We are not in the land of the living headed towards the land of the dying. We are in the land of the dying going to the land of the living. When you were born, you were squalling your head off and everybody was happy. So live your life so that when you die, everybody is squalling their heads off and you are rejoicing. Shawn is rejoicing today in the presence of the Lord.

The Funeral Service for Kimberly Jones

Kim's funeral was at 2:00 P.M at Gambrell Street Baptist Church in Fort Worth.

Ken Hemphill: Kim was one of those people everybody knew and loved, even though she had only been at Southwestern a short time. My greatest claim to fame now from her family is that after hearing me preach in an opening chapel service, she called her folks and said, "Listen, I think the president loves Jesus as much as I do." That's a wonderful word.

Revelation 12: 10-11 (NASB) tells us, "Now the salvation, and the power, and the kingdom of our God and the authority of His Christ have come, for the accuser of the brethren has been thrown down, who accuses them before our God, day and night. And they overcame him because of the blood of the Lamb."

Dax Hughes: Father, we come today, proclaiming your goodness. Lord I thank you for the life and testimony of Kim Jones. How it has penetrated us, affected us, brought us closer to your throne. Lord, I thank you that we do not have to live only by our circumstances, but that we have hope in you. I know that Kim will be happy, Lord, that you are going to bring goodness and that you are going to be glorified—Kim's one desire. Lord, she is with you now. She is rejoicing. While we grieve, we rejoice. Thank you for your servant. It's in the precious name of Jesus that we pray, amen.

Al Meredith: I knew Kim Jones for the last two years. She was converted through a college Bible study, through friends witnessing to her. Most of us come to know Christ and then the process of sanctification is gradual as His grace works out in us. But with a few, it's as if that process of sanctification is instantaneous. Kim came to know Christ and was filled with the Spirit the next moment. I never saw her but what her face wasn't beaming beyond description. She longed to impart the joy that God had given her to those around her. One of the reporters asked me on the street the other day, why is it that when these things happen it seems the best are always chosen? I don't have an answer for that. I can't think of people more crucial to our ministry and to the kingdom of God than these. Kim was so supportive. She'd light up a room when she walked in. She'd light up my heart. You never shook Kim's hand. She just hugged. She had a passion for Christ and for people. That was what she was training for. She'd already done ministry and realized she needed some more training

Of all the wonderful things we could say about Kim, the most critical thing, the only thing that counts today, is that a few years ago, as a co-ed at college she recognized what a hopeless, helpless person she was. She cast her life on Jesus Christ, who died for her, and Christ transformed her life, and that alone makes all the difference today.

You read in the paper that Kim Jones died several days ago. Don't believe it. She is not dead. She lives today. These are her remains. And this stuff doesn't matter. She was a nut. When you go to the ballpark, and your boyfriend buys you some peanuts, what do you do with the shell? You throw it away. In a few moments, you are going to go to a graveyard, and everything there will say this is the end, this is final. Don't you believe it. The devil is going to whisper in your ear, "That's Kim you are lowering in the ground." Don't you believe it. That's just the shell. The nut has gone on.

Stephane Jones: Kim would want to say, "I love you. Thank you for coming." I don't know a lot of you, but a lot of you touched her life. As you know, we live in Saudi Arabia, and one of the hardest things for a mom is to be away from her kids. And so, I prayed a lot. And I prayed, "Lord I can't be there, so You are going to have to bring people into her life to take my place." And He was faithful.

Kim told me this summer, "Mom, can you wait to see Jesus?" And I said, "Kim, I can wait." And she said, "Well, I can't. I can't wait. I'll be so excited to see Jesus."* And so, she is there, and she is rejoicing. This is only a journey here, and she would tell you that this is not our home. Thank you.

Clyde Glazener: Father, we do thank You. We can never thank You appropriately, adequately, but we want to do so. We thank You dear God for calling us into being, for the gift of life. Thank You dear God for choosing to give us that gift. And thank You dear Lord, that in our rebellion, You kept on loving us. So much that You sent the Lord Christ to die for our sins. We thank You dear Lord for the assurance, the victory, the celebration that's ours when we come to this time of transition for one who has been promoted to the Father's house and who knew Jesus as Lord and Savior. Our Father we thank You for the life of Kim. We thank You for the input into our identity that she had. We thank You for the confidence we have that she is in Your Presence. In Jesus' name, amen.

The Funeral Service for Sydney Browning

Sydney's funeral took place at 4:00 P.M. in Truett Auditorium, Southwestern Baptist Seminary.

---

*A 12-minute video of Kim's testimony is available from Student Discipleship Ministries, 800-880-8736.

Ken Hemphill: We have had a long-standing tradition at Southwestern Seminary in the first chapel of the year. Perhaps no one could do it as well as our president emeritus who is now gone on to be with the Lord, but Dr. Robert Naylor would always declare our new students "Southwesterners." He would tell the students of the great history and heritage of this institution. He would tell them that there had been those who had gone before them, those who had given their life for the faith—martyrs who died on the foreign fields. Then he would end his statement with a sobering reminder that someone would rather die than bring shame to the name Southwesterner. I want to say to you today that Sydney Browning, one of our wonderful alumni, brought honor to the name Southwesterner. And more importantly, she brought glory to the precious name of her Savior.

Brett Cooper: As we've been talking with so many old friends, it occurred to me how Sydney would dearly love to see all these friends and how she would love to dispense a little bit of that unique Sydney wisdom to all of you. She would be gloating to the point we could hardly stand her if she could see how many people showed up today. We have been heartbroken all week over the fact that someone who was so dear lost her life at so young an age. But isn't it a wonderful thing to look around this auditorium and see the impact that God made through this wonderful lady in just thirty-six years?

We are here today to remember and to celebrate the life of Sydney Browning, and celebrate is the operative term for what we want to do here. Yes, we do mourn. We grieve and we cry today. That's as it should be and frankly as it needs to be. That's part of the process that helps us with this. But as we go through the mourning, there are some other things that we need to do here today. We're not going to understand the tragedy that befell us on Wednesday night, but there is one thing that we can do—we can understand that the tragedy is ours; it's not Sydney's. Sydney has gone home to be with the Lord that she served so faithfully. She has never had it so good as she has it right now, and we're going to see her again one of these days.

There's something else that we hope to establish through what we do as we meet here today. Let's remember from this point on how Sydney lived her life rather than how she left it. It's rather ironic that the one thing that got Sydney on CNN was one of the least remarkable things about her life. The way she lived her life—the joy, the laughter, so much that she brought into our lives that made them immeasurably richer—that's what we should remember Sydney for.

We have an adversary as we well know. And he would have us focus today on death and darkness. But we have news for him today. We serve an almighty God of life and light. We serve a God of joy and peace beyond understanding. This, make no mistake about it, is a very dark hour. But the light of Jesus Christ shown very brightly through my friend Sydney Browning. And it continues to shine brightly, maybe even more so, in her passing, and the darkness will not overcome it.

Raymond Scott: Father God we've joined together here today to honor and remember Sydney Browning. Each of us was deeply and indelibly changed by the humor in her heart, the touch of her teaching hand, the outpouring of obedience to your church that she loved so dearly. This day and more days to come bring hurt, sorrow and grief, though we do not grieve as those without hope. But we know and we are convinced that nothing can separate us from your love. Jesus, mend our hearts as only you can. Holy Spirit, unify us in this time of adversity. Father God, find some time for Sydney because I know she's got some questions. We pray this in your Son's name, amen.

Shannon Carter: I just want to bring honor to God today as my sister did. I'm sure I'm surprising her because she never thought I would do this. But I do want to share some things that I found just in her apartment in these last couple of days that I think show Sydney's intimacy with her God and with those whom she loved. Selfishly, the first thing is a letter that I had written, dated September 14, and obviously she didn't get it. And I really wanted her to because I was trying to finally sit down and take the time to tell her some of the things I felt about her. So I feel compelled now to read it in her honor.

Thank you for sending those tapes (of Brother Al's sermons). You knew that one on grappling with guilt would be so good for me. I wept. I felt free. Thank you for loving me and praying for me and lifting me up spiritually. You have done so much for my walk with the Lord. Thank you for being that kind of sister. I bow in my heart in true thankfulness to the Lord for you and who you are. I'm so proud of you, and I'm so happy that the Lord has given you good friends and a good church and a pastor and a place to serve and a job that uses your specific talents and personality. God is so good.

This may sound funny, but I want to go on record saying that I'm especially proud of you in a world where singles are sometimes misunderstood or stereotyped. You have risen above the prejudice to be the woman God made you. You're accepting of that and being who you are and having a wonderful influence in the lives of many people. I guess I say this because I know that indirectly you may often feel people think that you are not quite whole yet or whatever. But I do not think that and forgive me if I have or will ever make you feel that way. You are not unfinished to me. You are a life yielded to God, doing what He wants you to do. Oh, if we could all be that way more. Thanks for being an important and wonderful part of our family.

Sydney was very spiritual, but she was very real, and she lived in the real world. She loved God's Word and she loved the Lord. It was evident that she knew the hope and peace that made her life complete. I always believed that she felt she was tasting heaven in the real world, and I know that she would love every man, woman, boy, and girl to experience that same joy right now.

Al Meredith: We gather today to celebrate the home going of Sydney Browning. Sydney defined the concept of faithfulness. In a generation where faithfulness is unheard of, she was rock solid. You could count on Sydney. She defined commitment. If you ever wanted a tithing testimony, Sydney was there. Faithfulness in prayer and attendance? "What do you mean," she'd ask, "that Sunday is your only day off? It's the Lord's Day. What are you doing skipping Sunday night church?" She knew and loved the Lord. And God says "precious in the sight of the Lord is the death of His saints" (Ps. 116:15).

You might have read in the paper this week that Sydney Browning died Wednesday night. Don't you believe it! This is not Sydney. These are the remains. This is the stuff that was pumped with caffeine and couldn't sleep at night and couldn't stand still and had to sing all the time. This is not Sydney. "Absent from the body, present with the Lord." When that gunman thought he was doing her in, he was giving her wings. She flew away—her spirit, her soul. And the stuff that's left is unimportant.

Sydney loved. She loved her kids in the choir. I don't know who came up with TBCCINT. I think I just said it once when I was trying to get folks to be sure to come to the evening worship service. "You're going to hear The Best Children's Choir in North Texas." So T-shirts started coming out "TBCCINT—The Best Children's Choir in North Texas." She loved her kids. She loved the senior adults. She loved her students that she taught. She poured her heart into those kids. She would give me their names and tell me to pray for so-and-so and, oh, this one is so lost and I don't know how we can reach him, and this one is about to slip over the edge. She would tell me horror stories and yet she was right there.

We have a logo that some genius designed long before I got to Wedgwood. You see it on our litera-ture. It is a heart and it's the word *be-loved.* Join God's family and be loved. We're the beloved ones of God. Sydney was a wonderful, godly, precious, be-loved Wedgie. Sydney was one of the best of us.

The Funeral Service for Justin "Steggy" Ray

Steggy's service took place at 2:00 P.M. at Westcliff United Methodist Church, Fort Worth.

Ruth Huber-Rohlfs: Dear family and many, many friends who have gathered here, we've come to praise God and to witness to our faith as we celebrate the life of Justin Michael Stegner Ray. We come together in grief acknowledging our human need. May God grant us grace and in pain might we find comfort; in sorrow, hope; and in death, resurrection.

Matt Henson: Justin and I had a production studio together; we had just started it. It was what Justin loved most of all besides his mom and grandmother. I was one of Justin's many best friends, and he had a lot. He was always there to care about people, always watched over people. I know we're all going to miss him a lot. One thing to think about is that the next thunderstorm we have, we'll know it's going to be him running lights and sounds.

Bree Simonson: I was one of Justin's friends as well as many of you are. I was lucky enough to get to grow up with Justin. I was blessed to play with him in elementary school, socialize with him in middle school, and watch him become the man who he would have become. He told me numerous times that he was happy with the way his life was going, and he was so happy to be graduating in December. He brought much to everybody's life that he touched. The thing I learned the most from Justin was to never take life seriously. He taught me to laugh at things that made me cry; to always wear a smile; and to live life to the fullest. I'm glad to say that Justin lived his life to the fullest one can when it is cut off at seventeen. I am more proud to know that he will be waiting for me on the other side. I'll see you in sixty or seventy years Justin.

Tim Hood: Today we're here to remember Justin—"Steggy" as a lot of us remember him. I remember a young, skinny, redheaded kid walking into production class. He had so many dreams about what he wanted to do. He was great at video, but we all know his love was audio. Anything that could make a sound or mix a sound he would get hold of, and he loved it. Every time he got a new piece of equipment, he'd carry it around with him. He'd be carrying it around saying, "Look what I got." His talent for fixing things was phenomenal. Many times we crawled in and out of dumpsters looking for stuff. He said, "Hey, this place is throwing some stuff away, man, let's go over there." So we'd go and look for stuff and have to bring it home late at night when Judy wasn't there. Sometimes, he'd brag about it and say, "Hey, it lights up! It doesn't do anything but it lights up!"

If you needed him to carry out a favor or a job, he would complete it. He was responsible way beyond his years. I could count on him for anything I'd ask him to do.

We went on a choir tour this summer with the Wedgwood youth. He had a blast; he really did. He was my right hand and my support, and I appreciate your letting him go with us. It was just incredible.

We had some great talks on that trip, just he and I. He enjoyed being part of the Wedgwood group; he said he felt as if he'd been a part of them since he was growing up. We talked about decisions and commitments he made in this very church. His servant attitude had become more and more apparent throughout that trip and throughout that summer when we got back. He wasn't the same skinny, red-headed kid that had been in production class. He had blossomed into a mature young man. He had purpose and meaning in his life. He had put away old, childish things and become a young adult and embraced life. He had a change in his life, and I knew he had made peace with God.

Charles Hundley: What do you say about a young man named Steggy? What do you say when Jesus says, "love one another as I have loved you"? It seems to me that you might say that's what Steggy did. He loved us unconditionally, accepting us just as we were even when we were the weird ones. Justin loved us. Take just a moment, in your mind, in your heart, and remember some of Justin's acts of love. You remember that smile? That smile appeared out of nowhere, and that smile was for everyone. He was a servant to everyone, to anyone, at any time.

He loved each of you with a passion. He cared deeply for each of you. Something else—Justin's joy is now complete because he heard the call of God on his life. And he answered that call, he said, "Here

I am. What may I do?" And God spoke to him in his heart of ways that Justin could serve other people.

Justin has a new name. He had trouble with his name, it seems, when he went to get his driver's license. He thought he could just make it Justin Stegner and they said no, it's got to be Justin Michael Ray. A lot of us have different names, name changes. But what I want to leave you with is this: Justin heard God say, "I've called you by a new name and it is my child, my son." And so Justin is now with God the Father, celebrating for all eternity the fullness of what it means to be a child of God.

On Wednesday night, Justin was doing what he loved so much, serving God in a way that his gifts and talents just meshed together. God was there, and he is with God right now. But you need to know this: God is here, too, with us. And that is why we can really celebrate. Even with heavy hearts we can dare to shout, "Hallelujah." We can say, "Praise the Lord" because we know that God is with us and we can carry the memory of a life that was really lived well.

Steven Curtis Chapman and many other celebrities contributed to the Sunday memorial service at the stadium.

Photo by James Morris.

7

Sunday's Light

"As the First Day of the Week Began to Dawn" (Matt. 28:1)

On the Sunday morning following the greatest death known to mankind, our Lord Jesus Christ came out of His grave in resurrected form, offering humanity its greatest hope. "As the first day of the week began to dawn" (Matt. 28:1), great strength and encouragement was on the way for believers. In the hours immediately following Wedgwood's tragedy, Pastor Meredith voiced the hope that members could worship in their own buildings on Sunday morning. So, on Sunday, September 19, the members of Wedgwood were filled with anticipation of God's presence and power.

Early Sunday Morning

On Sunday morning more than two hundred church members met for prayer at 6:00 A.M. According to Kathy Holton, "We prayed over the whole building, but especially the sanctuary and areas where people were shot or injured."

Wedgwood member Aaron New wrote of those early hours:

> Walking into the auditorium that morning was extremely difficult. I prayed through my tears as I walked around the auditorium, lobby, and Sunday school classrooms. It was that morning that I began to feel for the first time an intense anger. I'm a Ph.D. student in psychology and counseling at Southwestern Seminary, so I was quite aware of the "normal" place of anger in grief and loss. However, this anger built up within me as thoughts ran through my head. "This guy walked into my church and shot and killed my spiritual family." It was then that God ministered to me very quietly yet very clearly. At no other time in my life have I felt so sure that the words of the Lord were echoing in my mind, "Aaron! This is my church. This is your family, but it is your family because it is my family." The peace that passes all understanding began to settle within me. I am sure God knows what sorrow we have all experienced because this terrible event took place at his church and to his family.

Jonathan Gardner, Wedgwood minister of music and worship, had arrived early that Sunday morning:

> As I walked into the building a few minutes after six o'clock, I felt God's presence in a mighty

way. In the worship center it was so strong you could almost touch it. The only way I know to explain it is that thousands of Christians had been praying for our Sunday morning services ever since Wednesday night, and God responded with His presence.

Entering the building, members walked under a banner that read, "Let the Healing Begin." Sunday school classes were turned into group therapy sessions led by trained counselors. Other counselors lined the hallways to assist those in need. Everywhere, there were signs of the intent to heal, and indeed the healing began as members shared their emotions with each other.

That Sunday morning, worshipers stepped on concrete floors where blood-stained carpet had been removed, and sat in pews that bore evidence of bullets. Draped over two chairs in the alto section of the choir were the white and maroon robes of Sydney Browning and Kim Jones. Their parents were in attendance. Matt Henson, who had lost his best friend Steggy Ray, went to the front of the church and spontaneously addressed the congregation urging them to speak out for the Christian faith and not let the deaths be in vain. As the tears flowed, the contribution of a local store was greatly appreciated. They donated hundreds of boxes of tissues.

At the conclusion of the Sunday morning services, seven people professed Jesus Christ as Savior and Lord while others came forward for prayer and counseling. Bob and Debbie Beckel, parents of Kristi, joined the church. During the second of two morning services, people laid hands on and prayed for the parents of Cassie Griffin. During the offertory, deacons laid hands on and prayed for Pastor Al Meredith.

The service itself was a familiar mix of traditional and contemporary music. Regardless of the song, the congregation stood spontaneously in affirmation, including the choir music "It is Well With My Soul." In the children's sermon, a specialty of Pastor Meredith, the object lesson was hard-boiled eggs and the story of Humpty Dumpty. "Our church," said Meredith, "has had a great fall, but unlike Humpty Dumpty, we know how to get up. What all the king's horses and all the king's men couldn't do, God can do. God can put us back together again."

A United Methodist church in Fort Worth sent fifteen people to Wedgwood that Sunday morning to cover the church's childcare needs so that no adult members would have to miss the service.

Some members of a church in Tulsa, Oklahoma, drove for five hours so they could walk around the church that Sunday and pray during the services.

Joanne Crawford was in the prayer meeting on Wednesday evening and passed two of the wounded on her way to warn the Girls' Auxiliary workers and to get her own granddaughter. On Sunday morning, four days after the shooting, a reporter put a micro-phone in front of her on her way out of the worship center. "Why were you here?" asked the reporter. Expressing the feelings of many Wedgwood members, Joanne replied, "This is my church. This is Sunday. I belong here."

The Perspective of the Building

One of the most interesting pieces of writing done by Wedgwood members in the days immediately following the shooting was by long-time member Warren K. Barber. How did the church building feel as Sunday approached? With Barber's permission, we include here "The Building":

> I stand on this corner as a lighthouse for this community. Whenever storm clouds rise and great turbulence threatens, anyone who is upon the raging waters can look to this light-house to guide them safely into my harbor of refuge. Throughout the last forty-one years, my doors have opened wide for those who are seeking refuge from the storms of life. You see, the Holy Spirit of God resides here within my walls. The peoples' hope and love come from God and His precious Son, Jesus. I am just a building, but a building where God's people congregate to worship the Risen Savior, Jesus. I

am just a building, but I serve here as a light-house, a refuge and a haven for people traveling down the pathway of life.

On Wednesday evening, September 15, 1999, I was doing what I do best—I was playing host as the people were meeting and drawing closer to God. I was so excited seeing all the happy faces as they worshiped the precious Savior, Jesus. Suddenly, shots rang out. Within minutes, a pipe bomb exploded and pandemonium reigned in my hallways, my rooms, and my sanctuary. Those who had come to seek refuge under my roof were screaming and running out of my doors. I was horrified as I looked down in total despair as I saw people dead and others crying out in pain.

Sirens screamed through the early evening dusk. Within moments the police, the firemen, the medics, and the emergency response teams were everywhere. I looked down and wanted to shout out, "This should not happen here—never ever here. This is a refuge, a haven. This is holy ground!"

Quickly, yellow police tape was placed all around me, and I was standing in complete and total loneliness. All of those whom I had grown so accustomed to seeing were gone. No longer did joy fill my hallways; no longer did joy fill my rooms; no longer did joy fill my sanctuary, and I cried bitter tears.

The next few days were hard for me. Cameramen were everywhere and as their cameras rolled, my face was splashed again and again all around the world. All I wanted was for the people to come back. I wanted to tell them that I can still be a lighthouse, a refuge. I can still be a haven.

During this time, I cried many tears. I cried for the families of those who died on my floors. I cried for those who were injured in my hallways. I cried for the young people who earlier in the day had so boldly met at the pole to pray and to stand up strong for prayer and faith. I cried for the police, the firemen, the medics, and the emergency response teams. I cried for our pastor and his family. I cried for our staff at Wedgwood and for their families. I cried for all the people who had come seeking refuge within my walls.

Soon, workers were ripping out my carpets and removing some of my pews. Seeing all of this, I could not help but wonder what was to become of me. I could hear the hushed whispers as reporters and others wondered, "Maybe this building really is not a strong tower. Maybe it really is not a refuge. Maybe it really is not a haven." I wanted to shout out, "I am still the same. I have just been violated."

During those first dark days, I must have sagged down a little under the weight of doubt and hopelessness. I looked out from my highest perch, up near where the cross stands atop my roof, and my eyes scanned the horizon searching for a glimpse of my fellow church buildings. Somehow they seemed to be standing taller. They even seemed to look stronger, and I think I saw them smiling at me. I could only surmise that they were telling me in their own way, "You must stand tall. You must stand strong for God's people. Wedgwood, you must always be a lighthouse for those in need."

About this same time, I happened to hear our pastor say, "We are not going to allow the kingdom of darkness to outshine the kingdom of Light." Then he continued, "We intend to hold services in this building Sunday morning." When I heard those words, I was happy and excited. "Hey, I am still going to be a lighthouse; I am still going to be a refuge; and I am still going to be a haven." Then I tried to stand a little straighter. I tried to stand a little taller and I smiled my brightest smile.

I could not help but wonder, however, after all of the bullets, all of the mayhem, and all of the pain, would God's people return to worship once again? Would they return to worship in my distressed, but beautiful, sanctuary?

I closed my eyes in prayer and I prayed. "Dear God, please send down your Holy Spirit to fill my rooms, to fill my hallways, and to flood my sanctuary. Lord God, I realize that I am only a building but I, too, humble myself before your awesome power. I pray, dear God, that you will send your Son, Jesus, down in power and glory to bring comfort and healing to your people, and they will love you. Your children will reaffirm that as for us and our house, we will serve God.

When I opened my eyes, I looked and I saw my church sign that had so boldly told the world my name, Wedgwood Baptist Church. All around my sign were beautiful flowers and many, many notes of love. The outpouring of love for those who had died and for those who are hurting was beautiful to behold.

Sunday dawned a beautiful day. At 6:00 A.M., I became excited when well over two hundred people came to pray. As I looked down, they were praying over the pews, over the chairs, over the pulpit, over the choir loft, over the organ, over the piano, over the orchestra, over my hallways, over my rooms, over my vestibule, and yes, even over the bullet holes.

I was still a little apprehensive, still afraid that God's people might think that I was no longer a safe haven. I was afraid that somehow they would think that I had let them down, that I was no longer a refuge. If only the people knew how I needed them under my roof once again. Oh, if I only had some beautiful chimes or some bells, I could ring out to call God's people home.

It was now about 8:00 A.M. and as I looked out once again, I saw cars coming from every direction. Praise be to God, the people are returning. I looked down, and I saw the children, I saw the young people, and I saw the families. They were coming. They did not care that I was not pretty. They did not care that my carpet was gone. They did not care that many of my pews were missing, and they did not even care that my walls had bullet holes. Then when I glanced down again, I saw the children, the young people, and the families all entering my sanctuary. Glory be to God, I am still a refuge, a haven, and a lighthouse for this community.

When I heard the singing and I heard the prayers, I lifted my eyes toward heaven and prayed, "Dear God, listen to your people singing and listen to your people praying."

I had heard the whispers that I was not going to be any good as a refuge, or as a haven, or as a lighthouse. Those whispers were wrong. God's people have returned and I know this for sure: Satan lost and God won. The poster is exactly right: Satan, the prince of darkness, shall never outshine Jesus, the King of Light! Not in my hallways, not in my rooms, and not in my sanctuary.

Sunday Afternoon

The community-wide memorial service on Sunday afternoon drew 15,200 people to the Amon Carter Football Stadium on the campus of Texas Christian University, including Texas Governor George W. Bush and Fort Worth Mayor Kenneth Barr. Outside the stadium stood fourteen horses and their riders, members of the Fort Worth mounted police. Near them sat Fort Worth Fire Department engines Q21 and Q26 with a large American flag hanging from their ladders.

Participating pastors brought this message to the multitude:

> As tragic as the deaths of these seven believers were, we know that the blood of martyrs is often the seed of revival. Since this tragic and dreadful night, students have found the eternal hope that only Christ can give. Many students have accepted Jesus Christ, and rumors of revival are already starting to be echoed in homes, schools, and churches. . . . While we will mourn with the families of the victims, we can rejoice as God takes what Satan meant for destruction and turns it into life. We can rejoice as we experience the comfort of knowing that one day in His courts is better than a thousand elsewhere. We know that when these seven believers were brought into His presence, He reached out with the most lov-

ing arms that exist and gave them life forever. We can be certain that He wiped away every tear, took away every hurt, and replaced every sorrow with the peace of His presence. We can be sure that they will never hurt again . . . for they are with God. . . . God never makes mistakes and He wastes nothing.

Don Browning stood in the ninety-five degree Texas sun to tell of the first solo his slain daughter, Sydney, ever sang: "When my daughter was six years old and in the first grade, she sang her first solo, 'This Little Light of Mine.' She didn't sing the Anglo version. She sang the song with an African-American flair." Browning then led the crowd in singing the same song.

Thanks was offered to the hundreds who assisted the victims of the tragedy—firefighters, police officers, medical technicians, school personnel, churches, businesses, and individuals. Media experts estimated that the program was viewed by approximately 200 million people worldwide.

Responses from Other Area Churches

The tragedy at Wedgwood affected many in the Dallas-Fort Worth metropolitan area, as evidenced by some of the comments and activities from other churches on this Sunday:

Alliance United Methodist Church, Fort Worth, Reverend Jerry P. Galloway: "A broken heart is not the same as a broken hope. This has been a heavy week for all of us. You can't be a living, breathing, healthy human person without being affected in some way by the horrific events that have taken place."

Pantego Bible Church, Arlington, Reverend Randy Frazee: "My son was crying in fear. I said, 'Well David, what do you think we should do? Do you think we should shut the doors because that would keep them out?' We decided that the church must remain open and welcoming to everyone."

Oak Cliff Bible Fellowship, Dallas, Reverend Tony T. Evans: "Our prayer has to be for those who lost loved ones in Fort Worth. Evil took place, and we sorrow hopefully, not hopelessly. You can't have enough policemen. Your trust has to be in the Lord."

Westminster Presbyterian Church, Fort Worth, Reverend Donald Hogg: "God gives hope to see beyond Wedgwood Baptist. God has led us to this place; He will lead us through this place. The good news is that we are not alone in life. We are not expected to do it all by ourselves. We can and will survive life with God's help."

University Christian Church, Fort Worth, Reverend Scott Colglazier: The entire worship service was dedicated to the memory of the shooting victims. A bell tolled once for each of those killed at Wedgwood.

First Baptist Church, Colleyville, Reverend Terry Washburn: The congregation joined hands and prayed in support of the victims' families and for the three Fort Worth police officers who were among the first on the scene at Wedgwood.

Sunday Night

By Sunday night, the worn, yet optimistic face of Pastor Meredith was as recognizable to TV audiences as many talk show hosts. Yet, unlike most of the hosts, Meredith's message was always one of hope. Whether on network news, CNN, *Larry King Live,* or some other media, the message was always one of hope and victory in the midst of tragedy. Jesus Christ was glorified through every media appearance. Light was shining in the darkness.

Memorials to all who died were left at the church.

Photo by James Morris.

8

Three Monday Funerals

*"Blessed Are the Dead Who Die
in the Lord" (Rev. 14:13)*

There is always grief and shock when a young life is brought to an unexpected end. People talk of what life might have held for them if they had lived. Yet Jesus makes no distinction as to the age of death when He proclaims from Heaven, "Blessed are the dead who die in the Lord" (Rev. 14:13). It is true, we do not know what future these young dead would have had, but we do know that because they died in the Lord, they were and are blessed.

The Funeral Service for Kristi Beckel

Kristi's friends and family gathered at 10:30 A.M. at Bethesda Community Church in Fort Worth.

Al Meredith: Lord Jesus, it is true that you alone are worthy of our worship and our praise. We lift up and magnify the name of Jesus on this dark day. We claim the victory that was won when you conquered sin and death and hell two thousand years ago. Though we grieve today, Lord, it is not as those that have no hope. We worship and magnify and praise the Lord Jesus Christ today. As Kristi tried to do in her life, so we will do in her death. And on this day especially, this memorial day, Lord Jesus, be honored, amen.

On behalf of the family I want to express my sincerest thanks and gratitude to you for coming today. This is not an easy thing to do. They are grateful for all the support that they have received, for the prayers, and words of kindness. This is how the body of Christ works. Those of us who have been comforted try to comfort others in their sorrow and loss. That is why we need each other. None of us ever expect to bury our children. Kristi's two grandmothers are burying their grandchild.

Kristi had a tender heart. She was easily disciplined. All Mom had to do was look crossways at her and she would break into tears. She loved her friends. She was a giver. She had a contagious laugh. You know how it goes: she starts laughing, you start laughing, and you don't know what it was about but she made you laugh. She watched her favorite "I Love Lucy" shows so often that she would memorize them. She would mouth the words as they said them. She loved to sing in choirs. She was a volleyball player who loved her friends, loved her life, and her Lord.

Today, we celebrate her homecoming, though in our schedule it seems out of time. There must have been some mistake. I encourage you to do what I have to do almost daily. That is to resign your position as general manager of the universe and let God be God.

We grieve today, but not as those who have no hope. We grieve with hope and even a tinge of joy. We don't mourn. We are not crying for Kristi; she is with the Lord. She can spike every ball that comes over the net now. She can sing bass if she wants to and first soprano. Her joy is unspeakable. She is with Him. Let's rejoice and praise our Savior that makes it all happen.

Vicki Vaughn: Kristi was a model student. She was a member of the National Junior Honor Society. Her favorite flower was the pink rose. Her favorite color was purple. You have already heard that Kristi loved volleyball. She loved her friends, her family. It has been said that every night Kristi would go into her parents' bedroom and say, "Goodnight, I love you." And then she would leave their room and go into hers and shout through the walls, "Goodnight, I love you."

When we consider Kristi's life, let's consider a tapestry that she has woven. Woven into the tapestry are simple but significant letters: JESUS. We will start with the letter J. I see this color as yellow. It stands for joyful. Joy is the emotion expressed by well being. Kristi was happy. All was well with her. The next letter in her tapestry is E. I see this color as green, because she was an encourager. 1 Thessalonians 5:11 asks us to encourage one another and build up one another. The third letter in her tapestry is S. I see this color as purple, her favorite color. It stands for servant. Kristi gave of herself to others—not only in life but also in death. The fourth letter is U. It is white and it stands for upright. Kristi's character exemplified Christ. She walked in the way of the Lord. The final letter is S. I see it as golden in color and it stands for smile. Proverbs 15:13 says, "A joyful heart makes a cheerful face." Her effervescent smile brought warmth and acceptance to all around her. Her life was and is a tapestry. It is beautiful and rich in design. It reflected and reflects Jesus. Kristi lived up to her name, Christlike, follower of Christ. Kristi was truly an ambassador for Christ.

Al Meredith: Of all the wonderful things that we could say about Kristi, the most critical fact is that when she was a nine-year-old girl after talking long with her mom and dad she gave her life to Jesus Christ as her Savior and Lord. She realized no matter how tender her heart was, no matter how simple and seemingly sinless her life was, she was still born in sin and self-centeredness and was in need of a Savior. The only one who qualified was Jesus Christ. So by simple faith, she turned from her sin and gave her life to Christ. That is why we have hope and that is why we have joy. We don't weep for her; she is with the Lord.

God provides grace to us for salvation, for living in the light of these dark days. God also provides peace for us. You need to understand that peace does not mean the absence of conflict.

It is wonderful to be a Christian. It is an abundant life. But if God should allow anyone or anything to take us from this life, to die is gain. And that is what gives us peace—not that God is going to remove all conflict from life, but that He gives us peace and confidence amid the storm.

The Funeral Service for Joseph Daniel "Joey" Ennis

Joey's service took place at 3:00 P.M. at First Baptist Church, White Settlement.

Jim Gatliff: Our heavenly Father, even though we have come to this place willingly, there is not a single one among us who comes here by choice. Father, we come here compelled to be here by the circumstances that we have faced at the loss of our beloved friend, Joey. Father, there is not a single person here who, if he or she had the wherewithal to do it, wouldn't rewind the tapes of time and eternity and go back to Wednesday night and stop the outcome that has brought us here. But Father, that is not within our powers. Father, we come here as broken people. We come here as helpless people. We come asking you just to do a few things here in this place today. Father above all else we pray that you would wrap your arms of compassion around this sweet family. I pray that you would give them the grace that they need to withstand not only this hour but the days that lie ahead. Father, I would pray, that above all else that you would somehow, in your grace, put the minds at ease of Joey's friends that are asking questions that are impossible to answer. Lord Jesus, we ask that you would be glorified here in this place by every word that is said and by every song that is sung. We ask all these things for Jesus' sake, amen.

Jason Ferguson: Today we are here to remember and honor Joey Ennis. I would like to take this time to share a few thoughts and reflections about Joey. Joey was your typical fourteen year old when it came to participation in youth Bible studies. But as the months and days went on, he began to tap into the studies and apply them to his life. He would come to me after a session and talk about what he had learned and would tell me he would try to act better the next time. And Joey did just that. It was an honor and a pleasure to teach Joey about the Bible because he wanted it, and he talked about it. Joey, we'll miss you. We know you can't be with us physically, yet we know that the memories we have of you will forever be etched in our hearts and minds. We will never forget you, Joey. We love you. Donna, thank you for letting your son attend this church and for the opportunity to meet him and get to know him.

Chris Belsher: I am just going to speak from my heart. Joey was my cousin, and I spent a lot of time with him. I appreciate everything you in this church have done. You have sat with my Aunt Donna and comforted her in her time of need. And now you're helping my family through this. I see everyone out there, and I see people of different races, and I wish that some way, besides this tragedy, they could have come together.

Just because this happened to my cousin, I don't think any one of you should ever stop attending your church. Even though, if I had never brought him to church, this might never have happened, I am still glad I brought him so he had the chance to get closer to God and to know Him better. We lost something last Wednesday, my family and his friends and everyone else. But we also gained the strength of our community and it has brought us more together than ever.

He was my cousin, my friend, and he felt like a brother. No matter how many times we fought, we could still make each other laugh. We just had fun together. I'll see you later, Joey. Bye.

Jim Gatliff: Joey got here early Wednesday night. He came early to play basketball. He was running around downstairs in our fellowship hall where some of you who are listening are seated now. I saw him there. He said, "Hi Pastor." Little did I know, and little did you know that the last time you saw him would be the last time.

To those of you who were his friends, he was the one who kept his promises. He was the one who was trustworthy. He was the one who had an outrageous sense of humor. My heart goes out to you. I know the sense of loss that you feel. Those of you students here, collectively, you will never be the same again.

What can I say to Donna, his mother? I could talk about heaven until I could talk no longer. I could talk about love and hope. I could talk about faith, and not a single one of those words would fill the void that is inside because Joey in so many ways was all that you had. But the one thing that I can share with you, his dear mother, is that God knows how you feel. He does. He saw his only son die on the cross. In that moment in time, as the Father in heaven looked down on his son on Calvary, he understood exactly how you feel. He has promised in his Word to give a compassionate comfort, a loving comfort, not just in words, not just in ideas and thoughts, but in His presence. And He has promised in his Word that He, Himself, can fill the void, the emptiness, that is left by the loss of this sweet son.

What can I say that somehow gives an answer to the questions that you are asking? Why did all of this take place? Neither Joey nor any of the other victims of that crime were victims because they were good or bad, or because they were in church or even because they were Christians. Satan knows that it is just a matter of time until he is ultimately and totally defeated. It has been often said that the blood of martyrs is the seed of the church. In every sense of that word, a trail of innocent blood that began in Genesis and flows through Calvary came to Wedgwood Baptist Church last Wednesday night.

Our heavenly Father, we thank you for the life of Joey Ennis. And Father, I thank you that not one, not two, but dozens of his fellow students already this week have accepted Jesus Christ as their personal Savior. Father, I pray that the torch has been passed to this family, to this school, these students, and to this community, the very light of Christ, that we would carry it proudly and powerfully, by your grace, to the ends of the earth. For Jesus' sake, we pray these things, amen.

The Funeral Service for Cassandra "Cassie" Griffin

The gathering for Cassie took place at 2:00 P.M. at Wedgwood Baptist Church.

Ronald Guest: Our Father God, our minds are filled with hope, hope that you have fulfilled your promise to Cassie; that you, Lord, have come again and taken her to be where you are. How our hearts rejoice in your faithfulness and your steadfast love for her and for us also. Father, our hearts are also saddened because she is not with us. We are already missing her—her smile, her conversation, her creativity. We are missing the way that she loved you. And Father, we find it hard for our spirits to rejoice totally. So, Father, we call on you in our time of sadness to strengthen our lives, to strengthen our hearts this day. You are our only hope, in Jesus' name, amen.

Don Robertson: Heaven is real. It is a good place. It is not very far away. For some reason, unknown to us, God has chosen to take back Cassie to be with Him in heaven. But Cassie's life is not over, although we certainly were ill prepared to have it taken from us. Our faith embraces the concept of something that eyes have not seen, ears have not heard, which has never entered into the imagination of man. As you know, she died at the age of fourteen on Wednesday, just a few feet from where her casket is placed today. I had the privilege of baptizing Cassie as a seven year old in June 1992. She impressed me with her ability to carry on conversations with adults even in her younger, grade school years. She was pensive and thoughtful, fluently verbal. She took the initiative to start relationships and keep them current. She was loving, warm, strong, and like a sister to my own daughter, Alesha. I baptized Alesha on the same day I baptized Cassie. They were the same grade in school and for that reason, the parsonage at College Heights Baptist Church was familiar territory to Cassie, and the Griffin family was familiar territory to Alesha. Cassie's commitment to Christ was genuine. She matured greatly in her faith after moving to Fort Worth. She also became an outspoken witness for her Lord. There are many in this room no doubt who have been helped in their life of faith by this young lady whose body lies before us but whose spirit lives on. The fact that Cassie became that kind of witness is no surprise to us who knew her well in her younger years. She was a Christian soldier, killed in the line of duty. Jesus died for her. She died for Him.

Kristen Dickens: Anybody who knew Cassie as well as I did knows that she was and still is a compassionate person who loved life to its fullest and was kind to anyone who crossed her path. Every time she saw that one of her friends was sad, alone, or angry, or maybe all three, she would always find a way to make them smile, to get them in a better mood. She would always keep trying until they would crack a smile. Cassie made friends everywhere. She always had people around her. She was so loved. She loved life. You just don't know what a special angel she was. I love her casket because it has the cross where Jesus was crucified and the other two who were crucified with Him and the clouds around it. It makes it look like she is in heaven, and she is.

Christina Charpia: The role Cassie took when she was here on earth was the role of an angel. Whenever I had problems, she was always deeply concerned and affectionately involved. She would put everything aside and try to make me feel as though I could work out my problems. She prayed all the time for people that she knew were going through a rough time. When I would cry, either in front of her or on the phone, she would always cry, too. This sweet angel who is in heaven will never be forgotten because I saw how great she was when she was with us. I want to be more like her.

Jay Fannin: Each time I got to be before the youth group, which was usually every week, I could always look out and see these big eyes looking back at me, the eyes of Cassie Griffin. And every time I have thought about her over the last couple of days, the eyes are what I remember—the way I could look at her and know that she was so happy. She was not the most vocal person in the youth group, but she was always there. She was so faithful to all the activities that we had. For the last couple of days, thinking about Cassie, I have heard her louder than I have ever heard her, saying to her friends: "Be sure you are going to heaven when you die." She loved Jesus, and she wanted to make sure that her friends knew Him.

Al Meredith: That first morning when the press stuffed the microphones in my face, someone asked, "Where is God in all this?" I remember saying, "God is right here. He is at the same place He was when His own dear Son lay hanging from the cross." He is here. He weeps with us. He mourns with us. He groans in His spirit with us, and His heart is broken for every broken heart here. Psalm

56:8 says God stores all of our tears in a box and He treasures each one. I don't know why tragedies like this come, but I know this: God loves us and He weeps for us. Calvary settled that once and for all. Don't ever doubt God's love.

Don't focus on what you have lost. Be grateful and thank God for fourteen wonderful years with Cassie. God was not out to lunch Wednesday night. He was not on vacation. He didn't wake up Thursday morning, slap his forehead, and say "My stars of darkness. Who is the guardian angel who let Cassie down? Take his union card away." God was in control—not the author of every event—but in sovereign control over the universe, and he can cause even little things to work together for good. He already has. Hundreds of young people have come to faith in Jesus Christ. The flesh is mortal; we are all going to die. But Jesus said, "I am the resurrection and the life." This gives us confidence and assurance that rises above the cries of the mourners.

Lord Jesus, we are so thankful that Cassie is with you. We pray that you will reap a great harvest as a result of her. We don't understand, Lord Jesus, but when we get to heaven we will ask. Until then, we will trust that You love us and that You are in control. And all God's people said, amen.

Mourners continued leaving mementos at the church for weeks.

Photo by James Morris.

9

The Days Become Weeks

"I . . . Wept and Mourned for Many Days"
(Neb. 1:4)

Each person passes through the stages of grief at his or her own pace. When Nehemiah heard the tragic news of Jewish grief in the days following the captivity, he exclaimed, "So it was, when I heard these words that I sat down and wept, and mourned for many days" (Neh. 1:4). As the Wedgwood tragedy moved beyond its first days, the majority were still mourning.

Monday and Tuesday

At Cassie Griffin's funeral her grandmother would write on the casket: "Cassie, our firstborn. What a precious gift we give back to God. Our days will be long without you. Gramma C." Remembering that "with the Lord one day is as a thousand years, and a thousand years as one day" (2 Peter 3:8), a friend wrote on the casket that he would see Cassie in about fifteen minutes.

At the Monday funeral service for Joey Ennis, Dr. Jim Gatliff, pastor of the First Baptist Church of White Settlement, shared the plan of salvation with the overflow crowd. With heads bowed, Gatliff prayed a prayer of salvation asking anyone wishing to invite Jesus Christ into his or her life to repeat after him or use similar words. Following the prayer he asked all who had prayed that prayer for the first time to raise their hands. "I'd say easily one hundred hands were raised," said Gatliff.

On Monday night a memorial service for Sydney Browning was held at Success High School. Planned by former students, the service drew approximately 250 students plus faculty and other friends. In addition to the sharing from fellow Wedgwood members and the recollections of two fellow teachers, several Success High School students shared their remembrances.

On Tuesday evening, September 21, Wedgwood Pastor Meredith met with the family of the gunman. They spoke of God's grace and prayed together that healing would come and God would be glorified. Then they asked if they might donate the proceeds of the sale of the family home—the residence of the gunman—to the ministry of Wedgwood Baptist Church. It was agreed, and a meeting was later held at Altamesa Church of Christ for the gracious donation. Weeks later, after the donation was made, members of both churches joined with members of the gunman's family in a circle around the altar. Holding hands, they sang, "Blest be the tie that binds our hearts in Christian love; the fellowship of kindred minds is like to that above."

The Handwriting on the Floor

Perhaps the greatest writing about the Wedgwood tragedy and the greatest therapy was done on the bare concrete floor of the worship center and the surrounding hallways. Because the blood-stained carpet had to be removed, and before the new carpet could be installed, Wedgwood members, beginning with the teen-agers, wrote messages on the floors. Listed below are just some of the messages written on the floor of Wedgwood Baptist Church:

✦ "My God, my God. You are sovereign."

✦ "Cassie,
    I saw your eyes,
    they were open.
    I looked at your body
    I couldn't help.
    We will miss you
    For awhile.
    Save a spot for the Wedgies."

✦ "Although Satan may have cut short some lives, he did not prevail!"

✦ "Don't ever forget! God is in this place. He mourns with us."

✦ "God spared me on this day so I can tell others about Christ. Gen. 15:25"

✦ "Justin—I love you now and for always. Mom & Grandma Diane"

✦ "Thank you God for sparing my son."

✦ "Satan you are defeated. God ended it 2000 years ago."

✦ "Satan can't hurt God's children."

✦ "Cassie, it's so hard to believe you are gone. I know you like it where you are because you have always loved worshiping God."

✦ "I was here. I can't believe I'm still here. Don't shoot please."

✦ "God was here Wednesday, September 15, 1999. He was watching over everyone. He sat right down here. He wept with us. He rejoiced with us. We will see Him soon."

✦ "Lord, say hi to Shawn."

✦ "Almighty God, thank you for saving my wife and my daughter."

✦ "Jesus died praising His father and the seven who were killed died doing the same thing."

✦ "Father, thank you for your love, peace and wisdom. It was at this spot the joy of my spirit and salvation became real again."

✦ "Sydney, you always brought a smile to my face, now a tear to my eye."

✦ "Someday we'll sing with Sydney in heaven."

✦ "To all who lost their lives, I hope you're having fun up there. I bet you are. I know we will see you again some day. I love all of you. I can't wait to see your beautiful smiles. I guess it's good-bye for now."

✦ "Hey, Mr. Gunman, I forgive you."

✦ "Justin—a good friend, the son I never had! Love, Hood."

✦ "He tried but he couldn't defeat the power of God."

✦ "Kim, thank you for your love and witness in planting seed with the students from Japan. The Lord will bring His flock home."

✦ "Thank you, God. I will let all the people at school know of your love. Thank you for saving me both spiritually (4/29/90) and physically (9/15/99). I love you Lord."

✦ "Keep on preaching Bro. Al. We love you."

✦ "Mr. Gunman, I haven't ever had any anger toward you. In fact, I feel sorry for you. You allowed yourself to be taken over by Satan and then Satan took full advantage of you. I forgive you and through Christ's love toward me, I can say that I love you."

✦ "Lord, this is where he was when I saw him. That was the instant that my life changed. This is where my all in all became real to me. Lord, I am now yours fully."

✦ "Kim, forgive me for bringing you in."

✦ "Evil has come here, but the platoon of Wedgwood Baptist has fought back and will fight again if necessary."

✦ "I am my beloved's and my beloved is mine." Song of Solomon 6:3. I love you, honey, so much. "Peace I leave with you. My peace I give to you, not as the world gives do I give unto you. Let not your heart be troubled, neither let it be afraid." John 14:27. Kathy Jo

✦ "You will never win, Satan. Don't try it again."

✦ "Fully Rely On God—FROG!"

✦ "Satan, you tried to take our church. You failed!"

✦ "I won't be shaken."

✦ "Lord, I am struggling in dealing with this tragedy, but You are in control and will help us through."

✦ "This is My Father's house."

✦ "Thank you, Lord, for sparing Kevin and Jeff. We love them."

✦ "Dear Lord, my Mom stood right over there

by the Coke machine. I thank you for protecting her. I don't tell her enough how awesome she is. Thank you for possibly using her to warn others. You have blessed me with a wonderful mother. She is definitely a prize. I hope I can be like her. Help me remember how I felt Wednesday when I couldn't find her."

✦ "May we never forget. May we never stop telling people what happened and may we never stop telling people about You. Thank you, God."

Wednesday, One Week Later

Southwestern Baptist Seminary student and Wedgwood member David Laningham tells this story:

One week after the tragedy, on my daughter's tenth birthday, I called her from work to wish her a happy birthday. During our conversation she expressed a fear of going to church that night. This was the testimony as well of other children at our church. However, she went. That night church members wrote encouraging notes on the floor where the carpet had been removed. The one that really stirred my heart was, "He didn't scare me away. God's Peace."

This one was signed by my ten-year-old daughter! In response, I wrote these words to a song:

I'm just an ordinary guy
I've asked many a question why
Why did you have to die?
Did I hear you right
You died to give me sight
Sight into the light

The darkness can't hide the truth
When the light reveals what's right
I'll know what to do . . .
I'll follow; I'll follow the light!

I'm just an average man
I've asked many a question when
When will I die?
You take all the fright
I hear I'll go when the time is right
Right into the light

The darkness can't hide the truth
When light reveals what's right
I'll know what to do . . .
I'll follow; I'll follow the light!

Right into the light!
Right into the light!

That Wednesday hundreds of people attended

prayer services at Wedgwood, so many that the crowds were divided into several sites throughout the church facilities. Church members were invited to write messages on the concrete floors of the worship center and hallways alongside those already written by the teen-agers and others. These messages would soon be covered by new carpet, but would remain as permanent reminders of the events of the previous Wednesday. Pastor Meredith welcomed two visitors from another church who asked to remain anonymous. "We are from another church of another denomination," they said, "but that does not matter. Our pastor took up a love offering Sunday morning for Wedgwood, and we are here to deliver it to you with our love and prayer support." The check was for $42,000.

It was also announced that the architect in charge of the expansion of the Wedgwood Church had proposed a memorial for those killed and injured. It would be an octagonal structure with waterfalls and a reflecting pool. All materials and labor would be donated, and there would be no cost to the church. Appropriately, it will be called "A Memorial to the Light."

Weeks Turn into Months

At Cassata High School, Judy Stegner attended a service dedicating a flagpole in memory of her son, Justin

Ray. The staff and classmates arranged for the flagpole to be given. Said Stegner, "Cynthia Morton, director of Cassata, was concerned that they did not have a flagpole. Now the kids have their own flagpole to pray under next year for See-You-at-the-Pole."

As money continued to pour in to the various victims' funds, the Texas Rangers baseball team arrived with a presentation. The players had collected $52,700 among themselves. This amount was then matched by the organization and also matched by owner Tom Hicks. Thus, the Rangers presented Pastor Meredith with a check for more than $158,000. Rangers' General Manager Doug Melvin said, "This touched very close to home. We hope this small contribution can help Pastor Meredith, the families, and the congregation get through this time."

In early October, Jordan Grey, a close friend of Shawn Brown, reflected:

> It has been three weeks since a man armed with two semiautomatic pistols walked into Wedgwood Baptist Church and began a killing spree that left eight dead (including himself), seven wounded, and everyone changed forever. This tragedy affected all our lives, but for some of us, myself included, it turned our lives upsidedown. You see, Wedgwood is my church, and I was there in the sanctuary that night. I lost a friend in Shawn Brown, and several others that I knew and loved were shot at or injured. The

images and sounds that I saw and heard that night are just as real as they were three weeks ago. It is only by the grace of God that I am even here to write this tonight. I was one of the many who thought it was a skit the entire time until he shot himself. At no time did I dive down behind a church pew, and right up to the explosion of the pipe bomb I did not make an attempt to protect myself. Naive? Perhaps, but tell me which one of you is used to people coming into your church, your sanctuary—the place of refuge—and killing?

Nowhere in the front, back, or any other portion of my mind did I think for one second that this could be real. But it was real. In the weeks that have passed since that night, the reality of those events has hit hard. I have played in my mind time and time again the sequence of events trying to figure out at what point I might have realized that this was not a skit, and that those were real gunshots and people were really being shot.

In a letter, Angela Kay Fuller wrote of missing her good friend:

To my sweet Kim Jones:
Playing the guitar in the college group at Wedgwood and not seeing you singing in front of me is still hard to understand. The last time

that I saw you we were having dinner together, just laughing and talking about Jesus. When we got up to leave, you just gave me a big hug. I said, "Kim, you always give hugs to people, but I think that's the first one I've gotten from you." You exclaimed, "Angela, there are thousands more where that came from." You know I never got to hug you again. But I am certain the next time I see you, I will surely receive the most amazing hug a friend has ever given. I love you and I miss you and I'm waiting on my hug.

October 31, 1999

On Sunday morning, October 31, Wedgwood Baptist Church honored several hundred police officers, firefighters, emergency medical technicians, school personnel, and others who assisted the church in the time of tragedy. In an emotional scene at the conclusion of the service, Pastor Meredith called the teen-agers who were present in the worship center on that Wednesday night to come forward and lay hands on the community servants while a prayer of thanksgiving was offered for them. Fort Worth Police Detective Dave Walters said, "It was absolutely awesome."

On that Sunday night, Halloween night, Wedgwood held its annual Fall Festival. Whereas in past years this event had attracted around a thousand people, this year the estimated attendance was two thousand to twenty-five hundred. The fear was passing, even as people outside the Wedgwood family continued to offer assistance. A senior group from Arizona sent forty boxes of homemade cookies.

The Follow-up Concert by Forty Days

On Wednesday evening, December 1, 1999, eleven weeks after it was interrupted by gunfire, the concert by Forty Days resumed at Wedgwood. Whereas on September 15, approximately four hundred to five hundred people were in attendance, on this night the crowd would number approximately nine hundred. Many came to complete what they had begun to experience weeks earlier. Some came because they felt guilty for not being with their friends on September 15. Uniformed police officers were present to offer a sense of security to those who had experienced recurring fears. Present also were family members of some of the victims. Numerous Wedgwood teen-agers sported new T-shirts with their feelings boldly printed on them, "September 15, 1999. The darkness had no victory over the LIGHT."

As the concert began, emotions were high and almost everyone was on his or her feet, singing and clapping. As the evening continued, many were in tears and held on to one another for support. Small groups gathered in the aisles to pray. Others would leave the worship center to find a quieter place to talk and pray. It was obvious the healing had begun, but just as obvious that it was ongoing.

Christmas Eve

The first Christmas following a tragedy is traditionally a stressful time. At Wedgwood the stress would be intensified by the annual Christmas Eve family service. Because of the high number of seminary students, Wedgwood has often been known as "the church from which everyone goes home for Christmas." Several years ago, it was determined to have a brief Christmas Eve family service. No nursery would be provided. Bring the kids. Don't dress up. Sing a few Christmas songs. Have a children's sermon. Light candles. Have prayer. Go home within the hour. The first year only a few attended. Each year the attendance got larger, reaching several hundred. On Christmas Eve 1999, more than one thousand were present.

For many it was not easy to attend. As the youth drama team depicted a scene of Jesus' birth, one couldn't help but notice in the group a youth who had been shot and others who were traumatized in this same building just fifteen weeks earlier.

As the choir came out of the congregation to bless us with their music, several were there who had been seated next to or near the wounded and dead on that September Wednesday.

As the children gathered for the children's sermon, there were those who had been hesitant to re-enter the church for fear of dead bodies, blood, and guns. Yet, here they were, being children again.

In the audience there were many whose lives had been forever changed because of events near where they sat. Others, like out-of-town family members, were in the worship center for the first time since the shooting. They had missed the blood-soaked floors, torn-out carpet, blood-stained cushions, bullet-scarred pews, bullet-ridden walls. One wondered if even as they worshiped on this night they tried to imagine what it looked like on that night.

When Pastor Meredith stepped to the front, it was a testimony of God's grace. What amazing strength and wisdom God had given this man over the past three months. The television cameras were there again, not as many as before, but just as noticeable. There was still a part of the story to be told. On the Sunday following the shooting, these cameras had shown the world a congregation entering their church building under the banner, "Let the Healing Begin." This night, on the ten o'clock news they showed a banner that read, "Christ, Our Hope." Perhaps not as newsworthy by today's standards, but the healing that has happened and will continue to happen is based solely in Christ, our hope.

Those gathered that Christmas Eve sang of that hope. Finally, they lit candles as the custom always was on Christmas Eve, yet this time it was different. As the pastor lit each candle of his teen-age helpers, he called out the name of a Wedgwood member who had gone on to spend their first Christmas in heaven. Tears flowed, then "Silent night, holy night . . ."

It was still too easy to remember another, more recent night that was neither silent nor holy. For many of those present, life had become more and more a blend of both nights.

Even as our quick-fix, fast-solution society offered instant closure so that life might move on, the darkness had only just begun to turn into morning light as numerous shadows still lingered for those involved.

Pastor Al Meredith gave deeply of himself during this time.
Photo by Chip Gillette.

10

The Light Watchman

A Pastor Remembers

The Watchman Said, "The Morning Comes . . ." (Isa. 21: 11-12)

W here would we be without Brother Al?" asked a Wedgwood member. It was a good question. Where would the Old Testament people of God have been without the watchman on the tower? Isaiah stood on the watchtower at Jerusalem, looking around, eager to warn the faithful and lead them from danger. He was asking how much of the night had gone by and how much still remained. His reply includes both hope and warning: "The morning comes, but also the night" (Isa. 21: 11-12). Living in the night watch, there is always hope for the dawning of light.

In the dark hours of September 15, 1999, Pastor Al Meredith ministered to his people and others who had been gathered in his church's buildings. In the early hours of September 16, before it was fully light, this sleepless, worn watchman took the tower position and called out over national and international airways, "We will not allow the powers of darkness to overcome the power of light." In other words, "The morning comes!"

Who Is This Man of God?

Born and raised in Michigan, Albert R. Meredith graduated from Marine City High School in 1964. He attended and received a B.R.E. degree from Grand Rapids Baptist College in 1968 and M.A. and Ph.D. degrees from Michigan State University in 1971 and 1973. Further education was received at Grand Rapids Baptist Seminary, Erskine Seminary in Due West, South Carolina, and Exeter College of Oxford University in England. Meredith married his high school sweetheart, Kay L. Dubois, and they have two children, a daughter, Becky, and a son, Josh.

With his training in history, Meredith served as professor of history at Anderson College in Anderson, South Carolina, from 1974 to 1979 at which time he became pastor of the First Baptist Church in Elberton, Georgia. He has been pastor of Wedgwood Baptist Church in Fort Worth since October 1987.

That Night from the Pastor's Perspective

Pastor Meredith offers here his own recollections of the tragedy.

On the surface, this attack could not have come at a worse time for me. Just two days before, I had preached my own mother's funeral. My emotions were numb as I dismantled my childhood home in Michigan, stripping it down and leaving it empty for the realtors to sell, saying a last goodbye to this wonderful place of countless joyful memories.

But God has a way of anesthetizing our spirits in order to get us through difficult times. That was my emotional state as I returned to Fort Worth that Wednesday—anesthetized, numb from the grief of my mother's death.

But God intended it for good.

When the phone rang with the tragic news that our church was being shot up, I rushed to the site. Helicopters buzzed overhead like a swarm of angry bees. Police cars and ambulances were everywhere. The scene was chaotic! But I was calm. The numbness of my heart allowed me to move from crisis to crisis without going into shock myself. That night was a blur: praying over the wounded; holding sobbing staff members, parents and children; calming and instructing the crowd; going with the witnesses to police headquarters; visiting the hospitals; and then making trips to the morgue to identify loved ones—all the while praying, ministering, holding, hugging, and weeping.

Then I met with the press, answering tough questions, giving hope, explaining the truth of our faith. I have been asked repeatedly, "Brother Al, how did you hold up? How did you remain so strong?" The answer is, I was never weaker in my life. Emotionally numb, spiritually drained, I had nothing left to give. And that is when the Lord stepped in and ministered through me to His hurting, shocked, stunned people. His "strength is made perfect in weakness" (2 Cor. 12:9). The Enemy timed his attack at my weakest moment . . .

But God intended it for good.

Satan also timed his attack while I was not there. I am always there on Wednesday night. I am hardly ever away. But, due to having returned from my mother's funeral, I had arranged for someone else to lead prayer meeting that night. My plan was to slip into the back row of the concert and be with the youth. But I was running late. As I arose from the table, the phone rang. . . . I wasn't there; the sheep were temporarily without their shepherd.

But God intended it for good.

Had I been there, I surely would have been one of the victims. I would have been among the first into the hallway once the shooting started. I would have been an easy target. My absence from the meeting that night likely resulted in my preservation.

Since that night, here is what I have witnessed.

When the shooter came through the door, he didn't ask for the preacher, or for the choir, or for the youth. He asked, "Where is that d___ prayer meeting?" Instead of destroying the prayer power of Wedgwood, the tragedy only enhanced it, and now Wedgwood is the most prayed-for church in the world. Over 20,000 cards and letters and 14,000 e-mails have come from all over the world to tell of prayerful support and love.

God intended it for good.

As a result, the power and presence of God has been upon us as never before in our worship. The head custodian related that, before the shooting, not a Sunday would go by without a stopped-up commode, a broken air conditioner, or some other mechanical malfunction. Since the shooting, there has not been a single breakdown on our church campus. What the enemy thought would bring a stop or at least a disruption of our worship has only enhanced the sense of God's presence. Our attendance is at an all-time high week after week. More importantly, the power of God's anointing is evident as we praise His name.

Satan thought he would make a public spectacle of a church falling apart under the pressure of violence and death. Instead, God has strengthened us in a way that encourages the rest of His church and astonishes unbelievers. For some reason, we have found favor with the secular media and have been given a public platform from which to proclaim the riches of Christ—and all on the world's nickel! Over 200 million people around the world watched the memorial service from the stadium at Texas Christian University, and there they heard that only Jesus gives us hope, only He can transform a wicked heart. They saw us raise our hands in praise to the Father, pleading for the lives of our children (Lam. 2:19) and singing "Alleluia" to the King of creation.

As a result of the broadcast, a missionary in Lebanon has been besieged with requests to explain our hope and joy in the face of tragedy.

At one nearby prayer vigil, twenty-nine high school students prayed to receive Christ. At another school one hundred ten were converted; another school reported forty-two committed their lives to Jesus. In public school classrooms as children discussed the shooting, students would ask what it means to "give your life to Christ." Before the teacher could respond, fellow students were explaining the way to salvation.

The wicked one thought he would terrorize our youth into spiritual paralysis. Instead, they are bolder than ever, determined that they "cannot but speak the things which they have seen and heard" (Acts 4:20).

God intended it for good.

Satan thought he could send a crippling blow to divide and destroy the community of faith. The gunman came from a God-fearing, church-going family. His great-grandfather was a Church of Christ circuit rider and donated the land on which the family church now sits. As he was shooting, the gunman was cursing not only Christians in general, but Baptists in particular.

Rather than divide the body of Christ, the shooting has only driven the universal Church together. When there is a death in the family, it draws us together. Everyone has been praying for us, ministering to us—Catholics to charismatics, Mennonites to Methodists, Pentecostals to Presbyterians. Our brothers at the Altamesa Church of Christ just down the road held a community prayer service the next evening, and we sang and wept and prayed together for the first time. On Saturday they sent a work crew to help us clean up our building for the first worship service after the shooting. Satan thought he would drive the wedge of denominational dispute into the heart of the Body. But God knew better.

God intended it for good.

So often God brings our greatest triumphs

out of our deepest tragedies. And the very things we think will destroy us provide for our deliverance and blessing. As the disciples labored for their lives on the stormy sea, the waves they thought would bring their death in a watery grave brought the Savior walking on the water. Moses thought the Sinai wilderness would ruin him. Instead, it strengthened him into being the man to lead God's people out of Egypt. Jehoshaphat thought the armies of their enemy nations would overrun and destroy him (2 Chron. 20). Instead, as the people sang God's praises, the armies turned on each other and it took three days to bring home the booty!

William Cowper put it this way in 1774:

God moves in a mysterious way
His wonders to perform;
He plants His footsteps in the sea,
And rides upon the storm.

You fearful saints, fresh courage take;
The clouds you so much dread
Are big with mercy, and shall break
In blessings on your head.

The prince of darkness thought he would deliver a crushing blow to God's people that night, but God has brought untold blessings from the tragedy.

Satan intended it for evil . . . God intended it for good. Amen.

Pastor Al Meredith, Brother Al as so many know him, was prepared by God for ministry and for his special ministry on this night of tragedy.

A Testimony about Al Meredith

Kathy Jo Brown, wife of slain Shawn Brown, wrote of their feelings for their pastor:

> Brother Al has played a major role in the spiritual growth of both Shawn and me. We have always spoken of him to our friends. We loved going to church together. Having such a broad history background from his teaching days, Brother Al is able to convey God's Word in such interesting, applicable ways. Shawn and I loved to learn from him, and I am very thankful that God used him in our lives in such a big way. Brother Al often makes reference to the fact that he prays that God would take him home before he would have a chance to defile God or the ministry in any way. This was such an example to Shawn and me of how important it is to live above reproach. I am thankful for the way God is using Brother Al through our tragedy.

Each time he is able to share about God's love and grace to our very lost world, Shawn's death is less in vain.

An Editorial about Al Meredith

The following is an editorial by Jim Jones, the religion editor of the Fort Worth *Star-Telegram,* written on September 24, 1999. It gives further insight into the person of Al Meredith and is used here by permission:

> I've been covering religion for years and have dealt with some unbelievable scandals, emotional events such as the visits of the pope and upheavals in major denominations. But nothing prepared me for what happened last week when a gunman burst into Wedgwood Baptist Church and killed seven people and wounded seven others before killing himself.
>
> As fate would have it, I happened to be the one to call the Reverend Al Meredith, pastor of the neighborhood church, to ask him about police reports of shootings at his church. He had not heard. He was at home rather than at his church, because he had just returned from Michigan, where he had attended the funeral of his mother. His time of sorrow was to be extended.
>
> I have known Meredith for years. We are fellow tennis enthusiasts. He plays serious ad-

vanced doubles. His seniors' team has made it to the national finals for two years in a row. But there was no thought of that on that warm late-summer night.

Meredith lives near the church and was there before I could arrive from my downtown office. He was there to pray over the wounded and, later, to identify those in the county morgue. Like other reporters, I was on the outside looking in. I could never truly know the ordeal Meredith went through, even though we had long conversations later.

Meredith, a relatively unknown Baptist preacher before the tragedy, became known to millions as he talked of his faith on local and national television. He spoke at multiple funerals and at a mass community gathering at Texas Christian University's Amon Carter Stadium. It was always an upbeat message.

He seemed tireless and impressed even local and national news media.

"Where do you find the strength to deal with this?" a local television reporter asked him last Sunday.

Meredith takes care of himself physically and even managed to get in a brief tennis game during the terrible week. But he doesn't know how to explain his stamina, either, except in divine terms. Finally he said, "It's just God."

Several times he said of his church members: "We are just ordinary people with an extraordinary God." I was never more impressed by Meredith and his entire congregation than when I was assigned to cover their first worship service inside their church after the shootings.

Being inside the church where innocent people had died and in a sanctuary that still bore bullet holes and shrapnel marks from a pipe bomb did not seem to faze the worshipers. Many sat in folding chairs where at least a dozen pews had been removed because they bore marks of the violence. Many knelt in prayer on bare concrete floors, where bloodstained carpets had been ripped out. But they didn't seem to notice. They were too busy exorcizing the evil that had befallen their beloved church. They sang joyfully and prayed fervently.

Surprisingly, there were few tears. Most of those who were dabbing away tears were in the choir, where there were poignant reminders of the loss of two faithful choir members. Choir robes that belonged to two of the dead, Sydney Browning and Kim Jones, were draped across empty chairs in the choir loft.

The focus was on the future. But Meredith recalled briefly the words of the mentally disturbed man who burst into the church on the night of Sept. 15. "I've been told he was railing against Christianity," Meredith said. Witnesses said the man shouted, "You Baptists think you know everything!" and then began methodically shooting down people.

"We Baptists don't know everything," Meredith said. "But we do know God is in control and that we have hope." Then he and his congregation began singing:

> My hope is built on nothing less
> Than Jesus' blood and righteousness . . .
> When darkness veils his lovely face,
> I rest on His unchanging grace . . .
> On Christ the solid rock I stand;
> All other ground is sinking sand,
> All other ground is sinking sand.

God revealed His love and grace even through the questions.

Photo by Kathy Holton.

11

With the Weeks Come the Questions

"Satan Transforms Himself into an Angel of Light" (2 Cor. 11:14)

Entering a darkened auditorium, Satan's best strategy was one of deception. The stage had been set. An announcement had been made about an upcoming skit. The teen-agers present were looking forward to it. Then entered the gunman. "What a great idea for a skit!" thought one teen-ager. "They're making us think we are being attacked by a mad gunman, complete with the gunman shooting blanks. Then we'll think through our faith and hopefully realize that we will stand firm in the face of martyrdom."

The Bible tells us that "Satan transforms himself into an angel of light" (2 Cor. 11:14). Satan does this because so often light represents godliness and holiness:

✦ "God is light and in Him is no darkness at all" (1 John 1:5).

✦ "If we walk in the light as He is in the light we

have fellowship with one another" (1 John 1:7).

✦ "My eyes have seen Your salvation . . . a light to bring revelation to the Gentiles" (Luke 2:30-32).

✦ "In Him was life, and the life was the light of men" (John 1:4).

✦ "I am the light of the world. He who follows Me shall not walk in darkness, but have the light of life" (John 8:12).

On the other hand, darkness often represents evil and ungodliness.

✦ "The power of darkness" (Luke 22:53).

✦ "What communion has light with darkness?" (2 Cor. 6:14).

✦ "For you were once in darkness, but now you are light in the Lord" (Eph. 5:8).

✦ "For we do not wrestle against flesh and blood, but against . . . the rulers of the darkness of this age" (Eph. 6:12).

Satan is smart enough to know that if he had appeared at Wedgwood that evening in the reality of his dark nature, his presence would have been rejected by most of those present. Thus he disguised himself, not just as light, but as an angel of light. He entered as though he were a part of the program, a participant in the skit.

The sad commentary that some churches sink to such levels of reality to impress teen-agers was exceeded only by the horror that this was not a skit. The bullets were real. The profanity was not from an actor. The blood was not from paintballs.

Some at Wedgwood continued to think this tragic series of events was a skit. Teen-ager Laura Watson describes her experience in an article she wrote in the Southwest High School newspaper, *Raiders' Review:*

> When I got to the church with Rachel Milliron and my sister, Brittney, Justin "Steggy" Ray grabbed me, begging me to run a spotlight during the skit.
>
> I said, "Sure, let me find out what they need." Brittney went in and sat down, and that was the last time I saw her until we were reunited outside later.
>
> I found someone else to run spots and told Steggy. He said, "Aw man, you'd have been so good. But thanks, you're so sweet." Those were his last words to me.
>
> I went in and sat down in the right center section. We were singing "I Will Call Upon the Lord" when gunfire started. Rachel and I remembered hearing the pop, pop, pop of the

shots and looking around to see if the tech crew was setting off firecrackers. I kept telling Rachel, "It's just a skit. It will be over soon." Then I heard someone and saw Steggy lying on the ground next to me. I thought, *Oh he didn't tell me he was into acting.* I seriously thought it was still a skit.

I saw the blood flowing down the aisle, right between my foot and Steggy. Even then, I remember thinking, *This is a bit much for a skit.* I turned and buried my head in Rachel's back, praying. "Please God, make the skit end soon. I know it's a skit, but please, just don't let it turn out to be real." My prayer was cut short when I heard an explosion and saw a flash of light whiz down our aisle. I thought pyrotechnics had been set off by the crews. After that a few more shots were fired, then it was quiet.

I heard people start to move, but I wouldn't get off of Rachel because I could see the people in the balcony not moving, just looking. I didn't want people to panic, running out before Jay told us it was a play and those playing dead got up.

Jay ran in and yelled, "Run! Get out NOW!" I just stood there, looking. I saw the last person run out, and I saw Cassie Griffin lying in her pew, fifteen feet across the aisle. We had to run right by the shooter, dead, on the bench. I just remember all the blood. I saw the cops start pulling up and running in. It was like, "Wow, they even got cops to spend their off-duty time to make this look real." We headed across the street on the west side and sat in the front yard with others.

A woman was running around in panic, asking if anyone saw a little girl named Amber. She acted like a terrified mother, but I didn't believe her. I thought she was the star actress of the group. I tried to take it all in as the helicopters started to land. We saw some of the youth using the phone, and Rachel got in line. I was not going to call because I didn't want to scare my parents when it was all pretend.

Rachel dialed her number and started screaming. I wrestled it away from her and was eventually able to talk. I remember telling them "There was a skit or something, I think, about a shooting. It was really bad and it just really scared Rachel." I still refused to believe it was real.

Eventually Laura realized that she had been deceived. There was no skit.

In the midst of such darkness, when Satan's deceptions are so real, people look for enlightenment. Many questions are asked in times like these. Dr. Scott Floyd, associate professor of psychology and counseling at Southwestern Baptist Seminary, tried to help us understand our thoughts and feelings:

As humans we like things to make sense. Our

brains like to have connections between things. The problem with trauma and a traumatic situation is that it doesn't make sense. When you use a computer, you input a command and it searches for a document or a file and finds it and pulls it up. When it can't find a document or a file, it spins for a while before telling you it can't find it. I think that is what happens to our brains when trauma occurs. Something not a part of human functioning in a normal sense pounds itself into our lives. I think what happens to our brain is like that computer searching for a file that it can't find. A lot of folks who were at Wedgwood had that experience. Their minds were whirling but they couldn't make sense out of it. We don't have a filé folder for going to a concert and a friend getting killed or coming home from church with blood on our jeans. In the immediate sense and in the long term, what our brains are trying to do is to make sense out of this and make it fit because it is something outside of anything we ever expected to happen or anything that we've had happen before.

Why Did This Happen?

The immediate question that each of us asks is why. While our answer may not be completely satisfactory to some, it will have to last until we get to heaven and know more clearly. For now we must be content to see "through a glass darkly" (1 Cor. 13:12).

When God created the universe and came to create mankind, there were two choices available—to create humans as robots with no freedom of choice, or to create humans as creatures with freedom of choice and will. Not wanting to control every human choice, God created us with the ability and freedom to make decisions. Jesus indicated that love was present even before creation. He said of His Father, "You loved Me before the foundation of the world" (John 17:24). Perhaps it was this love that motivated God to allow mankind to have freedom.

Given this freedom of choice, the first people, Adam and Eve, made a bad choice. In so doing, they sinned against God and because of their sin, other people suffered. Through the remainder of the Bible and throughout Christian history, bad choices have caused suffering not only for those directly related to the person making the choice, but for others far removed from the scene of the choice. When God's gift of free choice is abused, people, frequently innocent people, suffer the consequences. Here are only a few of many incidents of random violence:

✦ In Killeen, Texas, a man made a bad choice in October, 1991, and crashed his vehicle through the plate-glass window of a cafeteria before opening fire on those eating there, killing twenty-three people, while many more suffered.

+ In Oklahoma City a man made a bad choice in April 1995, when he drove a rental truck full of explosives up to the Murrah Federal Building. Many people died in the explosion and more were injured and thousands suffered.

+ In Pearl, Mississippi, a sixteen-year-old boy made a bad choice in October of 1997 and his mother and two fellow high school students died while seven others were injured and many people suffered.

+ In West Paducah, Kentucky, some teen-agers made a bad choice in December of 1997 and three students were killed, five others were wounded, and many people suffered at the hands of an ambush at Heath High School.

+ In Jonesboro, Arkansas, two boys, ages eleven and thirteen, made a bad choice in March of 1998. Four of their classmates and a teacher were killed, ten others were wounded and many suffered.

+ In Springfield, Oregon, a fifteen year old made a bad choice in May 1998, killing his parents, then killing two teen-agers and injuring more than twenty others. Many people suffered.

+ In Salt Lake City, Utah, a seventy-one-year-old man made a bad choice in April, 1999, opening fire in the Mormon family history library, killing two people, wounding four, and causing much suffering.

✦ In Littleton, Colorado, two students made a bad choice and in April of 1999 twelve of their classmates and one of their teachers at Columbine High School were killed and many people suffered.

✦ In Atlanta, Georgia, a forty-four-year-old man, upset over bad investments, made a bad choice in July 1999, killed nine people including his wife and two children, wounded thirteen, and caused much suffering.

✦ In Los Angeles, California, a gunman made a bad choice in August of 1999, killed one person and wounded five, and many people suffered at the North Valley Jewish Community Center.

✦ And on the evening of September 15, 1999, a lone gunman in Fort Worth, Texas made a bad choice. Seven died, seven others were wounded, while families, friends, a congregation, and the world suffered.

Did God Cause This to Happen?

No. Many have laid responsibility for these events at

the feet of God. But God did not cause these deaths. Kathy Jo Brown, Shawn's widow, responds:

> Why did Shawn run back to the sanctuary doors? Every time I hear this question, my mind goes back to just weeks before when Shawn said to me, "Kathy, I asked myself the question today, if I were ever in a shooting situation like Columbine, what would I do? I know that I would have to help in some way—either by shielding someone from a bullet or stopping the shooter in some way." At that time, I remember asking him to please be careful and thinking that surely that situation would never occur. Well, it did. My sincere thought on why Shawn returned to the sanctuary doors was to help in any way he could. He knew that Jay had taken care of 911, and there was nothing else to do but help.

So did God cause Shawn's death? No. Shawn died doing what he had been called by God to do. When you die being faithful to your call, you don't blame death on the One who called you.

Could God Have Prevented the Deaths?

God could have stopped the killing. God can do whatever God decides to do. Why didn't He? God chose to honor his gift of free will. To have prevented the tragedy would have been in violation of the God-created, and God-given, freedom of choice. If there is choice, there must be consequences. In this case the choice was bad and the consequences were tragic.

Where Was God in the Midst of this Tragedy?

God was exactly where God was the day Jesus died a cruel death on a rugged cross. If, "God so loved the world that He gave His only begotten Son," how much more did God feel the sting of every bullet, the anxiety of every parent who heard the news and went searching for a child, the frustration of every teen-ager who asked why? God responded to the cries of people, answering their intercessions and petitions. God ministered to people through those who had been called to provide such ministry. God is today still grieving with those who continue to grieve, weeping with those who still weep, agonizing with those who are agonizing still. Just because God would not stop the tragedy does not mean that God is disinterested.

The observations of Fort Worth Police Officer Royce Hearn help us understand where God was:

My first emotions were shock and disbelief. My

mind kept saying that this could not be happening. I then thought of my own family, who were in services at my own church. This was way too close to home.

The reality of it all came when I saw the first body. I truly felt the loss of a fellow believer, but I had to push that aside. There was a job to do. The scene was chaotic with people running around everywhere. But I sensed a peace in the middle of the storm. Emergency crews barking orders, police setting up perimeters, fire trucks arriving, and everywhere I looked I saw groups of people on their knees in prayer, unashamed. I saw the church in action and I was proud. Peace was upon the place even in the midst of grief. This ordeal did not take God by surprise and He was firmly in control.

What Is God Doing Now?

Even though the decision was made not to stop this tragedy, God is still sovereign. God is not running up and down the corridors of heaven uncertain as to what to do next. God is busy working "all things . . . for good to those who love Him and who are called according to His purpose" (Rom. 8:28). While God did not cause the tragedy nor prevent it, God seeks to be glorified through it. Because of the

faithfulness of the people of Wedgwood and surrounding churches, God was glorified even in the
death and the suffering of innocent people.

As Pastor Meredith said, God used for good
that which Satan intended for evil. In his book, *The
Great House of God,* Max Lucado describes our adversary, Satan, as "the Colonel Klink of the Bible."
The old television comedy, *Hogan's Heroes,* was set
in a German prison camp occupied by American GIs
and led by the indomitable Captain Hogan. Stalag
13, as it was aptly called, was ostensibly run by the
bumbling idiot of a Nazi, Colonel Klink. In reality,
however, it was Hogan who ran the camp by stealth
and cunning, eavesdropping on every phone call,
intercepting every message from Berlin, and manip-
ulating the hapless colonel. Every time Colonel
Klink thought he was increasing the misery and discipline of the prisoners, he was, in fact, only giving
them aid to their situation, playing into their hands.

Lucado argues that every time the wicked one
thinks he has dealt a death blow to the kingdom of
God, our sovereign Father only causes it to work together for the benefit of His children (Rom. 8:28).

As Joseph explained to his guilty brothers after
Jacob had died, "You intended to harm me, but God
intended it for good" (Gen. 50:20, NIV).

That has been the recurring testimony of Wedgwood Baptist Church where, on September 15,
1999, an angry, deranged gunman entered the

church armed with two hundred rounds of ammunition and a pipe bomb, intent on wreaking havoc and destruction.

But God intended it for good.

Why Would God Allow This to Happen?

Sometimes God allows tragedy to happen in order to increase our patience, endurance, or perseverance. James writes, "count it all joy when you fall into various trials, knowing that the testing of your faith produces patience" (Jas. 1:2-3). Other times we are allowed to endure tragedy so that through it God may be glorified. Paul writes, "we suffer with Him, that we may be glorified together. For I consider that the sufferings of this present time are not worthy to be compared with the glory which shall be revealed in us" (Rom. 8:17-18). On still other occasions, God allows tragedy so that we may be strengthened. Peter writes, "may the God of all grace, who called us to His eternal glory by Christ Jesus, after you have suffered a while, perfect, establish, strengthen, and settle you" (1 Peter 5:10). Sometimes God allows tragedy so that we, like Jesus, may be able to minister to others. The writer of Hebrews writes, "For in that He Himself has suffered, being tempted, He is able to aid those who are tempted" (Hebrews 2:18). Finally, there are occasions where God allows tragedy in order to unify believers. Paul writes, "If one member suffers, all the members suffer with it" (1 Cor. 12:26).

Dr. Bob Garrett, professor of missions at Southwestern Baptist Seminary and member of Wedgwood Baptist Church, responds:

> My own conviction is that God allowed an event that would not add up by any reasonable nor rational criteria so that we would be required to understand that what occurred was essentially spiritual in nature. The only things that I can understand about this tragedy are discerned spiritually. The attack was an attempt straight out of the pit of hell to dump poison and hatred and death in the heart of our church and the lives of our young people in Fort Worth. It is clear that God intervened, midway along and said, "Enough!" There is no more reason that the gunman stopped taking others' lives and took his own than that he was challenged by a quiet young man in the name of Jesus, but that is enough.
>
> It is clear that Satan took advantage of a lonely, desperate, and unbalanced man to come and do his work. It is also clear that where sin abounded, grace abounded even more, and that even in the tragedy a sovereign God put limits on the evil, checked its flow, and intervened on behalf of the several hundred people in our church buildings that night. I do not pretend to under-

stand why God intervened to protect us when he did, nor why he allowed our friends to be wounded or die. Many of us have cried ourselves to sleep for more nights than we can remember asking, "Why my friend? Why not me?" There are no answers to those questions either, but it is crystal clear that we cannot understand what happened unless we see ourselves in spiritual warfare and know for certain that God was and is always in control.

What remains now is to recover and to look expectantly to God to see how this terrible tragedy will be turned into good purposes in the future of our lives.

Why Teen-agers at a Church Youth Rally?

Jim Gatliff, pastor of the First Baptist Church of White Settlement, answered this question at the funeral service of Joey Ennis. Here are his words:

Imagine if you will all the forces of darkness, and Satan himself, thinking about Wednesday morning—at schools all throughout the world teenage Christians were gathered singing praise to the Lord Jesus Christ and praying at the flagpoles of their schools. This represented a whole generation of teen-agers saying, "We will obey God rather than man." Imagine the agony the wicked one felt at that. Then at Wedgwood Baptist Church, they celebrated what God had done on that day.

I believe that the forces of darkness were shaking, seeing the power of God resting on a whole generation of teen-agers throughout this land.

There is a revolution taking place among the teen-agers of our land today. They are bearers of the light.

Why Did the Church People Handle This So Well?

Wedgwood is a praying church. The prayer room is adequately staffed, and the Watchman on the Wall Prayer Ministry involves more than 250 church members. Frequently on Sunday mornings, the pastor will pray not only for Wedgwood, but for sister churches—Baptist and non-Baptist—in Fort Worth. Half of the Wednesday evening adult service is devoted to praying in small groups. Various prayer groups meet throughout the week.

In times of crisis, those who pray best are those who have been praying most consistently. In other words, a time of crisis is no time to learn how to pray. In prayer, consistency is better than intensity. Wedgwood had been consistent in prayer.

In addition to being a praying church, Wedgwood became a prayed-for church. One of the wonderful results of the shooting is that Wedgwood has likely been the most prayed-for church in the world. From those who were led to prayer before they knew what happened, to those who responded with prayer after hearing the news, more people likely prayed for Wedgwood than have ever prayed for a single church before. So when people have asked, "How are you doing so well?" the answer has been, "only by the prayers of God's people."

Those prayers have been answered by an obvious outpouring of God's strength and grace upon the church as observed by Fort Worth Police Commander Kenneth Flynn:

> I had the same feelings as many others involved with the homicides at the Wedgwood Baptist Church: shock, sadness, and grief. As the commander of the policing district in which the church resides, I was at the church quite a bit in the days following the shootings and saw the way the church staff and members handled this tragedy. In the midst of their pain they were strong, even expressing concern for the welfare of the police officers, fire fighters, etc. I know this church body relied on God's grace and strength. Their strength and dignity helped me deal with my own feelings about this inci-

dent. Through their witness, what was meant for evil brought glory to God.

If God Is Sovereign Should We Still Pray?

We pray because prayer is God's idea, not ours. It is God's desire that we enter into two-way communication. Because prayer is a divine creation, it means more to God than it does to us. Therefore, especially in times of crisis, God is even more interested in communicating with us. Prayer was never intended to be based on our feelings but on God's desire to communicate with us. We should continue to pray, even in times of crisis, because God listens to our prayers and among other benefits offers strength, comfort, courage, wisdom, discernment.

Concerning Wedgwood's prayer ministry, Pastor Meredith stated:

When the shooter came through the door he asked for the prayer meeting. Satan, cunning as he is, knew that if he could destroy our prayer warriors he could cut our church from its power source. But that night the prayer meeting and the youth rally had switched locations. Prayer meeting was squeezed into the fellowship hall where the lights were brighter. The youth were in the sanctuary where the lights—except for the spot-lights on the stage—were turned off.

Instead of destroying the prayer power of Wedg-wood, the tragedy only enhanced it. We now have more prayer warriors than ever before in the history of our congregation. As an example, Sunday morn-ing (6:00 A.M.) prayer watch has quadrupled in size and intensity.

How Do We Deal with Tragedy?

One of the ways to cope with the uncertainty that tragedy brings is to focus on what is known. That is what Dr. Ken Hemphill did in chapel at Southwest-ern Baptist Seminary the morning following the shooting in which two current seminary students, one recent graduate, and the teenage daughter of an alumnus were killed:

> There are some things that we know for cer-tain. First of all, we know that God is still on His throne. I want you to listen to Psalm 46:
>
>> God is our refuge and strength. A very pres-ent help in trouble. Therefore we will not fear, even though the earth be removed, and though the mountains be carried into the midst of the sea: Though its waters roar and

be troubled, Though the mountains shake with its swelling. There is a river whose streams shall make glad the city of God. The holy place of the tabernacle of the Most High. God is in the midst of her, she shall not be moved; God shall help her just at the break of dawn. The nations raged, the kingdoms were moved; He uttered His voice, the earth melted. The Lord of hosts is with us; the God of Jacob is our refuge . . . I will be exalted among the nations. I will be exalted in the earth!

No matter what we see, in the culture and in current events around us, we know that God is still on His throne.

Number two, we know that death and destruction is the tactic of the adversary. Jesus in John 10:10, compared him with the thief. Jesus came that He might give life and give it abundantly. The adversary came to steal, to kill, and to destroy. We should not be surprised when evil comes to destruction and death

Number three, we know that the resurrection is a sure and certain reality. The apostle Paul, writing to a grieving Thessalonian community says, "Do not be uninformed brethren about these who are asleep. That you may not grieve as do the rest who have no hope." If we believe that Jesus died and rose again, then we also believe that God will bring with him those who have fallen asleep. In 2 Corinthians Paul affirms that in death, to be absent from the body is to be present with the Lord. We know that our fellow students are already present with the Lord. And they face a sure and certain resurrection, as do we.

The fourth thing we know is that our God is an ever-present help in times of need. Turn to Him and seek His face. While there are no easy answers, He is the answer. Turn to Him and He will bring strength and solace.

The fifth thing that we know for certain is that we stand in need of spiritual awakening. This makes us aware that time is short for all of us. We must pray as we have never prayed, and we must witness as we have never witnessed— that the world may know the hope that lies within us, the hope that is ours.

The last thing I want you to know is that these deaths have not been in vain. Sometimes we act almost as if God has been surprised by our circumstances. We might think, *Why were the lives of these young seminarians cut short when they had such a ministry before them?* God has so often used the death of martyrs to bring greater glory and witness than even the living witness of the saints. Let me remind you what Revelation 12:10-11 (NAS) says, "I heard a loud voice in heaven saying, 'now the salvation, and the power, and the kingdom of our God and the authority of His Christ have come, for the accuser of the brethren has been thrown down, he who accuses them before our God day and night.'" How was he thrown down? How has he overcome? Listen: "And they overcame him because the blood of the Lamb and the word of their testimony, and they did not love their life even to death."

I heard some of our students saying last night, "Dr. Hemphill, the blood was literally flowing under the pews at Wedgwood." That's been true for years. The blood of Jesus has been flowing under those pews for years. It is in the blood of Jesus that there's victory. It is in the word of our witness and it is in the life of those who did not love their life even unto death.

We know these things for certain.

Those who were grieving were comforted by messages of support.

Photo by Scott McIntosh.

12

With the Weeks Comes the Need for Counseling

"Walk as Children of Light" (Eph. 5:8)

What has Wedgwood learned that might be beneficial to those who in some future darkness must walk as children of the light? This chapter is an account of the counseling and caregiving dimension of the Wedgwood shooting.

The Dark Aftermath of a Trauma

In the dark days following the shooting, what became apparent was the extent to which the shooting had affected both those directly involved and those who identified with those who were involved. Not only had the church community experienced a tragedy of unthinkable proportions, but people connected by the common thread of wanting security for their children and a safety for their future found themselves in the same dilemma that was facing the church. How are we going to get through this? How can we help our children cope with a tragedy this close to home? What can we as parents, teachers, and community leaders do to protect our families? Engulfed by darkness, how can we "walk as children of light?" (Eph. 5:8)

These questions and others have been the focus of many sermons, community meetings, and school board gatherings. What emerged from the chaos brought about by a single gunman has been nothing short of the expressed provision of grace and peace by our Lord in the midst of a great storm.

The Extent of the Crisis

The community-wide impact of the shooting created a great need for professional personnel. Counselors, doctors, hospital staff, chaplains, ministers, and volunteers helped provide a sense of comfort and direction for hundreds, even thousands, of children and adults and for many of the emergency personnel who found themselves in an arena where they had never been before. Many of the police reported having gone home in the early morning hours of September 16, checked on their own children and wept, feeling grateful for their safety and yet deeply saddened for the families who would not see their children again this side of heaven.

By the end of the evening of the fifteenth, it was

apparent to members of the city and of the school district that the tragedy at Wedgwood would be greater than they could imagine. One of the slain was a well-loved teacher and the others were all students at different stages of their education. What kind of an impact would be made on the children whose teacher was not going to show up for class that day or ever after? or the children whose teacher suddenly and tragically lost her beloved husband? or the students whose friends and classmates would no longer be accompanying them to football games or weekend get-togethers?

Southwestern Baptist Theological Seminary was dramatically affected. Of the seven slain, three were either current students or graduates, and another victim's father was a graduate. Two other students were among the seven wounded survivors. What would be the response of this community?

The Provision of Many Counselors

From the moments immediately following the shooting to the present, the need for a multitude of professionals became very obvious. Throughout the county, counselors, pastors, chaplains, and crisis professionals began arriving on the scene, helping wherever and ministering in whatever capacity they could. Not much is known as to the exact nature of the counsel given by these professionals, except that many stayed through the night and assisted in helping church members get home, sat with children until a parent could pick them up, worked with emergency officials to keep crowds away from the buildings, and provided many embraces for those just coming to terms with reality.

One group of counselors who arrived at the scene came from the seminary led by Drs. Ian Jones, Scott Floyd, and John Babler. Along with the other counselors, these men worked through the night counseling and consoling from the elementary school across the street. Later that night Jones and Floyd began to discuss a plan to meet the counseling needs of the coming days. The next day a number of counselors met at the seminary's counseling center for the first of two training classes in crisis intervention taught by Professor Floyd. From there, counselors were sent throughout the city to churches and schools to help teachers and church leaders working with affected children and adults. The first schools and churches visited involved those of the victims and their families. The schools included four high schools and one elementary school as well as five churches.

Advice to Hurting and Helping Seminarians

On the morning after the shootings, Floyd stood before an overflow crowd in the chapel service at the seminary to offer advice to present and future caregivers. Many of those present were pastors, youth ministers, and children's workers in area churches. Preceding his advice to these caregivers, Floyd read that ours is the "God of all comfort, who comforts us in all our tribulation, that we may be able to comfort those who are in any trouble, with the comfort with which we ourselves are comforted by God" (2 Cor. 1: 3-4). He then offered this advice:

You will see groups around all through the day today talking. Talk about what you saw, what you heard, what you felt. That will be the beginning and working through of the grieving process. Allow others to talk to you. Allow them to tell you what they saw, what they heard, especially those that were around the church and those that were directly involved. If folks talk to you, don't attempt to solve their problems. Don't attempt to answer all of their why questions. A lot of times the why questions don't have answers. Make sure you allow folks to express their emotions as they go through this and don't attempt to keep your own emotions back. Look for appropriate places to share your emotions.

With younger children I would try to buffer them as much as I could from the things that have happened. With our own younger children, we have not allowed them to see newscasts or newspapers. We are not talking with our younger children about what went on. Children who are a little bit older are going to hear about these things in school, and so I would allow them to talk about what has taken place. Reassure these children of their safety. With older grade school children and with teen-agers, you need to make sure you are checking with them about how they are doing. You bring it up, you initiate it, and give them a chance to talk about what's happened.

Floyd went on to encourage the potential helpers to take care of themselves and their emotions—to not deny what they were experiencing. It was good advice.

A Weekend of Counseling Activity

The weekend immediately following the shooting became a whirlwind of activity. The first intent was to provide counseling and support to area churches and schools and second to reclaim the building where the worst church shooting in Texas history had taken place. On the morning of September 17, the seminary counseling center conducted its second crisis intervention training class for more than thirty counselors who would be attending the first worship service at Wedgwood following the shooting. These counselors would be available for members of Wedgwood coming back into the building. They would also be used that Sunday evening, when children and parents met in homes with their Sunday school classes. These trained counselors would assist parents in consoling their children.

Saturday the 18th, the crisis intervention training taught by Floyd was offered to the pastors, youth workers, and counselors of the Tarrant Baptist Association, the association Wedgwood is in. Attending the training from Nashville was the former youth minister of Wedgwood, Steve Hayes, who had come to provide counseling assistance and to support the present youth pastor, Jay Fannin, whom Steve had mentored. Throughout the week, Hayes worked on a crisis manual specifically for the youth and their families to use in assisting them through the grief process.

A Day of Triumph: Let the Healing Begin

The morning of the 19th began just like every other Sunday morning. But for the members of Wedgwood and community churches throughout the Fort Worth/Dallas area, it was to be the first major test as to the impact of a gunman leaving the sanctuary of a church as a killing field. How would the communities respond to the attack on what many believed to be the last safe haven? How many would stay home from Wedgwood because going back into that same building would bring back too many painful memories? How many would use this incident as the final acknowledgment of evil's victory in their life and drop church involvement altogether? How would the young children react, many of whom had not been back into the building since they were evacuated Wednesday night, running past the injured bodies of leaders in their church? How would the church respond to a frightened community still feeling the effects of the tragedy just four days old?

Armed with their courage and the boldness to be counted among those who were not going to be intimidated by evil, more than nineteen hundred members and former members arrived at Wedgwood to be present at a worship service that one reporter termed "TRIUMPHANT!" During the Sunday school hour, counselors from Southwestern Seminary were present in each class to assist in helping members come to grips with this tragedy. A number of other churches in southwest Fort Worth requested counselors from the seminary to assist them in dealing with the impact on their congregations. For many, the Sunday after became a rallying point to begin the process of healing and to come together as a body of believers for the purpose of comforting and helping each other get through this tragedy in the life of their church.

Searching for a New Normal

The staff meeting at Wedgwood on Tuesday, September 21, included Drs. Jones and Floyd from the seminary. There by invitation of the church, they were given six assignments by the pastor to assist the church membership and staff in helping them find a new normal, a point of reference within which to bring about an understanding of the tragic events. The first assignment was for the seminary to provide counseling during the day for passersby at a makeshift memorial being erected at the corner of the church property. As visitors and mourners would drive past and get out of their vehicles, counselors were standing by to speak to them, offering words of comfort and the message of the hope that is in Christ. This corner counseling continued throughout the week.

The second assignment involved the provision of individual and family counseling for members of the staff and support staff at Wedgwood. At the request of the pastor, staff members were instructed to seek out and attend counseling for themselves and preferably also for their families. This counseling was to be provided by members of the seminary staff and doctoral students at Southwestern, or a counselor of their choice. Many of the staff sought counseling at the seminary because of its reputation and closeness to the church.

The third, fourth, and fifth assignments involved seminary counselors maintaining a presence at the church for several weeks for Sunday worship services, Sunday school classes, and Wednesday night activities. The week immediately following the shooting involved the presence of counselors in numerous churches throughout Fort Worth, many of them provided at no cost by the seminary.

The sixth assignment given to Drs. Jones and Floyd involved providing a class for parents to help them work with their children in coping with the fear and anxiety of severe trauma. They were also to assist the parents in establishing certain safeguards for helping their children return to school. By September 21, families that wanted counseling had many avenues available to them through the Southwestern Seminary counseling center and other counseling centers throughout Fort Worth and Tarrant County.

Praying for One Another

The tragedy became for many a rallying cry for the church to come together in support and comfort for the victims. Not long after the story broke, communications of every sort, from all over the nation and literally all over the world, began to flood into the then ravaged Wedgwood building. Beginning with a few hundred e-mails, letters, cards, banners, and well wishes, there came such an outpouring of love and support that it literally covered the walls of the church buildings. With these messages hanging from the walls, members, visitors, and family members were able to see and read firsthand the fact that Wedgwood was in the prayers of many and would not be forgotten like yesterday's news. This flood of mail stood out to the church as a visual reminder that when one part of the body hurts or is grieving the whole body hurts as well. For many, these thoughtful gestures of love became a therapeutic opportunity to receive from those they had never seen. These words were repeated over and over: "I don't know what to say to you in this time of great sorrow, but I just felt that I had to write and let you know that I am praying for you and your church and for God's best in your life."

Individual prayer meetings sprang up all over the city as people began to hear the news of their fallen friends, family members, coworkers, and brothers and sisters in Christ. One group in particular formed on the third floor of the women's dorm at Southwestern Seminary, where Kim Jones had lived. Upon hearing the news of the loss of their friend and classmate, several women formed prayer groups of between ten and fifteen each. Many of the groups stayed up all night comforting others as they came in, fielding calls from family members around the country, and praying for the people that they knew were wounded. These prayer groups continued over to the next day and became a part of class time for many of the students in the seminary.

Comforting One Another as unto the Lord

As the days moved on, many of the youth present at the church the night of the shooting became convinced that the horror witnessed by them firsthand could not be understood by adults, not even by their parents who were not there. Numerous counselors and youth workers in those days following the shooting found themselves sitting in silence surrounded by youth still unsure of the impact of the trauma on their lives. For the youth who were there that night, the source of comfort came primarily from their own ranks, other teen-agers who were there and could help validate the fear and horror that they felt. According to Minister of Youth Jay Fannin, the teens counseled each other—getting each other to open up.

Going back into the building following the shooting became a catalyst for many of the youth to break down the denial of the loss that many were feeling but unable to process. By the second day of the cleanup process, the building was released back to the church for use and was soon visited by Fannin, Steve Hayes, and many of the youth. With the initial shock of the event still fresh in their minds, many youth and youth workers wept openly, remembering the events of two days before. This initial visit to the church made attending the worship service that next Sunday an easier transition for many. Fannin believes that these events in the days immediately following the shooting were instrumental in moving the youth toward a measure of sorrow necessary in the initial stages of grief.

One event, however, that Fannin recounts as the most beneficial to the overall processing of grief and healing occurred late Tuesday night at the conclusion of a youth meeting. The youth were encouraged to express their thoughts and feelings in a way that was to be a lasting remembrance to the lives of their friends, children's choir director, and Sunday school teacher. Armed only with their grief and felt-tip markers, the youth were led to the now stripped floors of the sanctuary and outer hallways of the church. They were instructed to write messages of farewell, appreciation, love, grief, forgiveness, and confidence in God in the midst of what for them was a time of fear and confusion. After all the messages were inscribed, the result of this exercise was nothing short of inspirational. As youth, parents, and other members of the church eventually discovered, the power of their words and expressions of love and sorrow provided a beginning in the healing process.

This exercise, scheduled for a brief time that Tuesday night, kept many of the youth at the church late into the night and again at church the following

Wednesday to continue the writing. According to Fannin, several of the youth came to the church straight from school, asked for a marker and continued where they had left off the previous night. On Wednesday evening the youth were joined by other church members in completing the task. By the time the carpet installers were ready to lay carpet in the sanctuary and hallways of the church building, several hundred square feet of concrete floor was covered with the well wishes and farewells to the fallen and words of forgiveness to the gunman. Although now covered, the record of these messages continues to be an inspiration to parents and others of the church.

Identifying the Problems

Tragedy and trauma have been a big part of the human condition throughout history. The problems facing the professionals who were working with the victims of the shooting were:

1. the nature of the trauma—a gunman heavily armed with intent to kill helpless individuals;
2. the victims (those directly involved) of the trauma—whether by mistake or by design, the victims were children, many in middle school or younger;

3. the location of the trauma—a church sanctuary, a place historically known for its safety and security, now a refuge for children no longer; and

4. the number of people affected either directly or indirectly by the shooting—400 to 500 individuals present in the worship center, many more who were evacuated from the building, and friends and family members who waited for the news of their loved one's safety.

These problems as well as many others created a huge challenge for professional counselors and social workers to assist families and communities citywide in dealing with the fallout of the crisis. What emerged from many planning meetings was a multiple approach that would encompass as many of the victims as possible. The following information came from many different models used in helping the victims.

One of the first opportunities for individuals to deal with the trauma in their lives came in the form of a class offered by the seminary at the church on Sunday evenings. Entitled "Parental Responses to Violence: The Wedgwood Tragedy and Grade School Children," the class was primarily designed for parents whose children were at the church the night of the shooting. Dr. Ian Jones offered this advice.

Know your Family

How involved was your child? The level of response to a crisis depends upon how directly involved one was with the traumatic event. In the case of the shooting, there were five levels of involvement:

1. Those actually in the area of the shooting at the time of the shooting. This group would include all the adults in the south foyer and east hallway and the youth and adults in the sanctuary itself.

2. Those in the building but not in the proximity of fire from the gunman. This group included the adults in the fellowship hall as well as office personnel in the office at the time of the shooting.

3. Those either in adjacent buildings or in the neighborhood within sound of gunfire. This group included children attending mission activities upstairs, adults attending teachers' meetings, adults and children in the nursery area, and adults in the church library.

4. Those neighborhood friends and passersby who arrived on the scene just after the shooting had occurred. This group included emergency personnel along with other professionals who became involved

in tending to other victims. (Some of the emergency personnel who went into the building immediately after the shooting should be placed in either groups one or two due to the type of exposure and direct involvement with the crime scene.)

5. Those counselors, media personnel, and people watching the event from their homes all over the country who were affected by the shooting as a violation of what they considered their own personal boundaries.

The affect on the children would also depend upon how it related to other events in their lives. For many of the families at Wedgwood, the shooting became the most traumatic event in their lives, especially the lives of the children involved. Families were encouraged to sit down with their children and allow them to talk about the event in their own words from their own perspectives. Depending on how the family typically dealt with stress, families were encouraged to assess the level of stress facing them and to focus on the family strengths used to work through stressful events. Suggestions for dealing with stress included: family days off for mini-vacations to refocus and family nights that may include playing games, having a favorite meal together, or other popular activities.

Know Yourself: The Parent As the Model

How have you personally dealt with the tragedy?
What is known about how families deal with any
type of stress is that as the parent goes, so goes the
child. Parents who tend to deal with trauma hon-
estly and openly set a tone of openness for their
children to follow. In cases where families are not
willing to deal with tragedy directly, the message
sent to their children is that tragedy is a phenome-
non that will deal with itself in time and should have
no significant impact on their lives. This "out of
sight out of mind" mentality can be devastating to a
child who may be re-traumatized by not having a
safe environment in which to discuss private fears.
For parents, giving a child a safe place to talk about
their hurt reinforces the role of the parent as a protective influence. In many ways in order for the
child to receive comfort in dealing with a tragedy,
the parent must have comfort and security to pass
on. For the parents, it is crucial that they know
themselves well enough to identify significant
changes in their personalities or behaviors that prevent them from appropriately working through the
tragedy.

Know Your Child

Just as it is critical for the parents to know themselves in the event of a trauma, it is equally important for them to know their children. The first step is to know the developmental level of the child. Often in response to a traumatic event, a child may regress to an earlier developmental stage that reflects a more secure time in their lives. In some cases, a child may regress two or more developmental stages due to the severity and the exposure of the event. Reports in the days following the shooting revealed that many children and youth were sleeping with their parents or in their parents' room. Too afraid to be by themselves, many of the youth would not stay home or go anywhere by themselves, even to empty rooms in their own homes.

Parents must also be familiar with their child's personality and temperament. Any dramatic changes other than what would be considered a normal response to trauma, may be an indication that the child needs more than the security of the family to help him or her. The parents must be aware of the way in which the child talks about the tragedy and if the child is seeking to include the parents in the discussion or trying to leave them out. Some children may be more inclined to speak with their parents than others. In the case of the Wedgwood shooting, as mentioned above, many of the youth did not talk in great detail to their parents. This was due in part to the children's sense that their parents could not understand if they were not at the church that night. Parents in this situation had to be even more alert to changes in behavior, personality, or school performance that might indicate a need to consult a professional. If no dramatic changes occurred, the parents would look for opportunities to talk with their child or to encourage others with whom the child may be sharing.

Know Your Church and the Community

When an individual or family finds themselves in the middle of a tragedy that is too great for them to handle on their own, it is extremely important for them to be aware of various church and community resources to which they may turn for support or needs. It is important for families to know that they can turn to their church or community for help. In the case of Wedgwood, the victims' needs were met by the overwhelming response of area churches, community leaders, and professionals who provided support and stress relief.

Helping Those Who Help Others

Jeremiah was called the "weeping prophet" because his emotions were continually being affected by the conditions of his people. On one occasion he lamented, "I am a man who has seen affliction. . . . He has made me walk in darkness and not the light. . . . He has surrounded me with bitterness and woe. He has set me in dark places" (Lam. 3:1-6). Those who offered hour upon hour of counseling and care-giving in the aftermath of the shooting felt at times that they had been set in dark places.

Those working with victims of severe trauma have their own needs for counseling and debriefing. The first step in working with helpers is to assist them in identifying their needs. Once the needs have been identified, the individual must begin appropriately dealing with the grief associated with the loss. The next step is to determine the role of God as the ultimate Healer in the context of tragedy. In incidents where professionals become overwhelmed with the task of ministering to traumatized individuals, they must keep in mind that it is God who heals, and the professional is only the helper through which God can work. The last step involves assisting the helper in finding an acceptable context from which to begin a new understanding of the tragedy along with a new perception of themselves and their responsibility to the event.

Both professional counselors and lay people learned much about grief and healing in the wake of the Wedgwood shootings.

Many stories told of miracles of survival.

Photo by Kathy Holton.

13

Angels in the Auditorium and Elsewhere

"In the Presence of the Angels of God"
(Luke 15:10)

While watching *Angels in the Outfield,* we might fantasize about the supernatural, but on the evening of September 15, 1999, there were reports of angels in the auditorium ... and elsewhere. It would be incomplete and unfair to tell this story without relating the supernatural. Not everyone will understand the accounts contained here, but let those who have ears to hear, hear and let those who have eyes to see, see.

Angels in the Bible

In the Bible angels are "ministering spirits sent forth to minister" to God's people—those who "will inherit salvation" (Heb. 1:14). They are mentioned in the majority of the books of the Bible. Examples of when God responded to prayer by sending an angel are numerous:

+ Genesis 19, angels sent to Lot
+ 1 Kings 19:5-7, an angel sent to Elijah
+ 2 Chronicles 32:20-21, an angel sent to Hezekiah
+ Zechariah 1:8-9, an angel sent to Zechariah
+ Matthew 4:11, angels sent to Jesus
+ Matthew 18:10, angels sent to the children
+ Luke 1:11-13, an angel sent to Zacharias
+ Acts 12:5-10, an angel sent to Peter
+ Acts 27:22-24, an angel sent to Paul
+ Revelation 1:1, an angel sent to John

This much we know about the activity of angels in the Bible:

+ Angels protect God's people (Gen. 32:1; 2 Kings 6:16-17; Dan. 6:22)
+ Angels deliver God's people (Acts 12:1-11; Acts 27:23-24)
+ Angels deliver messages to God's people (Luke 2:9-14; Matt. 28:2-7; Acts 10:1-7)
+ Angels deliver punishment on behalf of God's people (Acts 12:23; 2 Chron. 32:20-21)
+ Angels renew physical strength (Luke 22:43)

✦ Angels are sometimes accompanied by light—the glory of God (Luke 2:9; Acts 12:7)

✦ Angels, on at least one occasion, accompanied the dead to heaven (Luke 16:22)

Believers often say, "When God has a person He doesn't need a miracle." It has been observed in these days, when Satan has a person, God's people need a miracle. On the evening of September 15, God's miracle-working power was present, and angels reportedly were sent forth to minister to God's people.

Light and Darkness

Perhaps the most visible evidence of the supernatural was the experience of light and darkness. There are those who testify with absolute certainty that at the first gunshot, the worship center was filled with light. Others, like Chip Gillette and Jason Ferguson, testified that the lights came on suddenly just as the gunman shot himself. Still others, like Laura Mac-Donald and Jeremiah Neitz, testified with absolute certainty that after the shooting ended and those present began to leave the worship center, they did so in almost complete darkness. In between these extremes, there are perceptions of varying degrees of light and darkness, including the testimony of flashes of brilliant light and the testimony shared by Tammy Applegate: "My son Chris told me that while they were in the church during the shooting it was very bright and in the back it was very dark."

The concrete facts are as follows. Tim Hood was in charge of the lights, assisted by Brian Burkett. They were seated in the balcony during the concert. According to Hood, "on a scale of one to ten, the lights were on one to one and a half." When they realized that this was actually a shooting, they decided to bring the lights up slowly so as not to cause further panic. "When we got to full ten, there was no more shooting and people began to leave the worship center." So what is the explanation of the various perceptions of light in the worship center?

First, Satan masquerades as an angel of light just as the Bible says (2 Cor. 11:14). This may explain why some people thought they saw light, when in reality it was dark around them. It may have been a masquerade.

Second, there were reports of those who say they actually saw angels in the auditorium. Angels are sometimes accompanied by the glory of God, described in the Bible as light (Luke 2:9; Acts 12:7). In locations where angels may have been active—protecting someone, delivering someone, delivering God's message to someone, delivering God's punishment to the gunman, or renewing physical strength—there could have been light. Some may have seen this angelic light even though the auditorium was dark. Others may have seen flashes of light as angels passed by them. Where there was no angelic activity, people may have seen darkness.

Sometimes in experiences of great sorrow, darkness comes while it should still be light. As Jesus was being crucified, God the Father turned out the lights, sending three hours of darkness in the midst of the day (Matt. 27:45). There are some things that God does not want us to experience and even as they are happening, our eyes are blinded with darkness. So, why did the lights go out in the nursery of the church at the precise time of the shooting? The power was on, as evidenced by the functioning of the tape player, but the lights were not. Perhaps God, the Father, was offering comfort and protection to the youngest of His children and those who cared for them. In the darkness, the children were not able fully to see the panic on the faces of the nursery workers.

The Presence of the Demonic

Some will likely prefer to explain away the darkness and light with other, more logical, less supernatural theories. Still, we must consider the presence of the demonic. How do we explain the testimonies of those present who saw faces in the balcony smiling at them and heard laughter coming from the balcony? The psalmist said, "our enemies laugh among themselves" (Ps. 80:6). There were only five, then four people in the balcony that night. All have testified that no one was laughing or smiling. All were confused. They could hear the shots. They saw people crawling under the pews and saw band members running off the stage. They saw the effects of the pipe bomb that exploded straight up into the air toward the balcony. But, because of the way the balcony hangs over the lower floor, they could not see the gunman. They certainly were not laughing.

So what was the source of the laughter? Again, some will excuse it as the imagination of teen-agers or the confusion of noises in the auditorium. However, if Satan was present and if this was indeed spiritual warfare, he would have been delighted at the fear and confusion he was causing, not to mention the loss of lives and the injuries.

Another "Why" Question

If there were angels in and around the auditorium and if God sent them to protect people from the demonic, why were seven killed and why did others suffer such traumatic injuries? Remember this escalated into spiritual warfare. Even in battle, some who are obeying the commander-in-chief still lose their lives while others in obedience are wounded. But Scripture tells us, "The last enemy that will be destroyed is death" (1 Cor. 15:26). What our foes meant for destruction only ushered these seven saints into the presence of God, and "to live is Christ . . . to die is gain" (Phil. 1:21).

It was the popular theology of Jesus' day that said that favored souls received the special privilege of being accompanied to heaven by angels (Luke 16:22). If angels were present at Wedgwood and were looking for favored souls to transport to heaven, who would be more likely candidates than young Christians killed in the act of praising the Lord?

The Weapons of Our Warfare

So, in the possible presence of the angels of God (Luke 15:10) and in the midst of the battle between the powers of darkness and the power of light, much of what was experienced was of a supernatural nature. Consider the testimonies of those present as well as those not present but affected.

Jason Ferguson recalled:

The gunman came down the middle aisle on the organ side, but he only came down about four pews. It was as if he was going to chase this lady filming or chase someone on stage. He came as far as four pews, then he stopped. He was obviously frustrated, and he was trembling. All the way down the aisle he was shooting until he stopped about four pews from the back. He waved his gun and then went back. This is when he really began to curse.

Stacy Grey remembered, "the gunman was confined to the back of the sanctuary. He had plenty of ammo to walk down every aisle, but something kept him at the back."

Amy Galloway recalled watching the gunman's feet from her position under the back pew. "I saw him go down at least three different aisles, but he always went back."

In 2 Corinthians 10:4, Paul writes, "The weapons of our warfare are not carnal but mighty in God for pulling down strongholds." There were no carnal weapons readily available in the worship center. Police Detective John Baker rehearsing with the church orchestra in the choir room did not have his weapon on him or in his car, a very unusual occurrence according to Baker. Police Officer Chip Gillette came running from his home across the street, was met by a church member, then returned to make a call on his police radio and get his gun and police vest. The delay caused him to not be in the worship center while the gunman was still alive. Various people in the worship center considered rushing the gunman but could never find the appropriate angle or timing. However, no carnal weapons were needed. This was spiritual warfare. God had a mighty weapon ready.

One possible reason why the gunman kept turning back relates to light and darkness. Standing at the back of the worship center, under the balcony, with the lights dimmed, it was very dark. Walking down any aisle from the back, a bright light would appear as the fourth pew was passed. With the early evening sun shining through the stained-glass window above the choir loft, the stained-glass cross would have shone very brightly. At approximately the spot where the gunman kept turning back, he would have seen the brilliance of the light shining through the cross.

There are other theories as to why the gunman stopped in each aisle exactly four rows from the back, but the supernatural explanation is that "the weapons of our warfare are . . . mighty in God."

A Bullet in the Hymnal

Police Officer Chip Gillette related the following:

> One specific thing took place that changed me forever. I walked back into the worship center on Thursday morning through those same south doors. I was retracing and reliving the whole shooting event in my own effort to make some kind of sense of the shooting. When I got to the rear doors of the worship center, I could see the ATF agents busily mapping out every

minute detail of the crime scene. I walked on in. I was fully expecting someone to ask me to stay out of the area until they had finished their work, but no one said anything. There was a strong feeling of the presence of God that came over me and I began to pray, "God if there is anything left in here that I can take as proof that this really did happen, please show it to me."

I began looking on the floor for a bullet, bullet fragment, or shell casing that might have been overlooked. I stepped over tape outlines of where bodies had laid and over blood trails. Nothing was there. The crime scene search guys had picked it clean.

On the last aisle, as I was walking toward the rear of the room and was heading for home, I saw where three bullets had struck the end of a pew. Thinking that there might be a bullet embedded in it, I reached for my pocket knife and was planning how I could check this out without drawing the attention of the ATF guys. I touched the hole and felt on the backside to determine if it had gone through or was still in the wood. It was a through hole. I touched another hole. It, too, was a through hole. I had a sinking feeling as I reached farther down to the last hole. It, too, was a through hole. As I was bending forward, I saw that there was a corresponding hole in the last bullet path that had hit the wooden hymnal rack. The hymnal in the rack was pushed over to the side. My heart began to pound as I took it out of the rack.

The bullet was still there. I could feel it when I touched the front of the book. I sat down in the pew and opened the hymnal. It fell open to hymn number thirty-seven, two pages into the Hallelujah Chorus. There was a great feeling of joy and excitement as I saw the bullet there stuck in between the pages. A great outflow of emotion came over me as I read the words of the chorus where the bullet had come to its final rest. " . . . King of Kings and Lord of Lords and He shall reign forever and ever." I began to cry and to realize that Christ was telling me that "He is Lord"—before the shooting, during the shooting, and forever more.

Testimonies of the Supernatural from Those Present

For Southwestern Seminary student Lana Bull, the church scene was all too familiar. When she was a child, a missionary had visited her home church and told of a church shooting. From that time until the present, Lana had experienced a recurring dream of being in a church during a shooting.

According to Lana, "When the shooting began, I knew it was real. My mind told me I had been here before." A psychology major, Lana remained calm and memorized everything she heard. She would become a valued witness of the proceedings inside the worship center and would testify as to the supernatural element present.

Kaye Dehlin Wilke had taken her children to their classes and was sitting in her parked car on the north side of the church enjoying her Bible study. She remembers:

> A short time later I felt uneasy. The unusual feeling caught me by surprise. I suddenly did not feel safe. I reminded myself that I was parked at Wedgwood and there was probably no safer place to be. I wondered if I was just being paranoid or if God wanted me to pay attention—so I locked the doors, sat bolt upright, and looked around. I thought, maybe I should go inside the building. Things just didn't feel right. Within a few minutes, a panicked young woman and her two children ran from one of the east doors to their car. I noticed one police car and then another. I saw preschool and nursery workers running with their tiny charges through the open construction area next to me. I saw a man in a blue shirt running from the church up the street towards me. Things were not right. He said, "There's a shooter in the church!" He kept running. I ran. East doors opened and a frightening exodus

was underway. Pounding tennis shoes . . . pounding hearts . . . fervent prayers . . . a sea of little girls . . .Grace's class. I looked for the boys and found Jon. I held both my children and my heart was okay.

Several days later, I picked up my Bible study workbook from the floor of the car and resumed at the point where I had abruptly stopped. What I read nearly took my breath away. The commentator wrote: "It seems a paradox that the death of Christians could be the key to church growth. Yet as surely as the cross of Christ was essential to our salvation, the sacrifice of believers is crucial to world evangelism. That is as true today as ever." God had indeed spoken in the midst of tragedy.

When Wedgwood Children's Minister Kim Herron got the children out of the building, she took them across the street to the elementary school—the back door of the school where they could not see all that was happening in the street. But the door was locked. To no one in particular, Kim said, "How are we going to get inside to safety? We need someone to go to the front and unlock these back doors from the inside." At this point, a well-dressed man walked up and said, "I can do that." He left and in a few minutes the back doors of the school opened and the children entered. No one recalled ever having seen the man before. No one saw him again after he opened the back doors. He was not an employee of the school and thus had no key to the back doors. No one knows who he was or why he was behind the school building. Could this be yet another angel delivering God's people?

During the shooting, Aaron Clark was sitting in the front row next to Robert DeBord, who was injured. Aaron dropped to the floor when he realized the shooting was real. He then felt a sensation on his shoulder and thought he had been hit. But a bullet had passed through a pew and landed on his shoulder. He wasn't injured and carries that bullet with him as a reminder. "To me, it's God's promise that He has something greater in store for me," Aaron said.

Long-time church members Johnnie and Lahoma Loar had spent the day sitting with the family of a church member who had been taken to the hospital with chest pains. The afternoon had ended with successful bypass surgery. After running by their home to freshen up, the Loars arrived at Wedgwood after the prayer meeting had begun. They recalled:

> As we walked in the south foyer door, we made note of the fact the prayer meeting was being held in the old fellowship hall because a youth rally was in the auditorium. We struggled with a desire to be with our friends in prayer meeting and give a report on the surgery or sit in the

foyer and visit with other friends who always meet there prior to choir practice. The desire to remain in the foyer was strong and further motivated by the fact that we were leaving in a few days on an extended trip. The Lord's still, small voice seemed to tell us to "go to prayer meeting. That is your appointed place on Wednesday nights." Obedience is not always easy, but it is always right. No one knows what would have happened had we not obeyed, but I do know where we would have been and it was there three of our friends were shot.

Longtime church member Jane McDonald wrote:

On September 15th a friend called to see if I could come visit her as she had recently lost her husband. I told her that as soon as we finished eating I would. I also wanted to go by the church to pick up the church prayer list, "The Gap," as my granddaughter was listed on it. When I left my house and came to the four way stop, two blocks from the church, I decided to turn right and go to Gracie's as she sounded so depressed on the phone. I know God protected me that night, because right after I entered Gracie's house, the phone rang and it was my husband calling from home to tell me about the news reports that Kevin Galey had been shot and the gunman was still in the church.

Other Supernatural Occurrences That Have Been Verified by Wedgwood

✦ The gunman entered the worship center occupied by four hundred to five hundred people, armed with nearly two hundred rounds of ammunition. He fired between sixty-five and one hundred rounds and only five people were killed and four wounded in the worship center.

One church member explained this amazing statistic as follows:

The angels were placing shields of protection around people so that the gunman could not even see them. Angels were saying, "You can't have this one. . . . This one is found faithful and is ready." Finally, the angel of the Lord said, "That's enough. You can't have any more," and the curtain dropped leaving only one person visible to shoot, the gunman himself.

✦ The homemade pipe bomb, which could have had devastating results, did not explode as the gunman had planned. Instead of landing in the crowd, where it would have been devastating, the bomb sailed over the youth, landing on the floor of the sanctuary. The force of the explosion went up, not out, so that the shrapnel landed harmlessly in the balcony rather than ripping through the crowd.

✦ On Sunday afternoon CNN broadcast portions of the memorial service from the stadium and because one of the victims, Kim Jones, was born in Saudi Arabia, a portion of the program was carried there as well. The coverage was viewed by Kim's friends who live there. The gospel was heard clearly in this Muslim nation where it is against the law for a Muslim to convert to Christianity.

✦ Because one of the first calls for help came on a police radio from Chip Gillette, emergency vehicles were dispatched immediately without spending precious time to verify that the call was real.

✦ One of the people in the church at the time of the shooting was a paramedic. There were also several nurses present. These trained medical personnel were able to assist in stopping the bleeding of the wounded and in offering early assistance to those in shock.

✦ All seven victims who were killed were Christians. God did not allow any non-Christians present to be taken.

✦ Because of the hurricane bearing down on the eastern coast of the United States, numerous schools postponed their See-You-at-the-Pole activities until Thursday morning. With the students arriving at the services fully aware of the Wedgwood shooting, many schools reported conversions and re-dedications. One school reported 110 students accepting Jesus Christ as Lord and Savior. Another reported a teacher led twenty-two of her students to faith in Christ.

✦ Christian teachers have been able to share their faith in the classroom because students are asking questions. In many cases non-Christian teachers have allowed the Christian students to share their testimonies in response to questions posed by other students.

✦ In a nearby community, prayer and Scripture reading is once again occurring over the public school intercom.

✦ A caller to local Christian radio station KLTY said he didn't know what those people had, but he wanted it. The DJ led him to faith in Christ over the air.

✦ On most Wednesday nights, children are playing on the church playground near where the gunman parked his car. Due to delays, no children were on the playground on this beautiful fall evening. Therefore, they did not become targets nor did they have to see the people running from the church buildings in panic.

✦ Now, at Wedgwood, "worship services end, but the people don't leave," states Wedgwood's minister of adult education, singles and prayer, Chris Shirley. "They stay and talk with one another," continued Shirley. "I hear a lot more people telling one another, 'I love you.' I see a lot more people hugging."

Testimonies of Those Not Present

Why was God so protective of the people present at Wedgwood that Wednesday? Why did God send angels? The response was fueled by the intercessory prayer of people not even present at the church. Consider these testimonies.

✦ I am a twenty-six-year-old Christian in Tulsa, Oklahoma. I was in my own church at 7:00 P.M. The feelings coursing through me were that of fear and being alone. I have no reason to feel this way in my life. I continued crying in a back room. I just could not be comforted. This continued through most of our worship service. I finally collected myself and went back in to finish the service. When I got home I saw the report on the local news as to what happened. I truly believe I was crying for the victims and those left behind. I just wanted you to know someone who had no idea what was going on at the time it happened was praying and crying over these people because God knew. K.M.C.

✦ I woke up that morning to go to our own See-You-at-the-Pole rally here in Borger, Texas, at Frank Phillips College—to videotape it for our youth minister. I had an overwhelming sense to pray for all See-You-at-the-Pole and Saw-You-at-the-Pole rallies. I have four children and knew two of my sons would be leading at two different rallies. I knew with the recent Littleton experience, anything could happen, so I prayed all day for everyone involved in all the rallies all across the nation. I had a heightened sense of awareness, you might say. B.D.

✦ Early the morning of the shooting, I was driving by Southwest High School thinking and praying about the See-You-at-the-Pole rallies that were happening across the city. KCBI radio was giving interviews about the event. Suddenly I had this strong impression that there was going to be a shooting. I dismissed the thoughts, but they kept returning. I thought I should call KCBI and give them a warning but reasoned that they would consider me crazy. I then thought I should contact Wedgwood, but again I convinced myself that I would be causing panic for nothing, even though I was a former member of Wedgwood. All day long I relived in my mind a shooting. My prayers and thoughts have been with you. I have wished a thousand times I had called KCBI or contacted the church. Please forgive me for not acting at God's prompting. G.L.B.

✦ From the time Pam Minatrea woke up September 15, she felt an inexplicable need to pray for the safety of the young people around the state who were gathered in schoolyards for See-You-at-the-Pole prayer meetings. She told her husband, Milfred, about her uneasy feeling. About twelve hours later, Milfred, director of church ministries for the Baptist General Convention of Texas, was coordinating the Baptist response to hurting families at Wedgwood.

✦ I am not a member of Wedgwood but my roommate and I have been visiting the church since the shooting. On that tragic evening, we were already engaged in intercession. We had no idea what or who we were praying for. My roommate was weeping and said that the Scripture that was going through her mind was Matthew 2:18: "Rachel weeping for her children." It was only later that evening when she checked the Fort Worth Star-Telegram's headlines on the Internet that she found the news from earlier that night about the shooting at Wedgwood. Be assured that our God does see and move people to pray in times of trouble. G.E. & K.G.

✦ Seated in a worship service in her church in North Carolina, Darlene Heaton, the aunt of Kim Jones, recalled, "When the pastor was praying during our Wednesday night prayer meeting, I was praying along with him. A scene flashed through my mind of a gunman walking into a church and shooting. I didn't understand where this image came from. It was approximately the time of the shooting at Wedgwood. Now I feel as if the Lord was preparing me."

✦ I work with a high school group in McKinney, Texas. I had taken some of our kids to See-You-at-the-Pole and did not know until we heard the news about Wedgwood that several of them expected someone to be shot somewhere that day. But they went on anyway! G.B.

✦ That day, in my heart, there was a special tension of inner peace and worldly turmoil. The day before I was thinking about Columbine. The night before the tragedy I dreamed or had a nightmare about the anti-Christ. I got chills. I sensed the anti-Christ or at least the spirit of the anti-Christ was already alive and well and ready to attack again. I had a sense of fear as though this killer was entering my dreams, yet I felt protected by God. When my parents called to tell me of the shooting, it was as though I already knew. Warrensburg, MO

✦ A group of adults had our own See-You-at-the-Pole rally at the Carson County (Texas) Court House at the same time the kids were praying at the school. The Holy Spirit prompted me to pray for the safety of all our youth and for the Saw-You-at-the-Pole rallies that night. All the adults agreed in this prayer. C.C.

✦ My twelve-year-old daughter came home from her youth group that night at the same time the news broke the Wedgwood story. Before we knew any details my daughter told me she had had a strange experience while sitting in her youth group. She told me that she had a very vivid thought, and in her mind had seen a man walk in the back of the youth group and begin shooting a gun. When she then heard the news update, she felt as though God had been speaking to her heart and now feels that God has used this to show her that in the future she should pray for others immediately when she has thoughts. C., Georgia

✦ Early in the morning here in Japan, when it would have been the afternoon of the shooting at Wedgwood, I had a strange dream. I was in a large building with a lot of people and there was a gunman trying to shoot us, especially me. I don't remember much else about it now, but if I remember correctly, it was related to religion. When I have dreams about people out of the blue, I always pray for those people, assuming that at least part of the time God is prompting me to pray. R.C.

✦ Something happened that Wednesday night, September 15, 1999. I had experienced a perturbing day, but nothing too much out of the ordinary, and had gone to our church's prayer meeting (in Brazil). As we began praying, I can't explain the sudden overwhelming sense of burden that I felt. I looked at my watch and it was 8:47 P.M.—6:47 P.M. in Fort Worth. I felt that I needed to leave and pray on my own, so I did. Some of those around me noticed that I left and had special prayer for me. On the way home I felt a great need to cry out to the Lord in an attempt to find peace. Knowing what I know now, I think this was God's way of getting me to intercede for those suffering so greatly at Wedgwood. I was shocked to find out next morning what had happened and that we knew several of those hurt and killed. I'm still in awe of the way this unfolded. I haven't shared it with anyone until now, but here it is. B.H.

What was happening? Knowing the shooting was about to occur and knowing the suffering that was near, the Holy Spirit began to alert the prayer warriors, those with the spiritual gift of intercession. The letters above are from some of the thousands of people who talk to God on a regular basis. The Holy Spirit got on what one author calls God's S.O.S. Emergency Prayer Network and raised up intercessors on behalf of those present at Wedgwood Baptist Church. Were it not true that intercessors prefer the prayer closet to the spotlight, we would have been inundated with letters like those above. It is yet another part of the supernatural dimension of September 15, 1999.

The cross shows us the way.

Photo by James Morris.

14

How to Get to Heaven from Wedgwood

"Light to Those Who Sit in Darkness"
(Luke 1:79)

For days and nights immediately following the shooting, hundreds of people gathered around Wedgwood Baptist Church—in the parking lots, near the church sign covered with flowers and messages, across the street at the elementary school, and in neighbors' yards. Among these were hundreds, then dozens, of news media, grieving church members, supportive friends, and burdened strangers. But there was still another group. These were the non-believers who came to investigate, observe, even marvel at the faith of God's people. It seemed to them that these Wedgies had a faith that was contagious. No matter how dark their nights, their faith seemed to be "new every morning" (Lam. 3:23).

During another dark night many centuries ago, Zacharias, the father of John the Baptist, prophesied concerning his son that he would give "knowledge of salvation" and "light to those who sit in darkness" (Luke 1:77, 79). The purpose of this chapter is to offer light to those who are still in the dark. To not include the way out of this darkness and into the light would be a guilty silence. Our Lord said, "A little while longer the light is with you. Walk while you have the light, lest darkness over-take you; he who walks in darkness does not know where he is going" (John 12:35).

Steps to Peace with God

The Billy Graham Evangelistic Association and World Wide Publications offer the following "Steps to Peace With God." We share it here with permission:

Step 1. God's Purpose: Peace and Life

God loves you and wants you to experience peace and life—abundant and eternal. The Bible says . . .

> ". . . we have peace with God through our Lord Jesus Christ." Romans 5:1

> "For God so loved the world that He gave His only begotten Son, that whoever believes in Him should not perish but have everlasting life." John 3:16

". . . I have come that they may have life, and that they may have it more abundantly." John 10:10b

Since God planned for us to have peace and abundant life right now, why are most people not having this experience?

Step 2. Our Problem: Separation

God created us in His own image to have an abundant life. He did not make us robots to automatically love and obey Him, but gave us a will and freedom of choice.

We chose to disobey God and go our own willful way. We still make this choice today. This results in separation from God. The Bible says . . .

"For all have sinned and fall short of the glory of God." Romans 3:23

"For the wages of sin is death, but the gift of God is eternal life in Christ Jesus our Lord." Romans 6:23

Through the ages, individuals have tried in many ways to bridge this gap . . . without success. . .

The Bible says . . .

"There is a way that seems right to a man, but in the end it leads to death." Proverbs 14:12

"But your iniquities have separated you from God; and your sins have hidden His face from you, so that He will not hear." Isaiah 59:2

Step 3. God's Remedy: The Cross

Jesus Christ is the only answer to this problem. He died on the cross and rose from the grave, paying the penalty for our sin and bridging the gap between God and man. The Bible says . . .

" . . . God is on one side and all the people on the other side, and Christ Jesus, Himself man, is between them to bring them together. . ." 1 Timothy 2:5

"For Christ also has suffered once for sins, the just for the unjust, that He might bring us to God. . . " 1 Peter 3:18a

"But God demonstrates His own love for us in this: While we were still sinners, Christ died for us." Romans 5:8

Step 4. Our Response: Receive Christ

We must trust Jesus Christ and receive Him by personal invitation. The Bible says . . .

"Behold, I stand at the door and knock. If anyone hears My voice and opens the door, I will come in to him and dine with him, and he with Me." Revelation 3:20

"But as many as received Him, to them He gave the right to become children of God, even to those who believe in His name." John 1:12

" . . . If you confess with your mouth the Lord Jesus and believe in your heart that God has raised Him from the dead, you will be saved." Romans 10:9

Is there any good reason why you cannot receive Jesus Christ right now? How to receive Christ:

1. Admit your need (I am a sinner).
2. Be willing to turn from your sins (repent).
3. Believe that Jesus Christ died for you on the Cross and rose from the grave.
4. Through prayer, invite Jesus Christ to come in and control your life through the Holy Spirit. (Receive Him as Lord and Savior.)

What to pray:

Dear Lord Jesus, I know that I am a sinner and need Your forgiveness. I believe that You died for my sins. I want to turn from my sins. I now invite You to come into my heart and life. I want to trust You as Lord, in the fellowship of Your church.

Date_____

Signature_____

God's Assurance: His Word

If you prayed this prayer, the Bible says . . . "whoever calls upon the name of the Lord will be saved." Romans 10:13

Did you sincerely ask Jesus Christ to come into your life? Where is He right now? What has He given you?

> "For it is by grace you have been saved, through faith—and that is not from yourselves, it is the gift of God—not by works, so that no one can boast." Ephesians 2:8-9

The Bible says . . .

> "He who has the Son has life; he who does not have the Son does not have life. These things I have written to you who believe in the name of the Son of God, that you may know that you have eternal life, and that you may continue to believe in the name of the Son of God." 1 John 5:12-13

Receiving Christ, we are born into God's family through the supernatural work of the Holy Spirit who indwells every believer . . . this is called regeneration or the "new birth."

This is just the beginning of a wonderful new life in Christ. To deepen this relationship, you should:

1. Read your Bible every day to get to know Christ better.
2. Talk to God in prayer every day.
3. Tell others about Christ.
4. Worship, fellowship, and serve with other Christians in a church where Christ is preached.
5. As Christ's representative in a needy world, demonstrate your new life by your love and concern for others.

May God bless you as you do.

From Darkness to Light

Those who have placed their faith in Jesus Christ claim many benefits:

✦ Walking in the light ("Walk while you have the light," John 12:35) vs. walking in the darkness ("he who walks in darkness does not know where he is going," John 12:35).

✦ Life with meaning and purpose ("a lamp unto my feet and a light to my path," Psalm 119:105) vs. life without a valid purpose ("They grope in darkness without a light," Job 12:25).

✦ Looking to Jesus Christ for direction ("the Light of the world," John 8:12) vs. being led by Satan ("the rulers of the darkness of this age," Ephesians 6:12).

✦ Experiencing eternal heaven ("there shall be no night there," Revelation 21:25) where there will be eternal joy ("joy in heaven," Luke 15:7) vs. eternal hell ("outer darkness," Matthew 8:12) where there will be eternal agony ("weeping and gnashing of teeth," Matthew 8:12).

The Bible describes God as "light and in Him is no darkness at all" (1 John 1:5). Further, the Bible affirms that it is God "who commanded light to shine out of darkness, who has shone in our hearts to give the light of the knowledge of the glory of God in the face of Jesus Christ" (2 Corinthians 4:6).

In rebellion against this mighty offer of God, the Bible says we sinned against God rather than offered glory to God. "All have sinned and fall short of the glory of God" (Romans 3:23). We chose to walk in the darkness rather than in the "light of the knowledge of the glory of God . . ." Even in our rebellion, the Bible challenges us to "walk in the light of the Lord" (Isaiah 2:5). The alternative to walking in the light of the Lord is to remain in our life of unforgiven sin. The ultimate result is spiritual death. The Bible explains, "the wages of sin is death, but the gift of God is eternal life in Christ Jesus our Lord" (Romans 6:23).

To facilitate this, God gave us the greatest "gift." In one of the best-known verses in the Bible, this truth is proclaimed: "God so loved the world that He gave His only begotten Son that whoever believes in Him should not perish but have everlasting life" (John 3:16). This same truth is stated in another way: "God demonstrates His own love toward us, in that while we were still sinners, Christ died for us" (Romans 5:8). Thus, the alternative to walking in darkness is offered in these words from the Bible: "If we walk in the light we have fellowship with one another and the blood of Jesus Christ His Son cleanses us from all sin" (1 John 1:7).

Through the death of Jesus Christ, God's Son, a way has been offered to you for forgiveness of your sins and for life with meaning and purpose. Jesus said, "I have come that they may have life, and that they may have it more abundantly" (John 10:10).

So, you do not have to walk in darkness with sin. God has made a provision for you. The Bible says, "if you confess with your mouth the Lord Jesus Christ and believe in your heart that God has raised Him from the dead, you will be saved. For with the heart one believes unto righteousness, and with the mouth confession is made unto salvation" (Romans 10:9-10).

Confess to Jesus Christ that you have sinned against Him. Believe that He is who the Bible says

He is—the Son of God who came to earth in the form of a man to purchase your salvation through His death on the cross. Invite Jesus to come into your life as your own personal Lord and Savior. The Bible says, "He has called you out of darkness into His marvelous light" (1 Peter 2:9).

While you should not make this crucial decision without serious thought, there is an urgency to it. As we have all seen, no one is promised tomorrow. The Bible says, "The night is far spent, the day is at hand. Therefore let us cast off the works of darkness, and let us put on the armor of light" (Romans 13:12). Further the Bible urges, "now is the accepted time; behold, now is the day of salvation (2 Corinthians 6:2).

You may still have questions and be confused as to the validity of this truth. The Bible affirms that this may be the case. When Jesus came to earth He was rejected by those who did not understand. It was said of Him, "the light shines in the darkness and the darkness did not comprehend it" (John 1:5). Becoming a Christian is a step of faith. You will never be able fully to understand or comprehend it. That is why the Bible describes those who have already placed their faith in Jesus Christ as follows: "By grace you have been saved through faith, and that not of yourselves; it is the gift of God, not of works lest anyone should boast" (Ephesians 2:8-9).

It is as though God is knocking at the door of your life, desiring to enter. However, the door must be opened from the inside. God will never enter your life by force. God is awaiting an invitation. "Behold, I stand at the door and knock, If anyone hears My voice and opens the door, I will come in to him" (Revelation 3:20); "Today, if you will hear His voice, do not harden your hearts as in the rebellion" (Hebrews 3:7-8).

If you are ready to invite Jesus Christ into your life you might want to pray a prayer similar to this one. Remember, it is not the specific words of the prayer but your sincere intent that matters most to God.

> Dear God, I know I have sinned against You. In my rebellion, I have walked in darkness. I acknowledge that I cannot save myself, cannot bring to myself life with meaning and purpose. I desire to walk in the light. So, believing that You are who the Bible says You are, I invite You into my life to be my personal Lord and Savior. I will confess publicly that You have entered my life and saved me. Thank You for my new life. Thank You for light shining in my darkness, in Jesus' Name, amen.

If you prayed this prayer or one similar to it, you now need to share it with someone and eventually become a part of a Bible-believing church where you can be influenced and nurtured by other Christians.

Let us reiterate what we have proposed for you to do. It is as simple as ABC:

A = Admit you have sinned against God.

B = Believe that Jesus is who the Bible says He is the Son of God who died for you.

C = Commit your life to Jesus Christ as your own personal Lord and Savior.

If you have further questions or would like to share your decision with the Christians at Wedgwood, you may do so by writing:

Wedgwood Baptist Church
5522 Whitman
Fort Worth, TX 76133
USA

Or, send an e-mail to Wedgwood at:
thewedge@flash.net

Or, check out the Wedgwood web site for more information:
www.wedgwoodbc.org

The "healing bear" was passed on from students at Columbine High School.

Photo by Kathy Holton.

Challenge

Don't Wait
until Thursday

"Wonders . . . Known in the Dark"
(Psalms 88:12)

The story of the tragedy and victory of the Wedgwood shootings goes on. As this book goes to press, families are still grieving the loss of loved ones, others are still undergoing therapy, teenagers are still traumatized, children are still afraid to go to church. God is still at work.

In the midst of tragedy, God often reveals great wonders to believers. The tragedy at Wedgwood was no exception. In what may be the most tragic song in the Psalms, the psalmist writes out of a background of life-long trouble. Due to his affliction, the psalmist had been deserted by friends and felt that even God may have abandoned him. In the midst of his aloneness, the psalmist prayed and asked God, "Shall Your wonders be known in the dark?" (Psalms 88:12). Those present at Wedgwood on that night of darkness know the answer to that question. Perhaps the greatest wonder made known in the tragedy of Wedgwood is the certainty of the moment and the corresponding uncertainty of the next moment.

Those present at Wedgwood on September 15, 1999, did not expect to have a Wednesday like the one they had. Some said later that there were things they should have done before that terrible evening arrived. But they waited, and for some Thursday never came. For others, Thursday would never be the same again. We would like to challenge you to take action for your future. Don't wait until Thursday.

Don't Wait until Thursday to Show Someone Your Support

Dan Burdan, a minister of education and elder in a Texas church, sent an e-mail to his son, Evan, a youth minister in Kansas. The message was forwarded, perhaps repeatedly, until it reached Pastor Meredith at Wedgwood:

> I don't think I ever told you about the fourth member of my little gang that I ran around with as a teenager. The fourth member of our gang was really quiet. He was a loner. He didn't come to the youth functions very often. The youth group was over at his house a lot, visiting his sister who was dying of muscular dystrophy. When our preacher started his Preacher Boys' class, all four of us were in-

volved. The pastor took us on a tour of the area congregations where we preached, led singing, read Scriptures, etc. Our picture was made and published in *The Firm Foundation.* We joked about the way our number four guy looked. Even the pastor remarked that he looked more like a preacher than the rest of us. He stood posed for the picture with Bible in hand, held close to his chest, and sports coat unbuttoned. I lost track of number four over the years. I knew he joined the Navy for a while. His father died about three months ago. Funeral was at Pleasant Ridge. I saw the obituary in the paper and told myself to go—after all, I hadn't seen number four in a long time. Maybe I could be of comfort to him since I know what it is like to lose a father. Number four is dead now. He took a gun to the Wedgwood Baptist Church youth rally last night, killed seven people, and then killed himself. I should have gone to see him at his father's funeral.

Do you need to show support to someone? Don't wait until Thursday.

Don't Wait until Thursday to Tell Someone You Love Him or Her

Donna Ennis remembered the last words her son, Joey, said to her as he got out of the car to go to the concert that Wednesday evening, "I love you, Mom." Following the funeral she met with Joey's fellow students at Brewer High School to say to them, "Always tell your people you love them, because you may never see them again."

After being shot, Mary Beth Talley remembers thinking, *I can't die. I haven't told my mom I love her yet today.*

Do you need to tell someone you love them? Don't wait until Thursday.

Don't Wait until Thursday to Repent or Say You're Sorry

A pastor wrote:

> I pastor a small church in Coeur d'Alene, Idaho. Our midweek service is on Thursday night. When I asked for testimonies from "See You at the Pole," one young man began to share about his reaction to the news of the shooting. He told of how he heard the story as he was driving to work and immediately pulled his car over and wept. He wondered if it had been at his church if he would have been ready. Throughout the day he prayed with his main focus being on repentance. After he shared this testimony, people began to share their reactions to the news story and to cry out to the Lord in repentance. Needless to say, I

never preached that night, but the meeting went almost an hour longer than normal, with people praying for each other and the people at Wedgwood. That kind of meeting you could never orchestrate.

Do you need to repent, ask someone's forgiveness, forgive someone else, or pray for someone? Don't wait until Thursday.

Don't Wait until Thursday to Get Things Right with God

Wedgwood member Meghan Grubb wrote:

> During the evening of September 15 sometime after the shooting at Wedgwood, my son Benjamin started crying in response to seeing the tears rolling down my face. He asked why and then answered before I could: "I think sometimes what we want to do we don't do, and what we shouldn't do, we do." In a strange way, I heard Romans 7:15 from my son. The words gave Benjamin a sense of calm and helped me forgive the gunman. As we have heard, a great good has come out of this tragedy. Many have been saved as a result, including Benjamin. On October 13, 1999, he asked Jesus into his heart. Praise the Lord!

Someone else wrote to Pastor Meredith: "I was a backslider until I heard your sermon on September 19, 1999. I was going in the wrong direction and obeying fear. As I sat and watched the memorial service on TV, the Spirit of God came over me and filled my emptiness with great joy. I want to thank you for your sermon, for it was this sermon that brought me back to Jesus."

Do you need to make the same decision as Benjamin, asking Jesus Christ into your life and trusting Him as your Savior and Lord? How about the decision of recommitting your life to Jesus Christ? Don't wait until Thursday.

Don't Wait until Thursday to Get Things Right with God's Church

Danna Crawford Heiliger had not been actively attending church when she got the call that Wednesday evening:

> Just as I was getting home from work that Wednesday evening, I received a phone call from my dad. He asked if I had seen or heard the news and instructed me not to turn on the TV. He informed me that there had been a shooting at Wedgwood but not to go there because he would find my mom and my daughter, Whitney, and take them to his house. I was to

meet them there. In the next few minutes I received a blur of phone calls with the same information about Wedgwood.

I remember driving on Granbury Road as Whitney and I do every morning on the way to her school. We sing as we drive along. In the midst of my anxiety, I was trying to sing, "I'm a GA, GA cutie pie, and I'll be one till the day I die." No, don't say die. "Amazing grace . . ." No, that's a funeral song. I just started to pray, "God I know a ton of moms and families are praying right now for the same thing, but please hear me. I've overcome a lot and I'm a strong person. I've learned a lot of things the hard way. I know you have a plan for me, but please don't have it in Your plan to take away my little girl. She is my angel here on earth. I know that You know I'm selfish, but please forgive that. This guy in front of me is driving too slowly. Please help me Lord, I'm losing it." I felt as if I was in a dream, but it was no dream. I continued my prayer, "Thank you, God, for saving my little girl and my mom."

My parents have always taken Whitney to church. Now, I'm going to be there too.

Do you need to reacquaint yourself with one of God's churches and begin again to have fellowship with some of God's people? Don't wait until Thursday.

Don't Wait until Thursday to Take a Stand against Satan and Evil

Several versions of the following letter were circulated over the Internet and signed in various ways as people cut, pasted, added, and deleted, then signed their own names. As best we can determine, this is the original version with a few grammatical adjustments. The title of this version is "Standing in His Strength":

> Hey, Satan! You really shook me up last night! Having someone go into a youth rally and shoot people—that seemed cruel even for you. You almost had me discouraged and disheartened. Almost. Then I started to realize what was really going on.
>
> My main question was, why were you attacking Christian youth? Then it hit me, fear. You realize that these are the people that will turn the tide of your "battle." You are so afraid because these youth aren't afraid of your conventional weapons. Peer pressure, drugs, sex, greed are all failing as these kids are standing up and saying "No! I choose to honor God with my behavior." You tried cranking up the heat, making the culture more enticing to them, and they still said, "No!"
>
> So you tried to use the weapon that works with adults, fear. That's not working. You killed

them in Paducah, Kentucky, but still they pray. You shot them because they said yes in Littleton, Colorado, and they still choose to walk with God. Now you murder them in Fort Worth, and they still worship our awesome God. In case you haven't figured it out yet, it won't work!

Our kids won't cave in to you! They are going to do exactly what you fear most—they will pray for strength. And God will give it to them. He will give them strength to keep going. They will spark a revival in our nation that will turn millions back to God. Once again, Jesus' love will beat your hate!

Oh, and as for trying to make them feel that life is hopeless, that's where I come in. I won't let it happen. I will fight you every step of the way, showing the hope that is in the unconditional love of Jesus Christ. You see I know we have not been given a spirit of fear, but God calls us His children, and you don't mess with one of God's kids!

So take your shots and try, but we will not cave in, and we're finished being on the defensive. Jesus tells us that the gates of hell can't stop us, and we're claiming that promise. So get ready for the battle of your life. The problem for you is, you've already lost. You lost 2000 years ago when you tried to kill Jesus. Now the students that you killed are standing with Him, with no more pain, laughing at you and your feeble attempts at victory.

Try to understand, this is no less than a declaration of war. You may want to give up now, because our Dad is on our side and Jesus told us that if He is for us nobody can stand against us. So if you desire, we will accept your unconditional surrender. Otherwise, let's get ready to *rumble!*

Your sworn enemies forever,
the children of the Most High God

Do you need to take a stand against Satan, evil or ungodliness? Don't wait until Thursday.

Don't Wait until Thursday to Pray for Revival and Spiritual Awakening

Richard Ross, youth minister consultant at Life Way Christian Resources in Nashville, Tennessee, sent this statement after the shooting:

I perceive that Satan is making a shift in strategy. Perhaps he has grown weary of getting his work done in the shadows, limited by a need to stay hidden as the angel of light. He now seems more willing to be seen for the powerful, ugly, violent person he is. Now he has opened fire on a school prayer group, a church youth rally, and on individuals who gave testimony to their relationship with God. Now spiritual warfare begins in earnest. I sense we are in the last two minutes of the game, though only sovereign God knows. We may be moving toward the Second Coming faster than any of us can imagine. If Satan is already beginning to feel the heat from the lake of fire, it stands to reason that he would take off his mask and come out swinging. There is about to be a call to Christian students to share the gospel with every lost student in America by the end of the year 2000, and a call to college and older high school students to commit a summer, a semester, or a year to evangelize North America and the world. Perhaps this will be the final harvest and then the end will come.

There is no such thing as a safe place anymore. The only place that matters is being exactly where God wants you to be. Youth pastors and youth ministers are on the front lines as never before. They are in one of the most crucial positions in our society and deserve prayer, support, and respect. It is not about one-hundred-yard banana splits any more. It is about helping parents bury kids, and assisting the Great Physician in healing hearts, and calling a generation to be willing to die, and, more importantly, to live for the Lord Jesus Christ.

Have you prayed lately for revival in God's church

and awakening in the land? For the sake of the next generation, please don't wait until Thursday.

Everything about the tragedy at Wedgwood cries out to you, "don't wait until Thursday!" Is there something you need to do right now? Don't wait until Thursday!

The tragedy, the darkness, the evil, the grief of this tragic event all yield to God's victory, light, goodness, and comfort. These words have been sung by many generations. They are powerfully appropriate today:

> For the darkness shall turn to dawning,
> And the dawning to noon-day bright,
> And Christ's great kingdom shall come on
>   earth,
> The kingdom of love and light.

Appendix A

The Story of the Videotape

by Mary Evelyn Kirkpatrick,
seventh grade girls' Sunday school teacher

Wednesday, September 15, was See-You-at-the-Pole. For this yearly event, I offered to edit the video for our youth group who were praying around flagpoles at their various schools. This video would be shown at the Post See-You-at-the-Pole rally at Wedgwood that night. Our youth minister, Jay Fannin, had invited youth groups from the area to come and celebrate with us at the rally. Having filmed the events of the early morning, Jay and I started editing at 9:00 A.M. that Wednesday and finished by about 12:45 P.M. I'm so glad God allows me to edit video for students. It is a ministry to me and, I hope, to them.

I went to pick up my son, Caleb, at preschool and I'm not really sure what Caleb and I did after that, but usually we play and then he takes a nap. I remember being so excited about the rally, although I was nervous about the video showing. It was the first one I had done for the students, and I wanted them to really enjoy it. I wanted them to know how much I loved them and wanted their love in return. I remember going back and forth in my mind on whether to take my camera to the concert. I wanted to just enjoy the event with "my girls" from my class without having to stop and decide if I should videotape something. But the thought of students from other churches being there and the place being packed was a visual I couldn't pass up. I imagined a scene from up in the balcony with all of the students praising God and having a great time! What a wonderful piece of heaven this would be to have on tape. Unfortunately, that was not all that was on that tape.

I dropped Caleb off at the nursery and headed for the sanctuary. I remember looking at my watch; it was 6:27 P.M.

and I thought, *Great, I'm not late.* Youth events rarely start on time anyway! I ran into some of my girls outside the sanctuary and walked in with them. I think it was Brittany Watson, Erin Bodiford, Cherise Price, and Valerie Smith. We got our seats close to the front. We were on row three or four. I sat on the end so I could slip in and out to get video. I was on the end, then Brittany, then Elizabeth Hendricks and Sarah Denson. I didn't know that Sarah was there until later. Erin and Bethany were in the row behind us.

The rally started about 6:40 P.M. Jay got up first and welcomed everyone and introduced the band, Forty Days. When the band started playing the kids stood up and started singing and clapping to songs. I filmed Jay's welcome and started getting scenes of the concert. I can't remember the sequence of when I filmed what, but I remember getting a picture from up in the balcony. I also got a walking picture of the front row of students right in front of the stage. I then got scenes of the band members. I got very close to the stage and filmed from a very low angle looking up at them. Some of the band members were cheesing it up for the camera. We were all having a great time. I went back to my seat and sang for a little bit, and then realized I could film from behind the band if I went into the choir loft. That was a great scene. It really showed what the room looked like. I went back to my seat to enjoy the concert.

We were singing, "I Will Call Upon the Lord" when the shots were heard. I heard pops like a starter gun or cap pistol. It didn't sound like a real gun. Of course I hadn't heard a gun being fired inside a building before. I remember thinking *What was that?* and turning around. I saw the people behind me move like waves of water away from something moving in the back. The bang sounds were loud and really irritating.

I saw the gunman in the back of the sanctuary shooting with his right hand, with his left hand at his side with a cigarette. I thought it must be a skit. After about ten shots I thought all the kids were probably getting scared and that's not good. It was quiet in the sanctuary except for the gunshots. People were squealing at the loud bangs and laughing nervously. I remember saying or thinking, *Even if it is a skit, it's not funny.* I looked through my viewfinder and saw the gunman shooting. He had a short jacket on and moved very methodically. He would point, aim, then fire, move to another target, aim, and fire. I could not sense any emotion from his movements. He shot with one hand. I was videotaping him while he was shooting. When I would see him start to point in my direction, I would duck.

As the shooting continued it was as if I was expecting something else to start. But the gunman just kept on shooting. The noise of the gun and the repetition of the shots were getting nerve racking. After filming from my seat for awhile I thought I needed to go to a different angle, so I crouched down and went to the next set of pews to stage left. When I got him in my viewfinder to start filming again, he threw the pipe bomb. He threw sideways. I remember seeing the pipe bomb going through the air with one end red hot and the other end smoking. The bomb landed three feet behind me, and it was smoking. I thought, *Even if this thing is a skit, I'm not going to be this close to it.* I went back up the aisle in full sight of the gunman. I slipped in on the end of a pew on the opposite side of the aisle from where I started. The people in the pew were ducking down behind their pew. I noticed one guy sitting up in the pew and not moving.

I got the gunman in my viewfinder again and started filming. He put the gun to his right temple and I thought, *Oh! Now he's going to act like he's shooting himself.* That thought really disgusted me—that someone would pretend to shoot himself in front of students. Then he saw me and pointed his gun at me. I filmed him looking at me. Pure fear went through me feeling like a tidal wave. I felt pure hate from his eyes, and I ducked down. I felt a tingling on the right side of my head and realized something had hit me. The guy next to me pointed out that something from my camera had fallen off onto the ground. It was the battery off the back of the camera. At that point I thought, *If something from his gun hit my camera so hard, from that distance, that it knocked my battery off, he's going to hurt some kids by accident.* It was then I said to my-self, *This skit is going to stop right now!*

I crouched down and went out the door by the organ, stopping to pause for a second. I was so mad and confused I knew I needed to calm down before I talked to anyone about stopping the skit. Then the doors going into the sanctuary shook. I thought, *He's trying to come and get me.* I really freaked out at that point. The whole time it was like my body felt the fear, but my mind would not admit it could really be happening. I pushed and the other doors opened up. I was outside. What a relief! I could breathe.

Needing to know what was going on in the sanctuary, I walked over to the other entrance by the church office and looked through the glass doors. I could see the doors going into the back of the sanctuary and Mike Smith standing in the doorway. He was on the defensive, dodging, and moving around. That's when I knew this was real. That guy had a real gun. He was shooting real bullets at people. *My students! I left my girls in there!* The guilt came crashing down on me. In-stantly, I thought of going back in. That thought scared me to death. But if I went back in maybe I could do something. The best place to go in would be the back, and Mike Smith was al-ready there. He's a trained soldier. I couldn't do anything more than he could. So I waited.

Suddenly I was overcome with panic to find my son. As I rounded the church I saw Kevin Galey, who had been shot. I stopped and prayed over him and someone said he was going to be okay. I ran around the church to the nursery to see a trail of children holding hands crossing the street. I yelled to some-one, "Where are the kids? Are they all out?" They said they were on the other side of the school. By this time my heart was pounding, and I was running hard. I was hyperventilating.

I rounded the corner and was yelling for Caleb. He was sit-ting on the ground as calm as could be with his back on the school building next to a childcare worker. I really broke down at that point when I took him into my arms and cried. They then moved us into the school building just in case the gunman ran outside. Eventually we found out the gunman was dead.

I went outside with Caleb to find my girls and to be with the students. It was so great to see them and to hug them. The parents were glad to see me and needed a break from being brave with their children, so they could cry over their pain. The kids were in shock and many were crying; some were bleeding. Eventually I realized my camera had been shot and gave the camera with the tape in it to a policeman. I told him I had it all on tape and they needed to see it. The police then got everyone who was a witness to go to the school library to give statements. After some time, the police took all the witnesses downtown to give our statements. I was amazed at how many details I remembered. Now those details are getting foggy. I gave my statement and a policewoman took me home about 2:30 A.M. Thursday.

The next three or four days were a blur of pain, emotion, and numbness. I had the typical reactions to trauma. I was scared of the dark. I had trouble going down the hall at night without lights. Sounds would drive me to panic. The wind would blow a neighbor's gate, and I would be in the middle of fear again. I felt as if my body was reacting without my making any decisions. I would just start to panic in crowded places without being conscious of being fearful. The phone was ringing off the hook. I really felt the need to talk to people on the phone. I'm so grateful to be alive. Through the pain and emotion, I just kept saying to Jesus, "I trust you, Jesus"—even when I couldn't see any light at the end of the tunnel of pain.

The big thing we had to deal with was the videotape of the shooting. We received many contacts from the media concerning the tape. The decision was made to destroy the tape after I watched it. Seeing the tape was very important for my healing and knowing what I had filmed was real. Instead of just destroying the tapes at the church, I needed to see the video through an editor so that I could work the controls. Coming from the production background as I do, having the control of the shuttle knob and looking at the video field by field was very important for me. This gave me some control over the video I had filmed. My husband, Jerry, Pastor Meredith, and Steve Hayes were in the room when I was editing. Jerry needed to see the video so he could understand better what I had gone through. Steve needed to see the video to understand better how to counsel in trauma situations. Brother Al needed to see the video so he could understand better what his church had gone through.

After the editing Jerry and I took the video and copies to the church sanctuary and broke up the tapes and then took the beaten and torn pieces home and burned them in our trash can. There is no way anyone can put them in a video machine and play any images. What is left is a charred black chunk.

Appendix B

The Tragic Ties That Bind Forever

by Ted Parks, *The Christian Chronicle,*
a Churches of Christ periodical

The portrait of the shooter began to emerge soon after he killed eight people in a Fort Worth Baptist church—and the reports made clear he had grown up in Churches of Christ.

Mary Ann Lowry, now a member of the Malibu Church of Christ, Malibu, Calif., was about two years younger than the gunman as both of them were growing up at Glen Garden Church of Christ in Fort Worth. She recalls him as a "very quiet, nice guy." Lowry's father echoed her description, "He was very quiet, very passive."

It was the family that Lowry most clearly recalls. She had been in their "nice middle-class tract home," she said. "Not a peripheral family" in any sense.

The family had needs that Glen Garden tried hard to meet, Lowry explained. Disease had left a daughter in a wheelchair. The youth group often stopped by the house to see her. She died as a teenager, not long after Pat Malone began his ministry at Glen Garden in 1966. Malone is minister and elder at the Pleasant Ridge Church of Christ, Arlington. When Glen Garden church moved from southeast Fort Worth to southwest Arlington in 1977, the name changed to Pleasant Ridge.

People who knew the shooter's parents described them as faithful throughout life. After the gunman left home for the Navy, however, he "never had any interest in spiritual things," Malone recalled. The precise connection between the junior-high boy in the preacher-training class and the frustrated adult who opened fire at a Christian concert will probably forever elude the people who have grappled with what happened to him.

But the ties between Churches of Christ and the pain that this member brought Fort Worth did not, like the gunman himself, slip lifelessly into the pew after the final suicidal shot that ended the killing spree.

Appendix C

Where Is God in All of This?

Excerpts from a sermon by Pastor Meredith,
September 19, 1999

Let's remind ourselves of the truth that God gives to us as we read it together as a congregation, confidently, Romans 8:28:

> And we know that in all things God works for the good of those who love Him, who have been called according to His purpose.

This has been an unbelievable, traumatic, shocking time for us—for families who heard of the news, or somebody called, or they found out that their precious children had been shot. (No one ever expects to bury their children.) Our deepest sympathy and prayers go with these families. Friends sat in church and saw their good friends next to them have their lives snuffed out. This is a time of shock for this church, a time of shock for the entire community of God all around the world. What can be said when kids gather in the church sanctuary to sing and to pray and a gunman comes in firing and their friends are shot? There are many, many questions to be answered: Why? Why us? Why me? How could this happen? How could anyone have done such a thing? But the question I've been asked most as I walk down the street and microphones are shoved in my face is, "Can you tell us where God is in all this?"

If God really loves us, if God is really all-powerful, why in the world did He let this happen? Why does God allow evil to seemingly abound in this world of ours? Why Columbine? Why

Paducah? Why Pearl? Why is there pain? Why is there suffering? Why is there mental illness? The question is where is God when we hurt? If you're a Wedgie, maybe you've heard me say, "If I were stuck on a desert island and I could have only one book, I'd lose my ordination papers if I didn't say that book would be the Word of God." But if I could only have one book within that Book it would be the book of Romans. If I could only have one chapter in the book of Romans, that chapter would be Romans chapter eight. If I could only have one verse in Romans chapter eight, that verse would be the one we just read. "And we know that in all things God works for the good of those who love Him, who have been called according to His purpose."

Richard Halverson, for years chaplain of the U.S. Senate, once said that even the best preachers really have only two or three sermons. Wedgies knew that. They hear me repeat myself over and over again. They're just nice about it and they smile and say, "Amen pastor." The sermon of my life is this, God is in control and God loves us. Let me share with you from the verse a few thoughts.

The Confidence of the Believers

First of all, notice the confidence that believers have—"And we know." Gen Xers are a whole generation who want to know where the truth is, what is reality. They know that the world is phony. They know about computer-enhanced imitations of truth. Virtual reality means seeing is not believing any more. What is the truth? They tell me the most popular television show of the Generation Xers is *The X-Files.* In the opening scene the slogan comes out, "The truth is out there." Somewhere it's out there. What can we know? The world has no answers in the face of life's problems: doesn't know what to do about world hunger; doesn't know what to do about violence in American society; doesn't have a clue about AIDS or ecological problems. The world doesn't have the answers! I'm a child of the '60s. I love Simon & Garfunkle, the poet lords of the '60s, who sang, "I'm blinded by the light of God and truth and right so I wander in the night without direction." That's what the world has to say.

But God says, "And we know." Christians are an exclusive subculture of confidence and calm in a world of relativism and ensuing panic. I'm told that the shooter, as he was coming in, was cursing God and Christians and in particular Baptists. Someone said he said, "You Baptists think you know it all." No, we don't know it all, but we do know this:

> My hope is built on nothing less than Jesus' blood and righteousness;
> I dare not trust the sweetest frame but wholly lean on Jesus' name.
> On Christ the solid rock, I stand; all other ground is sinking sand.
> All other ground is sinking sand.

We know that God's word is absolutely true from cover to cover—even the cover that says "Holy Bible" is true. It is unshakable. It is certain. Some folks have said, "God said it, I believe it, and that settles it." I've got news for you—if God said it, that settles it whether you believe it or not. Your world falls apart when you have nothing to build upon. And when Christians come to crises like this, we run to the Word of God for the assurance and the hope that is the foundation of life. And we know! It's the confidence of believers.

The Covenant of God

Notice, secondly, the covenant of God: "And we know that in all things God works for good." That is one of the most precious promises in God's Word. Now here is how it works, as I understand it. I like the New American Standard Version because it says *cause:* "God causes all things to work together for good." Folks, the warp and woof of your life is not just blind luck. You are not a cosmic accident. It is not Karma. It is not fatalism. It is not blind chance. Hear me today. God is sovereign over every molecule in the universe. He is in control of the birds of the air. Do you remember Elijah by the brook Cherith? He was hungry. God sent a squadron of ravens to feed him. These were scavengers that would eat the food God placed in their mouths. They were sent in order for Elijah to have three square meals and a Big Mac for bedtime. God is in control of the birds of the air, of the fish in the sea. Do you remember rebellious Jonah running from God and cast into the sea? Was that just a lucky fish that came by and swallowed him? No, God said, "Buddy you are going here."

God is in control of the worms in the ground. How do you think Jesus said God feeds the sparrow? There are worms in the ground. It extends to every event in our lives, whether good or bad. It extends to my body. The Word of God says my DNA chain was fashioned and formed in my mother's womb before I was ever born. It extends to every event of my life. The Word of God says, "the steps of a good man are ordered by the Lord and he delights in his way." God is the one who is in control. God is the one who is working everything for good for those who love Him. Did you notice the comprehensiveness of the problem? He says, "in all things."

"Oh, come on Al, what good could possibly come from all this?" I was asked that this week. What good could possibly come from all of this? Don't argue with me; take it up with God. He is the one who said "all things." I have lived long enough to see what I thought was bad work for good.

As I walked from my car past our sign, Shanda New had just come out and picked up one of the many cards placed by the church sign. I haven't had a chance to read any of those. Here is what the unsigned card said:

> I am not sure exactly who I am sending this to. I just felt that someone would receive it. I have never believed in God or any sort of higher being. I was not raised in a

church. My fiancé and I agreed once that we should start going to church. It was something we were both interested in. One visit and now I can't get him to go back. He always has something to do Sunday mornings. Since Thursday night, I want to be a part of it. More than ever, something like this happens to you in church and all you say is that God has something bigger and better in store. It is all part of a place to draw Americans, neighborhoods, and families back together. Wow. How much confidence in your faith you have. I want that confidence. I want to trust my life to God. I want to believe there is a bigger picture. I am so sorry for all the families. I am so sorry for all of us that we don't all have the confidence you have, but I am now looking for it.

Signed with a heart.

If you wrote this card and you signed this, come and let us show you how you can give your life to Christ.

This tragedy that the devil wanted to use to stop the people of God has ended up strengthening us. Our church has never been more united. We have never been more praying. We have never been more singing. We have never been more in love with one another. There has been such an outpouring of love and support from all over the world. We can't say enough. Poor Mike Holton and our administrators have been overwhelmed. The police department here has been so wonderful. The city has been wonderful. I'm here to tell you Fort Worth is the best town in the world to live in. That is why we had to meet today. We will be stronger, we will be closer, we will be more united. There have been chances to share the love and grace of Christ to millions. Two days ago we had over 30,000 hits on our web site. We put up the plan of salvation and somebody did this (I don't know who it was, but God bless you) put it in Swahili, Chinese, Spanish, Russian, all the languages of the world, that the world could know why we have this hope.

God's covenant is that all things work together and the conclusion of the promise is for good. Now you have got to understand this. First of all, understand the negative. Let me tell you what this does not mean. When God says this promise, it does not mean that all things are good. That is idiocy—foolish naiveté. Cancer is an evil thing; famine is an awful thing. Crime and violence and divorce and death are horrible, obscene, evil things. But God says I can work them together for good. It doesn't mean that only good things happen to believers. Sometimes people will tell you, even Christian people, I believe mistakenly, will tell you that if you are right with God you are protected from all harm. One of the promises Jesus gave to his followers was this: "while you are in the world, you will have persecution." Why are we surprised? Jesus said don't be surprised. They persecuted me before they persecuted you. Did you think you were any greater than your Master? Abel was murdered; Jeremiah was imprisoned and thrown into a well; Elijah was depressed; Saints were martyred. Even Jesus, the founder of our faith, was crucified. Bad things do happen to good people. But God works them together for good.

Let me tell you the worst thing in all the world. The most obscene, despicable, evil crime in all the world happened 2000 years ago when they took the spotless Son of God and stripped Him naked, beat Him beyond description, nailed His hands and feet to a cross, and put that cross on a hill for everybody to see. It was the most evil, awful thing that ever happened! But out of that came my salvation and yours. The cross of Jesus Christ gathers together believers from all over the world because God took that evil thing and through the power of the resurrection worked it for the salvation of all who will repent and place their faith and trust in Jesus Christ. We rally around the cross.

> When I survey the wondrous cross On which the Prince of
> Glory died,
> My richest gain I count but loss, And pour contempt on all
> my pride.

The Holy Spirit is leading me to say this before I go on. People have asked me, can you forgive? Have they asked you that? I say forgiveness is not easy. It wasn't my child who was shot. It was my precious friends and my church members. But we must forgive. I hold no rancor in my heart for the family of the gunman. I hope God will move in every heart in every member of this church and the church community. The poor man was deranged; his mind had been twisted by heaven knows what. He was in the power of the prince of darkness. And when you think what God had to forgive in my life—it was my sins that nailed the Son of God to the cross. If He can forgive me that, how can I not forgive anyone anything?

But I have got to point out one last truth, and that is the condition of the promise. Romans 8:28 is a verse that divides humanity. It divides every one of us here. You see the promise is to the called who love the Lord. Let me ask you today, do you love the Lord? Is He your all and all? Jesus said the evidence would be if you love me, keep my commandments. Are you numbered among the called ones? Who are the called ones? I am so glad you asked. In Greek, the word is *ecclesia*— the called-out ones. We translate it into "the church." There is no such thing as lone-ranger Christianity. I have sure learned that this week. I need you. I need my fellow pastors. I need the family of God around the world that have been praying. We need each other, and the world will never believe that Christ is the Messiah until we are one. There are churches, though imperfect, that will love you, welcome you.

God is calling you to be a part of a church that preaches the Word somewhere, somehow, someway. Are you part of the called-out ones who love the Lord? Or are you part of the uncalled ones who love themselves? "Well, I don't hate God, preacher. I just want Him to leave me alone. I want to do my own thing." For you there is a promise. Nothing that ever happens in your life, no matter how good it is, is going to ever work out for good. The Word of God is clear, "The soul that sins, it shall die." "The wages of sin is death." What death means in the Bible is not that you cease to exist; it means separation—separation from good, separation from God, separation from one another.

Are you part of the called-out ones who love the Lord or the uncalled who love themselves? If you are among the latter and want be the former, I am calling for you today. Jesus is calling for you today. He is saying, come to Christ. You may have heard this message like the woman who wrote this card. Your heart is stirred. It is the Holy Spirit that does that. Your heart is drawn to God, drawn to Christ. Are you a troubled saint? Is your heart broken and you don't know how you are going to get through it?

Luther Bridges was a seminary graduate about 150 years ago. He had just gotten out of seminary and was called to a new church. Like most seminary grads, he had five kids. They were spending a weekend with his parents in Kentucky. That night, the house caught on fire and burned to the ground. His parents and he escaped. But his wife and five children perished in the flames, just as he was beginning his ministry. In his depression, he cried out to God: "Oh, God, give me a song. Somehow, give me a song to know that you are there." And God did:

> There's within my heart a melody,
>   Jesus whispers sweet and low,
> "Fear not, I am with thee, peace, be still,"
>   In all of life's ebb and flow.
> Jesus, Jesus, Jesus—Sweetest name I know,
>   Fills my every longing,
> Keeps me singing as I go.

The world doesn't understand it. But those who know Him, do. He is real, He is there. He is not asleep at the switch, and He loves me. I don't understand sometimes what God is doing. I said yesterday at one of the funerals, give up your right to the position of General Manager of the Universe and let God be God. He loves us.

Appendix D

God's Will—A Study of Romans 8:28-29

Excerpts from a sermon by Dr. J. W. MacGorman, distinguished professor emeritus of New Testament at Southwestern Baptist Seminary, preached in seminary chapel, September 21, 1999

And we know that all things work together for good for them that love God, to them who are the called according to his purpose." There is another manuscript tradition that inserts God as subject there and it supports the reading that you would find in other translations: "We know that in everything God works together for good with those who love him, who are called according to his purpose." Of course you recognize that as Romans 8:28, certainly one of the best known and most frequently quoted promises in all the Word of God. Men and women of faith have often turned to this great promise in God's Word for help from him and found it there. I suppose this is especially true during times of crisis such as our seminary family and our city have known since last Wednesday night.

I went to my New Testament class on Thursday morning. Kim Jones was not in her usual place. I turned the class over to a season of prayer, putting the lesson plans aside. Do you know we used almost that entire class period in prayer and one of the students in his prayer quoted Romans 8:28? Earlier that morning I had spoken with my sixteen-year-old grandson who had participated in a See-You-at-the-Pole prayer meeting at Paschal High School. When he came home, he said, that someone who was participating in that student prayer meeting at Paschal High School had included Romans 8:28 in his prayer. Yesterday for the first time since the tragedy, I went over to the Wedgwood Baptist Church. I was looking for someone on the staff there, and of course the media were present. I went to the pile of mementos—the flowers, the tributes, a teddy bear. People had come and left their tributes there. There was a tall white board and many had used it to put words of encouragement and greeting. Among them were several verses from Scripture, and as you would expect, Romans 8:28 was one of those inscribed on that board next to the sign of the Wedgwood Baptist Church.

I confess that this verse has been a significant part in my own personal pilgrimage of faith that now exceeds, by the mercies of God, six decades. I know that the promise of this great verse is true, and we find support and help from God in it.

But while affirming that it is one of the most quoted verses, one of the best known verses, you will be patient with me while I suggest that it is also one of the most misquoted verses. Misunderstood and misapplied and, yes, I have even met people angry with God because of what they misunderstood the passage to affirm. So allow me to follow a simple plan this morning. I want first to work with some of the misconceptions. I'd like to indicate some of the things that Romans 8:28 does not say and then, with the underbrush cleared away, we'll give the verse a chance to affirm its great promise.

What Does Romans 8:28 Not Say?

It doesn't say that all things work together for good for all people. There is no such Scripture. Ezekiel, the prophet, stood in the middle of the crises of his day and he said, "The soul that sins shall die" (Ezek. 18:20). Now, that's true in his day and ours as well. But it sure doesn't describe all things working together for good for all people. In fact, if we turn back just a couple of pages to Romans 6:23, we will find the passage reading, "The wages of sin is death." And that's true, in our day or

Paul's day. The pay envelope is always edged in black; the guaranteed cost of sinful living increases; you never have to strike for higher wages; but it doesn't describe all things working together for good.

All things did not work together for good for Achan and Jezebel in the Old Testament or Ananias and Sapphira in the New Testament. You don't have to move off the city block on which you live to know all things are not working together for good for all people in our city. Unfortunately, some of us do not have to move outside of our own families, those whom we love more than life itself, to know that all things do not work together for good for all people.

If the verse were quoted in its entirety, we would learn those for whom the promise obtains. It makes it perfectly clear, because it says "to those who love God." To those who have responded to God's gracious call and purpose in Jesus Christ, all things work together for good. To those who have responded to God's infinitely greater love for them with their own love for Him, and who have decided that God can be a greater architect of our lives than we can without Him, and therefore have responded gladly to His call and purpose. Oh, yes, it is for these that God can assure that He overrules all for good. God can do some things in the lives of those who trust Him and who love Him that He cannot do in the lives of those who are indifferent or hostile toward Him. It's pretty hard to walk with somebody going in the opposite direction. But to those who respond to God's love, so expressed in the idiom of a cross, the death of Jesus Christ, and His triumph over sin and death on the first Easter morning, the Lord can make this great promise prevail.

Another thing that Romans 8:28 doesn't say: It doesn't say that all things that happen are good. Nothing about taking Jesus Christ seriously asks us to be unrealistic about the world in which we live. The only world we know anything about found Jesus Christ, the matchless Son of God, intolerable. It nailed Him to a cross. It would do it all over again. The world: What an awesome mixture of that which is noble or good and that which is tragic or evil. It is a world in which there is sunshine and the beauty of changing seasons. There's a western sky, the wonders of birth and of growth and of strength. There are projects to feed hungry people. There are hospitals to cut diseased tissue out of bodies. There are schools to lift the blight of ignorance. There are technological marvels. There are skilled and dedicated people unselfishly committing themselves to lifting the lot of those all around them. That's reality too, isn't it? But it is also a world in which there are hurricanes. A world in which there are tornadoes, typhoons, earthquakes, volcanic eruptions; a world in which there is famine and disease, corruption in business and government, as well as integrity in business and government; mechanical failures, errors in judgment for which others pay large prices, and, increasingly, random shootings in our society.

Committing our lives to Jesus Christ provides no immunity to adversity. It does provide immunity against aloneness and meaninglessness, and the human spirit is capable of enduring vast adversity so long as it is never robbed of hope, meaning, and a sense of purpose.

I am going to push this one step further. There's nothing in Romans 8:28 that says that all things that happen are God's doing. Now you may disagree with me on this, but if you do, don't let it bother you. My wife and I have been married over fifty-two years and during the course of that time I've lost many an argument—I mean discussion. But you know all of us here this morning are united in a commitment to Jesus Christ as Lord. There's nothing so important as that. And as long as we are together at the point of the confession and commitment to Jesus Christ as Lord, we can afford to live with some differences in the family of grace. Sometimes people confuse unity and uniformity. But you never have uniformity without coercion, and coercion is a denial of unity. (You want to know the secret of living for over five decades with one lovely lady? Each of you has a mutual commitment to Jesus Christ as Lord, and you make very sparing use of the term *nonnegotiable*.)

I do not believe that God triggers the disasters that break

our hearts. The further down the pike I get, the less willing I am to attribute anything to the will of God that is not in keeping with the very highest that Jesus Christ has revealed about Him. And yet well-meaning people eager to console will often stand in the midst of stark tragedy and say something like this, "We may not be able to understand this now, but in some way beyond all of our understanding, we simply know this was the will of God." Be careful now, be careful. I can in no way take the transgression of the will of God and hocus pocus it into a carrying out of the will of God.

I have no trouble attributing every good gift to a loving heavenly Father, but it distresses me when that which is flagrant transgression of the will of God is sometimes spoken of as being the will of God in some way beyond all our understanding. The reasoning is a bit circular. "Well, now look, could not God have prevented it from happening?" You couldn't answer that in any way but to say, "Of course." Then the reasoning continues. "If God didn't prevent it from happening, it was his permissive will." But my flesh crawls when you hook the will of God up to the flagrant transgression of the will of God. Pardon me, I'd rather refer to it as the transgressed will of God. We must not take an overruling consequence of God's providential care and read it back into an original cause for the tragedy. I do not believe that God triggers the disasters that crush us. But I do believe that He promises to help us overcome. It's one thing to trigger a tragedy; it's another thing to pledge the power to overcome it.

What Does Romans 8:28 Say?

Now if Romans 8:28 doesn't say that all things work together for good for all people and does not say that everything that happens is good, what does it say? Well, if you read the whole passage, we find the answer, "We know that to those who love God all things work together for good" or "God works all things together for good to those who are the called according to his purpose. For whom He foreknew [verse 29] He also predestined to be conformed to the image of His Son, that He might be the first born among many brothers." The whole issue resides in the nature of the good that is promised in Romans 8:28. It's explained in Romans 8:29 as "being conformed to the image of Jesus Christ."

When Paul wrote this letter he didn't write it in chapter and verse divisions. Chapter and verse divisions were added centuries later. Most of the time they've been done well, and they make possible concordances and other tools of Bible study. But here was a division that never should have been made. Romans 8:28 needs to be quoted with Romans 8:29 because the good promised in verse 28 is described in verse 29. And what is it? Being conformed to the image of His Son, Jesus Christ. *Good* is an abstract term. What we tend to do is to read our value systems into the term *good* and then expect God to tune His providences to our faulty definitions. No! God our eternal Parent is far more concerned with what His children are and are becoming than with what they have.

There's nothing in Romans 8:28 that guarantees I shall finish 1999 with better health than I have right now. Or that I will move into an upper income tax bracket. That's not the good that is promised. The good that is promised is that if our faith resides in our loving heavenly Father, no matter what life demands of us, He promises to overrule even the tragedies, to make us more like Jesus Christ His Son.

The will of God for every child in the family of grace is essentially the same. Vocationally we may be differently gifted, but really now the will of God for every child in His family of grace is essentially the same. It's stated here—maximum family resemblance to our elder brother, the Lord Jesus Christ. And the Lord can use every good thing that happens to do that—the things that make us laugh, the things that warm our hearts, falling in love, the coming of a child, the marvel of watching a child grow, the achievement of a goal at great cost, all of these good things. Our heavenly Father can use all good things to make us more like Jesus. But this morning, aren't you glad that God isn't limited to a cloudless sky? Our heavenly Father has such a wonderful way of meeting us at the level of our crushing sorrows, the tragedies that break our hearts. And if we trust Him, He is able to overrule and make us increasingly after the likeness of Jesus Christ, His Son. I can live with that. And the hope expressed of course is that Jesus Christ might be the first-born in a large family with many brothers and many sisters!

I had a sabbatical year in the Middle East and had a chance to see the Arab and his children. To be the only child in an Arab home, to be the only son, is a great honor. To be the elder of two sons is a greater honor. To be the oldest in a family of many sons and many daughters? The more in the family the greater the honor in being the first-born.

Strength in Fort Worth

Because of the faithfulness of those who have sustained such tragedy in recent days, all of us have been strengthened. I attended the three funerals on Saturday. The one at noon here at the seminary honored the memory of Shawn Brown. On that occasion those closest to the one whose life was taken, his family, were bearing radiant testimony to the adequacies of God's grace.

Then at 2:00 P.M. I went to the service of my student, Kim Jones, and once again we heard the testimony of faithfulness at a time of overwhelming sorrow. I had an order of service in my hand, and it said nothing about Kim's mother going to the platform to speak to us, but she did. And in that service she bore a triumphant testimony to the grace of God and the hope we have in Jesus Christ.

At 4:00 P.M. I returned to Southwestern Baptist Seminary for the memorial service of Sydney Browning. When my grandson, Adam, now a junior at Paschal High School, saw her picture in the newspaper, he exclaimed, "That's my coach!" He took his grandmother and me to his bedroom where he had his collection of photographs on a bulletin board and showed us the picture of his first-grade baseball team. Sydney was one of his coaches, and now he's in high school.

Sydney's memorial service, like the others, was a celebration of a life intensely committed to Jesus Christ as Lord. A videotape was shown in which she was featured as soloist with the Wedgwood Baptist Church choir. It was followed by an audiotape in which she sang:

> Some glad morning, when this life is o'er,
> I'll fly away,
> To a home on God's celestial shore,
> I'll fly away.
> When the shadows of this life have gone,
> I'll fly away.
> Like a bird from prison bars has flown,
> I'll fly away.
> Just a few more weary days and then,
> I'll fly away.
> To a land where joys shall never end,
> I'll fly away.

And then the chorus:

> I'll fly away, O glory,
> I'll fly away.
> When I die, Hallelujah, by and by
> I'll fly away.

By means of an audiocassette, we heard Sydney sing at her own funeral. And while listening to her singing and looking at her casket, I was deeply moved by the testimony she gave in song to the hope of an eternal home which Jesus Christ promises to all who trust him as Lord and Savior.

These who have sustained such grief have been faithful and their affirmation has been "have faith in God." I want us to go on our way, singing the great hymn by that title, "Have Faith in God."

> Have faith in God when your pathway is lonely.
> He sees and knows all the way you have trod;
> Never alone are the least of His children;
> Have faith in God, have faith in God.
>
> Have faith in God when your prayers are unanswered.
> Your earnest plea He will never forget;
> Wait on the Lord, trust His word and be patient,
> Have faith in God, He'll answer yet.
>
> Have faith in God in your pain and your sorrow,
> His heart is touched with your grief and despair;
> Cast all your cares and your burdens upon Him,
> And leave them there, oh leave them there.
>
> Have faith in God tho' all else fail about you;
> Have faith in God, He provides for His own;
> He cannot fail tho' all kingdoms shall perish,
> He rules, He reigns upon His throne.

Appendix E

How Close Do We Even Want to Be?

by Danny Sims, minister, Altamesa Church of Christ,
Fort Worth

Wedgwood Baptist. How tragic when once unfamiliar words have horrible and heartbreaking images identified with them. Not too many knew of Wedgwood Baptist until this past week. But the church that was our quiet, friendly neighbor is now another place for flower memorials heaped along the roadside. Police and paramedics, red lights bouncing off the houses of our neighborhood, bright lights and cameras penetrating a dark Wednesday night and early Thursday morning. Teen-agers in shock, weeping and holding each other. Frantic adults racing across the lawn. These are the pictures we all have seen of Wedgwood Baptist.

The Altamesa Church of Christ, where I preach in southwest Fort Worth, is a growing Wedgwood neighborhood church of 1200. We're just blocks from the other growing Wedgwood neighborhood church of 1200, Wedgwood Baptist. Much of our membership lives in the Wedgwood section of Fort Worth. My home is in Wedgwood.

How close are we? Our teenagers were invited, but decided not to go to last Wednesday's Post-See-You-at-the-Pole youth rally where a gunman killed seven, critically wounded two more, and victimized a community. My schedule this week could easily have been filled with funerals.

How close are we? The gunman might just as easily have driven another dozen blocks to our sanctuary. The night the rampage took place, our own praise assembly had just begun. Not knowing all that had transpired, we dismissed quickly yet calmly when news of the shooting was phoned in by police. Just minutes later, news and police helicopters droned overhead.

How close are we? We hosted a community-wide prayer service just twenty-four hours after the shooting. Eight hundred people came, including two members of the House of Representatives and many families of Wedgwood Baptist, who wept in our pews. A deacon from Wedgwood Baptist spoke. Media from all the local Fort Worth and Dallas outlets were here. A church from Littleton, Colorado, sent flowers, as did the Jewish Community Center of Los Angeles, both of whom have also been targets of recent violent crimes. I remarked Thursday night that our community is larger than this corner of Fort Worth. We flashed across *Nightline* and *48 Hours* on prime time network television. Reporters called to get a viewpoint from a nearby preacher.

How close are we? Our youth ministers, Raymond Schultz and Hai Cao, spent much of Thursday at a local high school where one of the victims had been a student, consoling teens. Our counselor, Russ Bartee, was on the radio and coordinating activities with the Red Cross. Small groups minister, Scott Strother, was at the hospital. Outreach minister, Wade Weaver, was talking to local media. College and singles minister, Mark Aldriedge, was on the phone with area churches. Our team was on call.

How close are we? At the prayer service, our children's education minister, Patty Weaver, sang "Amazing Grace," dedicating it to Sydney Browning, Wedgwood's slain children's choir director. Sydney was the first one murdered. One of their little girls was described on television as lamenting out loud, "They killed my choir teacher! They killed my choir teacher!" I was overcome with emotion realizing, "It could just as easily have been Patty." What would our little boys and girls have said?

How close are we? My son, a first grader, came home Thursday telling us one of his tiny classmates was "at that church." Our children go to school together. Members of Altamesa are neighbors of members of Wedgwood.

How close are we? In another twist, some of our members know and long ago attended church with the gunman's family. In his childhood, one of our deacons knew the man who unloaded his two handguns into the crowd.

How close are we? That may be the most important question asked in the aftermath. How close are we to one another? How close are we to tragedy? How close are we to our community? How close are we to our friends and fellow believers in other churches? How close are we to God? How close are we to the end?

How close are we to reaching those, like this gunman, who reportedly grew up in the church but possibly and regrettably not in the Lord?

How close do we even want to be?

At our Thursday evening community-wide prayer service, we offered folks the opportunity to write a note to the families of the martyred, the injured, or write whatever was on their heart. Scores of pages were left behind for those who grieve, poems for the injured, prayers for the families devastated by that senseless deed.

Saturday I delivered the book of original copies to Wedgwood Baptist minister Mike Holton. Mike was deeply moved. In appreciation he tearfully said, "Thank you. All of us here love you over at the Altamesa Church of Christ. Thanks for what you did." As we visited, a young man came in. He immediately thanked me for our prayer service, saying his parents had come. Apologizing to Mike for his unavailability at two o'clock that afternoon, he explained his plan to attend the funerals (three were held that day for victims of the shooting). Mike assured him, "It will all be fine. Somehow God will provide." When I asked what was happening at two o'clock, Mike explained that chairs needed to be arranged for Sunday's service, and since most of their church was involved with the funerals he had no one to help.

Thirty members of the Altamesa Church showered Mike with supportive hearts and willing hands at two o'clock. We carried flowers and set up chairs. We quietly stepped inside the sanctuary. We prayed and sang a song: "O God, You are my God, and I will ever praise You . . ." I believe God did provide, as much for us as for Wedgwood Baptist.

Then Mike asked us to help carry out several of their pews—pews to be repaired by the manufacturer, who had traveled to be on site; pews with cushions and fabric removed; pews riddled with bullets; pews heavy with sorrow; pews where, as one of my church elders said, "Soldiers died." Thursday night the Wedgwood Baptist Church had come to cry in the pews of the Altamesa Church of Christ. Saturday afternoon the Altamesa Church carried out the pews at Wedgwood Baptist. Tears and service, service and tears.

We are close enough to do for a church that's experienced loss exactly what we do for our friends who experience loss. We're "just there." How often have we heard it said, "Just be there for someone grieving, someone in shock. Don't say anything. Just be there."

How close are we? Close enough to bear one another's burdens and practice the love commands of Christ: "Love your neighbor as yourself" and "By this all men will know that you are my disciples, by your love for one another." Close enough to emphasize for a rare moment all that we have in common, rather than practice the pattern of highlighting our differences.

How close are we? Close enough to love. Close enough to care, to "be there." Close enough to do something instead of talk. Close enough to do, we're convinced, the very thing Jesus would do and died for His church to do. Close enough to do what Jesus lives through us, His Body, to do.

That's how close we are.

Appendix F

A 911 Call to God

by Dr. Dan R. Crawford

"Until the Day Dawns and the Morning Star Appears" (2 Peter 1:19)

During the tragedy of the Wedgwood shooting, many 911 calls were placed and many others would have been placed except for overcrowding of the lines and busy signals. Why were people calling 911? It was a cry in the darkness. It was a call for help. It was an admission that assistance was needed. It was ultimately a yearning for the dawn of a new, less tragic day, a day heralded by the morning star.

Jesus is the morning star (literally "the one bringing light"). Numbers 24:17 says of the coming Messiah, "a star will come out of Jacob" and in Revelation 22:16 Jesus calls Himself "the bright Morning Star."

Many messages that arrived in the days immediately following the shooting said, in essence, "Don't worry. These are signs of the times. The Lord is returning soon to put a stop to all of this." Even though we at Wedgwood believe in the certainty of His coming, we also believe the timing is a mystery. While it may well be soon, the key word for us in our day of trouble is, until. What shall we do until our Lord returns and illumines all the darkness with morning star brightness?

Feelings of helplessness were rampant in the hours immediately following the shooting. The frustration of wanting to do something was exceeded only by the uncertainty of what to do. Of course, we knew to pray and we did much of that. We knew to offer help to each other and we did that. But, we thought, what about tomorrow? What can we do to prevent this from happening at another church, another school, another community center, another shopping mall, another office building?

There came an awareness that we could do little by ourselves. The problem was too enormous. The problem was not guns, or better security systems, or larger police forces, or better mental care. The problem was, at its roots, a spiritual one. It was a problem born and nurtured in the darkness. It was a problem that could be solved only in the light of God's presence. Thus, the problem could not be educated away, legislated away, counseled away, or preached away, but it might be prayed away. Increasingly, we came to believe that if God did not send a revival among His own people and a spiritual awakening in the world, our culture as we had known it had little chance of surviving. The solution, as we perceived it, was to ask God to revive the church and awaken the land. This alone would not solve all the problems of society, but it would be a beginning that might prevent the end. Since we are God's people, we invite you to join us at Wedgwood in taking the responsibility of praying for revival among the church.

First, let us look at a definition of corporate and personal revival. In his book, *Revival,* Richard Owen Roberts defines revival as "an extraordinary movement of the Holy Spirit producing extraordinary results." When applied to a person, this means an extraordinary movement of the Holy Spirit in your life. How long has it been since you experienced an extraordinary movement of God's Spirit in your life? A movement in which God's Spirit comes down and God's Word comes home and God's purity comes through and God's person comes alive? When this happens, there will be extraordinary results. God has given us a formula of preparation by which the Spirit can produce extraordinary revival in and through us.

The Preparation of Brokenness

The first step is the preparation of brokenness. Believers must be humbled before God will send revival to and through them.

Often God brings the believer to the point of brokenness so that he or she may be used more effectively as an instrument of revival.

The founder of Southwestern Baptist Seminary, B. H. Carroll, was preaching a revival meeting in Belton, Texas, when he became distraught over the lack of response. After several sleepless nights, Carroll got up one night, dressed, and went walking. He walked all the way to the town's cemetery. There he fell on his knees and in brokenness, prayed, "Lord, if you have called me to preach, I want you to show me what hell is like." That night, God responded to the broken, humbled preacher and revealed to him the horrible destiny of the lost. The next evening Carroll preached with such intensity that those present said it seemed as though flames of fire were leaping in his face. God revived the broken preacher, then sent revival through him.

Now there is a difference in being broken and being crushed. Stones are chipped and shaped to fit the purpose of the artist. Those stones that resist are crushed and destroyed. Being broken means to be obedient, not resistant to God's shaping of our lives. In *Finney On Revival,* Charles G. Finney said, "A revival is nothing else than a new beginning of obedience to God . . . a deep repentance, a breaking down of heart, a getting down into the dust before God, with deep humility, and a forsaking of sin." How then shall we humble ourselves? How shall we be broken? Only by placing ourselves up against the standard of God's Word will we be broken and humbled. Pray the prayer of the psalmist, "Search me, O God, and know my heart; Try me, and know my anxieties; and see if there be any wicked way in me, and lead me in the way everlasting" (Ps. 139:23-24). The following is a pretest for personal revival.[1] It may be helpful as you seek to humble yourself and be broken. Be honest with yourself as you answer each question. Agree with God about each need revealed in your life. Confess each sin, with the willingness to make it right and forsake it. Praise God for being forgiving and correcting. Renew your mind and rebuild your life through meditation on and practical application of the Word of God. Review these questions periodically to remain sensitive to your need for ongoing revival.

1. Genuine Salvation (2 Cor. 5:17)
   a. Was there ever a time in my life that I placed all my trust in Jesus Christ alone to save me?
   b. Was there ever a time in my life that I completely surrendered to Jesus Christ as the Master and Lord of my life?

2. God's Word (Ps. 119:97, 140)
   a. Do I love to read and meditate on the Word of God?
   b. Are my personal devotions consistent and meaningful?

3. Humility (Isa. 57:15)
   a. Am I quick to recognize and confess when I have sinned?
   b. Do I rejoice when others are praised and recognized and my accomplishments go unnoticed by men?

4. Obedience (Heb. 13:17; 1 Sam. 15:22)
   a. Do I consistently obey what I know God wants me to do?
   b. Do I consistently obey the human authorities over my life?

5. Pure Heart (1 John 1:9)
   a. Do I confess my sin by name?
   b. Do I keep "short sin accounts" with God (confess and forsake as God convicts)?

6. Clear Conscience (Acts 24:16)
   a. Do I consistently seek forgiveness from those I wrong or offend?
   b. Is my conscience clear with every person?

7. Priorities (Matt. 6:33)
   a. Does my schedule reveal that God is first in my life?
   b. Does my checkbook reveal that God is first in my life?

8. Values (Col. 3:12)
   a. Do I value highly the things that please God?
   b. Are my affections and goals fixed on eternal values?
9. Sacrifice (Phil. 3:7-11)
   a. Am I willing to sacrifice whatever is necessary to see God active in my life and church?
   b. Is my life characterized by genuine sacrifice for the cause of Christ?
10. Spirit Control (Gal. 5:22-25; Eph. 5:18-21)
    a. Am I allowing the Holy Spirit to "fill" (control) my life each day?
    b. Is there consistent evidence of the "Fruit of the Spirit" being produced in my life?
11. "First Love" (Phil. 1:21-26)
    a. Am I as much in love with Jesus as I have ever been?
    b. Am I thrilled with Jesus, filled with His joy and peace, and making Him the continual object of my love?
12. Motives (Acts 5:29; Matt. 10:28)
    a. Would I pray, read my Bible, give, and serve as much if nobody but God ever noticed?
    b. Am I more concerned about pleasing God than I am about being accepted and appreciated by others?
13. Moral Purity (Eph. 5:3-4)
    a. Do I keep my mind free from that which stimulates thoughts that are not morally pure?
    b. Are my conversation and behavior pure and above reproach?
14. Forgiveness (Col. 3:12-13)
    a. Do I seek to resolve conflicts in relationships as soon as possible?
    b. Am I quick to forgive those who wrong me or hurt me?
15. Sensitivity (Matt. 5:23-24)

    a. Am I sensitive to the convictions and promptings of God's Spirit?

    b. Am I quick to respond in humility and obedience to the conviction and promptings of God's Spirit?

16. Evangelism (Rom. 9:3; Luke 24:46, 48)

    a. Do I have a burden for the unsaved?

    b. Do I consistently witness for Christ?

17. Prayer (1 Tim. 2:1)

    a. Am I faithful in praying for the needs of others?

    b. Do I pray specifically, fervently, and faithfully for revival in my life, my church, and my world?

Brokenness comes with God's judgment and just as judgment must "begin at the house of God," it "begins with us first" (1 Pet. 4:17). There is a popular saying, "If it isn't broken, don't fix it!" In terms of personal revival, if it isn't broken, God won't fix it.

The Preparation of Prayerfulness

The preparation of brokenness must be accompanied by the preparation of prayerfulness. Just as the awakenings that have blessed the church in days gone by have usually come in response to the cries of an individual or small group, so likewise your personal revival must be preceded by prayer.

Beginning in September of 1857 and extending into the spring of 1858, more than 250,000 people were saved, and it all began in a prayer meeting. A businessman by the name of Jeremiah Lanphier announced a prayer meeting for laymen to be held in the North Dutch Reformed Church at the corner of Fulton and William Streets in New York City at noon on Wednesday, September 23, 1857. While only a few men participated on the first Wednesday, soon every room in the church was filled, not just on Wednesday but five days a week at noon. Then other churches became filled with praying men. The great Prayer Revival crossed into Brooklyn, then down the eastern seaboard and across the mountain ranges back toward the west. Miraculous, extraordinary accounts of revival were told, and it began in a prayer meeting.

Our forefathers, at protracted meetings, used to pray till the break came, then stand back and watch as God sent revival. They had time to wait and pray and so must we. William Carey preached, "the first and most important of those duties which are incumbent upon us (in the task of advancing Christ's kingdom across the face of the earth), is fervent and united prayer."

Andrew Murray speaks about this in his book, *Revival:*

> The prayer for revival is a most heart-searching thing. With it comes tremendous responsibilities. It needs great divine grace. It asks if we are ready to turn our hearts and lives from other interests and to bear the weight and sorrow of those in the city of God who sigh and cry because of the abominations that are done in the midst thereof. It asks if we so believe in prayer—in our right and power with God to undertake this great request—that God shall entirely change the life of some, of many, of His people from one of selfishness to one of entire self-sacrifice. It asks whether we will be the first to give the answer, to offer ourselves for the Holy Spirit to do His full work of convincing of sin and consuming what is of self. It asks if we will accept and carry the answer to our brethren and prove what God can do. Oh, this prayer for revival may mean much to us in more ways than one, but let us not fear. Let us unhesitatingly bring the whole tithe into His house; let us unhesitatingly expect to see the windows of heaven opened and floods of blessing poured out.

You must likewise pray for your times of personal witness, for out of our personal witness to God's reviving power, nonbelievers will be converted to Jesus Christ and the spiritual awakening of our society will be enhanced. Not only does the Bible instruct us to pray related to personal witness, it gives us many specific areas in which to pray.

Pray that nonbelievers will

- ✦ be drawn to God by the Holy Spirit (John 6:44)
- ✦ seek to know God (Acts 17:27; Deut. 4:29).
- ✦ believe the Scriptures to be true and accurate (1 Thess. 2:13; Rom. 10:17).
- ✦ not be blinded by Satan to the truth (Matt. 13:19; 2 Cor. 4:4).
- ✦ receive in their lives the work of the Holy Spirit (John 16:8-13).
- ✦ receive someone sent by God to show them the way to faith in Christ (Matt. 9:37-38).
- ✦ believe in Jesus Christ as his Lord and Savior (John 1: 12; 5:24).
- ✦ turn away from sin (Acts 17:30-31, 3:19).
- ✦ confess Jesus Christ as Lord (Rom. 10:9-10).
- ✦ yield everything in order to follow Jesus Christ (2 Cor. 5:15; Phil. 3:7-8).
- ✦ have faith that takes root and grows in Christ (Col. 2:6-7).

Our prayers for revival will have an impact. In his book *The Concert of Prayer—Back to the Future?* Robert Bakke, after giving a thrilling presentation of the history of the Concerts of Prayer beginning with Jonathan Edwards, encourages us to "recognize the enormous value of establishing a rhythm of prayer for the revival of the church and the advancement of Christ's kingdom."

The Preparation of Holiness

The preparations of brokenness and prayerfulness must be joined by the preparation of holiness. In 1734, four years prior to his conversion, John Wesley declared, "My one aim in life is to secure personal holiness, for without being holy myself I cannot promote real holiness in others." Neither can you. Before God will use you as an instrument in revival, you must be holy. Prior to every significant revival in Christian history, there has been a deep desire on the part of some for a return to holiness.

R. A. Torrey was said to have had what he called "A Prescription for Revival," which proposed:

1. Let a few Christians get thoroughly right with God themselves.
2. Let them bind themselves together to pray for revival till God opens the heavens and comes down.
3. Let them put themselves at the disposal of God to use them as he sees fit in winning others to Christ.

This prescription begins with holiness ("right with God"), and that's where our prescription must likewise begin. Isaiah (Isa. 35:8-10) prophesied concerning a highway of holiness:

A highway shall be there, and a road,
  And it shall be called the Highway of Holiness.
The unclean shall not pass over it.
  But it shall be for others.
Whoever walks the road, although a fool,
  Shall not go astray.
No lion shall be there,
Nor shall any ravenous beast go up on it;
  It shall not be found there.
But the redeemed shall walk there,
  And the ransomed of the Lord shall return,
  And come to Zion with singing,
  With everlasting joy on their heads.
They shall obtain joy and gladness,
  And sorrow and sighing shall flee away.

Likewise, the New Testament is filled with calls to personal holiness:

✦ "Behold, I send you out as sheep in the midst of wolves. Therefore, be wise as serpents and harmless as doves." (Matt. 10:16)

✦ "I want you to be wise in what is good, and simple concerning evil." (Rom. 16:19b)

✦ "Brethren, do not be children in understanding; however, in malice be babes, but in understanding be mature." (1 Cor. 14:20)

✦ "Therefore, 'come out from among them and be separate,' says the Lord." (2 Cor. 6:17)

✦ "But fornication and all uncleanness or covetousness, let it not even be named among you, as is fitting for saints." (Eph. 5:3)

✦ "Finally, brethren, whatever things are true, whatever things are noble, whatever things are just, whatever things are pure, whatever things are lovely, whatever things are of good report, if there be any virtue and if there is anything praiseworthy—meditate on these things." (Phil. 4:8)

✦ "Set your minds on things above, not on things on the earth." (Col. 3:2)

✦ "Pure and undefiled religion before God and the Father is this: to visit orphans and widows in their trouble, and to keep oneself unspotted from the world." (James 1:27)

✦ "Hating even the garment defiled by the flesh." (Jude 23b)

One of the ways the Bible instructs us to holiness is by encouraging us to seek God's face. The psalmist says, "Seek the Lord and His strength; Seek His face evermore" (Ps. 105:4). Then the psalmist asks, "When shall I come and behold the face of God?" (Ps. 42:2 RSV). Seek God's face in personal devotion, in prayer, in daily routine, in family life, in interpersonal relationships, in correspondence, in all of life.

The Preparation of Sinlessness

The preparation of brokenness, prayerfulness, and holiness must be complemented by the preparation of sinlessness. Prior to every great movement of God, the world has been marked by gross sinfulness. When Satan runs rampant on the earth, God begins to look for those who in bad times seek to remain good, those who in godless days seek to remain God-fearing, those who in careless days seek to remain constant in purity, those who in earthly days seek to have eternity in their hearts, and those who in sinful days seek to remain unde-feated by sin. The sinfulness of humanity, the lawlessness in the world, the permissiveness of society are not indications that revival is impossible. They are, rather, indications that re-vival is imperative and if history is to be repeated, inevitable. Flee, therefore, from sin, that you might be one whom God chooses to use in revival.

The beginning of the eighteenth century was a time of ma-terial prosperity and widespread sinfulness in England. While the colonies poured new wealth into the mother country, lux-ury, dishonesty, speculation, and extravagance reigned su-preme. It was a time of increased intellectual activity and expression. The freedom of worship secured during the Refor-mation had degenerated to the point that all authority, human and divine, was defied. The influence of Thomas Hobbes and John Locke had increased the popularity of infidelity. Edward Gibbon and David Hume were busy discrediting the church. In a spiritual chill, the church seemed helpless. The ministry became increasingly corrupt. The Sabbath was just another day, and God was openly defied. Just when the outlook seemed its darkest, God invaded history once again. In 1703, three men were born: John Wesley in England, Gilbert Tennent in Ireland, and Jonathan Edwards in Massachusetts. These three, along with George Whitefield (born eleven years later), would become the human instruments of the great spir-itual awakening that swept over England and America. God had raised up men who hated sin in the midst of a sin-crazed world, and God is again looking for those who will "turn from their wicked ways" and be used.

Ask God to use the following questions to help you identify the degree to which your attitude toward God is one of repentance from sin:[2]

1. Do I have a heart attitude that says, "Lord, everything I now know to be sin, and everything You show me in the future to be sin, I am willing to give it all up for Your sake"?

2. Have I ever experienced the repentance that characterizes genuine salvation? Was my "conversion" experience mere external reformation, rather than internal heart transformation?

3. Can I truly say that I am willing to forsake every sin in my life, including those which are not known to others?

4. Am I willing to call my wrongful acts sins, rather than characterizing them as weaknesses, flaws, or personality traits?

5. Am I more grieved over how my sin has offended a holy God (repentance) than I am over the consequences that I have reaped for my sin (remorse)?

6. Am I willing to accept personal responsibility for my actions, without pointing the finger of blame at anyone else?

7. Am I willing to take whatever steps may be necessary to make complete restitution for my sin?

8. Am I willing, if necessary, to confess my sin publicly before men, as well as privately before God?

9. Am I willing to face the possible consequences of public repentance, such as loss of reputation, position, or influence?

10. Am I willing, if necessary, to suffer the loss of all things in exchange for being clean before both God and man?

11. Am I willing to voluntarily yield privileges and positions of leadership to demonstrate a repentant spirit?

12. Am I willing to submit to the disciplines of man for my sin, as well as those consequences directly imposed by God?

13. Am I willing to be accountable to another believer in those areas of my life where I have experienced past failure, in order that I may develop new patterns of victory?

14. Have I at any time in the past year experienced genuine repentance, resulting in a change of actions, attitudes, and spirit? At any time since my conversion?

15. Am I willing to testify openly concerning where God found me before I repented?

16. Are there any specific sins in my life of which I have never truly repented? Am I willing to repent of those sins here and now?

Once you have repented of the big sins in your life, don't forget the "lilywork." When Solomon's Temple was constructed, the materials were of immense value. Cedar and cypress trunks were cut in the high mountains and floated on huge rafts down the river to Joppa, then thirty-five miles up to Jerusalem. The construction took seven years with the help of 30,000 Israelites and 150,000 Canaanites, and was completed without the sound of a hammer or the use of tools. Two bronze pillars sat near the porch. On top of these pillars— twenty-seven-feet high—where no human eye could see the details was the lilywork. The Bible says, "Upon the top of the pillars was lilywork" (1 Kings 7:22 KJV). The workers had given great care to that which was only to be seen by God.

"Do you not know that your body is the temple of the Holy Spirit who is in you?" (1 Cor. 6:19). Take care of the unseen, unknown, minute details of your life—the lilywork that is so hidden only God can see it. Your preparation is incomplete until you've dealt with the lilywork of your life.

In God's Hands

That's God's formula for personal and corporate revival preparation. Is it biblical? Good question. When God appeared to Solomon in response to Solomon's prayer, God made a promise with four prerequisite conditions. These conditions—and the promise—are still good. God said:

> If My people, who are called by My name, will humble themselves [the preparation of brokenness], and pray [the preparation of prayerfulness], and seek My face [the preparation of holiness], and turn from their wicked ways [the preparation of sinlessness]; then will I hear from heaven, and will forgive their sin, and will heal their land. (2 Chron. 7:14)

While visiting Ngaruawahia, New Zealand, in 1936 to conduct revival meetings, J. Edwin Orr was standing in line at the post office one afternoon contemplating his text for the evening, Ps. 139:23-24. In the background, he heard some Maori girls singing one of their native songs, "The Song of Farewell." The first line, "Now is the hour when we must say goodbye," captured Orr's attention and in five minutes he had set the words of his text to the native tune, thus capturing the genius of personal and corporate revival preparation:

> Search me, O God, and know my heart today;
> Try me, O Savior, know my thoughts, I pray.
> See if there be some wicked way in me;
> Cleanse me from ev'ry sin and set me free.
>
> I praise thee, Lord, for cleansing me from sin;
> Fulfill Thy Word and make me pure within.
> Fill me with fire where once I burned with shame;
> Grant my desire to magnify Thy name.

Lord, take my life and make it wholly Thine;
Fill my poor heart with Thy great love divine.
Take all my will, my passion, self, and pride:
I now surrender, Lord—in me abide.

O Holy Spirit, revival comes from Thee;
Send a revival—start the work in me.
Thy Word declares Thou wilt supply our need;
For blessings now, O Lord, I humbly plead.

Endnotes

1. "Preparing for Personal Revival," *Spirit of Revival* 18 (1): 37-39.
2. "Making it Personal," *Spirit of Revival* 21 (3): 29-30.

Appendix G

Editorial from the *Dallas Morning News,*
Sept. 22, 1999, by William Murchison

On the assumption that Satan, enlisting the help of a lone gunman (name deleted by choice of author), set out last week to intimidate Christians . . . well, did this unholy pair pick the wrong church!

Liberal Protestants of hazy theological outlook—that might have been one thing. But Southern Baptists! No one in his right mind would put forward the Baptists as subject matter for spiritual intimidation.

Confronted, menaced, jeopardized, Baptists reach for a familiar object—the Holy Bible. They open it, they brandish it, they thrust it right in the devil's face. Just how heart-warming it was to see them do so on a sun-splashed Sunday afternoon in Texas Christian University's football stadium, I beg here and now to report.

The Baptists, to every appearance, have it right: Spiritual warfare rages in our midst. The president of the United States (himself a Baptist, if not one in high favor with his co-religionists) insists that a deadly combination—evil and guns—is in fact at work. Addressing the Black Congressional Caucus immediately after the Fort Worth shootings, the president urged collective efforts "to make America a safer place." Translation: Let's control more guns.

The official Baptist position on gun control? I've no idea. We all know, nonetheless, the Baptist position on evil. It is that evil—resulting from the Fall—warps and corrupts human nature, turning it from God toward actions violative of His love and trust.

Secularism—a wholly new creed, as alien to the American as to the Western tradition—is often put forth as the foolproof response to modern "pluralism" and "diversity." It serves, just as likely, as a handy excuse for sleeping in on Sundays. The Baptists know all this. Their most engaging trait is that they don't care. They set forth the Truth as they have received it—that Jesus Christ died for your sins.

Case in point: The Fort Worth commemoration. The occasion is ostensibly civic. The mayor is a speaker; Governor George W. Bush and other officeholders have come as non-speakers just to reinforce the sense of public outrage and grief. A rabbi prays. I spot Muslims in the crowd. Yet the occasion is saturated with Christian joy.

There's an odd word—*joy.*

What's joyous about the desecration of a house of worship and the slaughter of teenage worshipers and counselors? Nothing is joyful about evil.

Joy, as the Baptists of Fort Worth would make known, comes with God's response to evil. Does He leave it to fester? Hardly. He points to the victory already won, and in the end to be lastingly consummated, through His Son's death and resurrection. It's right there in those Bibles waved under Satan's snoot. Nor does it stop even there, you dumb lunk with the pitchfork! Christians inside and outside the Southern Baptist Convention would affirm this reality.

Affirm? A mild word for what goes on at the stadium. What about the father of one of the victims, leading the audience/congregation in the singing of a song his murdered daughter had loved? What about the pastor of the desecrated church, the Reverend Al Meredith, whomping up a classic Baptist revival on the spot—a call to fasting, repentance and prayer? "Raise your hand if you want killing to stop—if you want to see the spirit of the living God sweeping over our land like wildfire." Up in the air—a forest of affirming arms, one of them attached to an Episcopal journalist.

Bad news for Satan. He's stirred up the Baptists—folk who take him with the deep seriousness his malice deserves. The culture wars may have taken a decisive turn.

Appendix H

How to Respond to the Violence at Wedgwood

Excerpts from a symposium held at Southwestern Baptist
Seminary, September 23, 1999

In the second week following the Wedgwood shooting, Southwestern Baptist Seminary offered this symposium. Excerpts are presented here.

Dr. Wes Black, professor of youth eductation, Southwestern Baptist Seminary: As I prepared for this symposium, I interviewed the pastor of First Baptist Church of Pearl, Mississippi, the Reverend Tommy Mitchell. He is also the police chaplain for the city of Pearl, Mississippi. He spoke of the way they have moved beyond the tragedy that occurred in their city two years ago. He said they have new energy and commitment to the Lord. To quote him, "Jesus is alive and in control. Don't panic. He is the God of life, not death." Pastor Mitchell offered several suggestions for us today. For one, he said the leaders must exhibit a confidence and calm. Youth can pick up on our panic and our anxiety and can become demoralized from that. Second, we need to control rumors. Tell everyone to speak only what they know to be the truth. Rumors can be rampant following a tragedy. Third, don't overreact and start crawling into a hole. Don't be afraid to face life and go on with normal activities. Fourth, after a while teenagers want to get on with their normal life. Don't drag out talking about the tragedy. Fifth, youth might need to talk months down the road. Just make yourself available to them. And finally, the three biggest problems you have to face are fear about what could happen, guilt because "someone else died and I am alive," and anger—wanting to get revenge for what happened.

Dr. Scott Floyd, associate professor of psychology and counseling, Southwestern Baptist Seminary: Let me tell you that when I think about what's happened at Wedgwood, I think of it in terms of how it affected people in concentric circles. The folks that were in the sanctuary would be in the inner circle. The folks that were out in the hallway would be real close—another real tight circle in the inner part of all this. Folks that were in other places in the church at Wedgwood would be in another circle. People who had friends there, members of the church who weren't there right at that time, would be a real close circle. And the circles would move out: other youth groups that were doing other things. I think being a Baptist you associate this tragedy with a Baptist church. So there are circles that move out from that inner circle of the people in the sanctuary.

Consider some short-term responses to folks that were in the inner circle and then short-term responses to folks a little bit further out in some of the outer circles. Folks that were immediately affected, directly affected, and folks that were less directly affected but still touched.

First of all, talking about short-term responses to those in that inner circle, those directly affected, I think there are a few things that we can attempt to do:

1. Be present for them. I think it is good to be able to be present, to be around, to be available. I think the best biblical example is Job's friends in the first week. If you remember what they did in the first week—they came, they sat, they did not say anything, they were just there. Then they opened their mouths and things went downhill, but they were there in the short term just sitting and being available.

2. Allow them to talk about what they have seen, heard, thought, and felt. Even things like getting them to talk about what is the hardest part about all of this for them.

3. Listen to what they say. I think we have to make sure in these situations we do not feel a strong need to tell them things or to correct what they are saying. I really think the value comes in them talking about what happened and us listening. I think that is an essential part of the beginning of the healing process.

4. Normalize their responses. Everybody responds differently to trauma. Some people shut down, some cannot stop talking, some want to be around others, some want to be away, some people cannot sleep, some sleep all the time. I think what we want to do is help folks become aware of what natural responses are to trauma situations and assure them they really are normal in the way they are responding and reacting.

5. Avoid the need to provide answers to questions. There are a lot of why questions that surface during trauma experiences. I think our tendency is to explain what happened, and I do not think we need to do that. I do not think that is what they are wanting at this point, neither is that what they are needing.

6. Provide opportunities for those directly affected to be around faith people. After a traumatic event, there are people that are safe and there are people that are unsafe. Those are really simple terms. Safe people are people that will allow the victim to be who they are and go through things at their own pace. Unsafe people are people who want to correct or tell the victim how they should be thinking or feeling, or want them to respond a certain kind of way. I think we need to help them find safe people.

7. Allow them to have rituals. They need to find rituals they can perform that are helpful. In the Wedgwood situation, the best ritual I saw was writing on the floor of the

sanctuary before it was recarpeted. Looking for opportunities to do things like that will help express the struggle and help them take a part in the grieving process.

8. Prepare for the long haul. One of the things that we have tried to say to our counselors this week is, whether we like it or not, we are pulled not into a sprint but into a marathon in dealing with this. This is long-term healing. You can hear the folks from Colorado even talking about some of their responses five months later: When they hear a loud noise, they are still reacting. I think we need to realize that this is a long process, and we need to be in it for the long haul as well.

With those less directly affected here are some suggestions for helping them:

1. Bring up the incident—let them bring it up, but if they don't, you bring it up.
2. Allow them to talk.
3. Provide an opportunity to respond by attending the memorial services, sending a card, etc.
4. Be aware that this incident may have a harsher initial impact on ones who have experienced any other recent trauma.
5. Provide opportunities for healing through natural relationship channels such as family, youth group, etc.

Chris Liebrum, director of human resources, Baptist General Convention of Texas: The checklist for youth events has changed. It once included food, T-shirt, van key, church credit card. Now it must include a safety checklist. We must give thought to safety for every youth event. This ranges from armed police to youth workers with cell phones.

Steve Hayes, minister of counseling, Two Rivers Baptist Church, Nashville, Tennessee; former minister of youth, Wedgwood Baptist Church, Fort Worth, Texas: The youth thought the gunman was part of a skit because this was the next item in the program and their minds could not believe that this was real. Other than attending the frightening judgment and hell house presentations such as those offered in October by some churches, this group was not accustomed to skits with violent content.

The youth now have a file in their mental computer for shootings in church as well as school. Let them know what plans have been made to increase their sense of safety.

This event at Wedgwood was not due in any way to a lack of supervision. The gunman was confronted by three staff members before he got to the auditorium: two of them were shot and wounded, the other was shot at twice.

Teach youth a correct view of God and His kingdom so they can create a faith file instead of a fear file in their mental and spiritual computers.

The greatest trauma and tragedy ever witnessed was the crucifixion of Jesus Christ. After the Resurrection, Jesus spent forty days with the disciples re-teaching the following from Acts 1:

1. The nature of God and His Kingdom, Acts 1:3
2. The ministry of power, comfort and healing of the Holy Spirit, Acts 1: 4-5, 8
3. God's authority and sovereignty, Acts 1:7
4. The certainty of Heaven and Jesus' return, Acts 1:11.

Ask yourself what type of faith foundation your youth would need to survive a tragedy like this. Is your church's youth ministry teaching them what they need to know?

Appendix I

To Wedgwood . . .
With Love

Messages From Around the World

In the book of Revelation, John describes heaven as a place that will not need the light of the sun or moon because the glory of the Lord will illumine it. Then he declares, "the nations . . . shall walk in its light" (Rev. 21:24). Ours was but a foretaste of this heavenly experience. As people of other nations walked in the light, the Light of the Lord was reflected to the Wedgwood community. Following is a sample of messages from every state in the United States and from fifty-four nations of the world.

An early e-mail from A.W. shared a poem from an unknown author:

> When nothing on which to lean remains,
> When strongholds crumble to dust,
> When nothing is sure but that God still reigns,
> That is just the time to trust.
>
> It's better to walk by faith than sight,
> In this path of yours and mine;
> And the darkest night, when there's no other light,
> Is the time for faith to shine.

And faith did shine brightly during the dark night of Wedgwood's soul. It was a shining faith, supported by many, many friends.

Messages from America

"We have been praying for you and your church continually."—*Crystal Cathedral Ministries*

"I think in a way it's sort of exciting to know that the devil finds your church so on fire for God that he has to attack it."—*Lauren*

"I am a Cuban Catholic exiled and living in Miami. I just read about the horrendous things that happened to your Baptist congregation. My wife and I run a radio talk show in Spanish. Tomorrow I plan to read your letter on the air in Spanish and we will pray for you again."—*L. F.*

"You now know that you have brothers and sisters up here in the Northeast."—*T.E.M., Riverside Assembly of God*

"I am a member of St. John the Divine in Houston and I send not only my sympathy but also my empathy."—*A. C.*

"I am writing this on behalf of the Seventh Day Adventist Church in Nowata, Oklahoma. We are a small community and a small church but we wanted you to know that we began praying as soon as we heard about the shootings and we will continue to do so."—*O.B.*

"A Christian teen is Satan's worst enemy!"—*Church of the Open Door, Ft. Washington, PA*

"As a Dallas Theological Seminary student in the D.Min program, I was really hit by how young and gifted those students were and the impact they made."—*B.T.*

"I am at the Appalachian Bible College in Bradley, West Virginia. I wanted you to know that I and our campus are praying for you."—*E.A.*

"This made me think that I need to spend a little more time with my son instead of going to another meeting or working late to meet a deadline. It made me embrace my own life and understand that we do not know when our time will be."—*T. D.*

"I was at your church the Sunday after the shootings. I had driven to Fort Worth to see my best friend who is a member of Wedgwood. God changed my life. I have started listening to the sermons online. I think God may be calling me to semi-nary."—*P.*

Jene Lindamen and Lon Thomas composed the following on the night of the shooting and graciously granted permission to reprint it here:

Please let the children pray

What is going on here Lord?
What can a mortal do?
Why can a child not even go
To church and worship you?

Must they always live in fear
That Satan will come in
And take away the very life
That you have saved from sin?

I know it must be Satan's way
To try to stop your own.
Surely he must realize
You take your children home.

He can take away their body
And spill their precious blood,
But to take them in a House of God
To kill them where they stood!

We cannot let him stop the kids,
Please let your children pray.
Please put your arms around them
From evil let them stay.

So Moms and Dads you taught them right,
The Golden Rule to live,
You shouldn't have to teach them
Their life they'd have to give.

And to the families in Fort Worth
Your child has gone to be
Wrapped in the cradle of His arms
For all eternity.

"I am a freelance TV director/cameraman, working mostly for ABC News. Thank you for speaking truth to the media. God uses the press, usually without their knowledge. Again, what is often a tool of the enemy has been used to confound him! God be praised!"—*J. E.*

"I'm not a Baptist, as a matter of fact, I'm not a religious person at all, but I don't feel that this is a denominational or even religious issue. It's a human issue. The strength of character and ability to transcend this horrible situation that your congregation has shown has been an inspiration to the rest of the nation. Thank you for showing the rest of us the higher side of the human condition and giving us the courage to face our own demons and hardships."—*G.*

"My father was killed and I was shot eleven years ago at Calvary Baptist Church in Emporia, Kansas. I was eighteen at the time and I know how horrible it is to deal with the pain and loss. My prayers are with you."—*B. H.*

"My wife and I lost our fourteen-year-old son four days after his birthday, so we've experienced (and still do experience) the awful pain. If there is any way we can walk beside you call us (even in the middle of the night)."—*M. & D. S., Wycliffe Bible Translators*

"I am seventeen and in my senior year. I myself was at a youth rally that same night. I want you to know that despite the casualties, your loss has helped me turn my life around."—*J. N.*

"I am a junior in high school. I know that nothing I can say will ease your pain, but I want you to know that I am consistently praying for you. I realize that if I do not do something personally, I will see my generation and nation die and go to a Christ-less eternity. This whole tragedy has drawn me back to the Savior and given me purpose in my life. I cannot straddle the fence any longer. The torch has been passed and with the Lord's help I will hold it high. I won't let your loved ones die in vain."—*A. R.*

"As a youth leader, do I have the faith it would take to stare in the face of death and say [that] . . . I don't understand but I believe in the sovereignty of my Lord Jesus and no one can shake that? You have encouraged me and inspired me. Your church has shown so much courage and faith."—*M. D.*

"As Christians we will be victorious over all these modern-day facets of persecution. Our ancestors were and so will we. Your loss and pain is our loss and pain also."—*J. C.*

"We are one body and we hurt together. The devil is stupid because we are made stronger through the fellowship of suffering."—*Rabbi D. S., Messianic Jewish Leader*

"I am thirteen years old and a member of First Baptist Church in Mandeville, Louisiana. We have prayed for your church since the shooting. The next morning I got on my knees in my room and my mom literally had to break into my room to get me to go to school."

"I have worked nonstop (as a nurse) since the shooting, and have treated some of the victims of this horrible tragedy at your church. I have not had time to watch TV or read the news, and now I finally have time to take a step back and my grieving process, though delayed, is beginning. Strangely enough, this tragedy hit me at a time when I felt so burned out and considered leaving nursing, but this week gave me a purpose. . . . I guess God must have been sending me a message. When I first moved to Fort Worth, your church was the first one I was introduced to and I visited. I recall the sermon was so powerful I had to leave before it was over. We are lucky to have you in Fort Worth."—*K.*

"We here at Carmen Ministries are praying for all of you and for the youth of your city and church that they may be empowered by this outrage of terror."—*V. A.*

"My husband is one of the Fort Worth police officers that was on the scene Wednesday. He cried last night for the first time after seeing the ceremony at TCU. Candy Skinner,

Nicholas's mother, told my husband that when she got to the church there was much chaos and the first person she saw was my husband. She said it was like seeing an angel in the midst of all the confusion."—*A. S.*

"On March 24, 1998, I lost my eleven-year-old daughter to a senseless shooting. She was the joy of my life. Times have been difficult and some days I am not sure how to survive. The one thing that has remained true is God's ever-present help. My heart grieves for your community. I will be praying for your strength and courage in the days ahead."—*S.*

"I am a sixteen-year-old girl living in a suburb outside Detroit, Michigan. My mom told me just before we left for school what happened at your church the previous night. I was devastated. In my Bible class that day we discussed what happened. I have to tell you that I have never seen such intense emotion about spiritual things. People were praying to use this as a springboard to a conversation about Christ with their unsaved friends. People in my school are getting real about their relationship with God. Things are happening that I thought I'd never see happen at my school. I don't believe this is the end, either."—*L. A.*

"I am a member of a Southern Baptist church on the coast of Virginia. I have been a member since I was a child, but for years I abandoned the church. Now I am about to be married. I feel I need to build a strong foundation for my future family, but I question my faith. Do I really want to do this without fear of criticism? This letter is to inform you that the ever-growing faith in the Lord professed by the members of Wedgwood, despite such a tragedy, tells me, "Yes, I do!"—*L.*

"I went to college as well as to seminary with Shawn Brown. My wife and I now live in Boston. We are seeing the effects of this tragedy up here as well. Our new church was strongly impacted and has begun to experience revival within the youth group."—*C. W.*

"I am a college student in Iowa and a Christian from a strong Christian family. However, since I've been attending college, I have sadly strayed somewhat from my firm commitment to God. I have given in to the 'too many things to do' syndrome. After seeing all the amazing things that have happened in the face of so much chaos and tragedy, I have been moved to reaffirm my commitment to the Lord."—*A. V. G.*

"Please know that our prayers and love are with you. Our son was one of the doctors at John Peter Smith Hospital that helped attend patients as they came in that night. He was praying for them and it deeply affected his walk with Jesus."—*R. & L. T.*

"We were at a See-You-at-the-Pole Rally when the news was brought to our attention. It was so awful, then God began to move. That night 127 students from area high schools were saved."—*C. H.*

"At our school, we had forty-three people get saved this morning because of the shootings."—*B. H.*

"I am fourteen years old and live in Laredo, Texas. I attend Grace Bible Church where my father is the Pastor. On Wednesday, September 15, 1999, at around 7:30 P.M. our church along with two others met to have a See-You-at-the-Pole post rally. We sang songs and had a great time. A testimony was given by a sophomore and while he was speaking the room went silent. His words stuck in the minds of many that night and seven people accepted the Lord as their Savior. In addition to those seven, ten others recommitted their lives to Christ. For Kim Jones, someone accepted the Lord. For Sydney Browning, someone accepted the Lord. For Shawn Brown, someone accepted the Lord. For Justin Ray, someone accepted the Lord. For Kristi Beckel, someone accepted the Lord. For Joey Ennis, someone accepted the Lord. For Cassie Griffin, someone accepted the Lord. For those who are injured and in the hospital, ten people recommitted their lives to Christ."—*M. R.*

"Be assured that your larger Baptist family is praying for you, asking that God will especially equip you for the demands being made upon you."—*Morris Chapman, president and chief executive officer, Executive Committee, Southern Baptist Convention*

"Our church lifts your church before the throne of grace

each week. I am grateful that God has already answered so many prayers. We stand ready for anything we can do."—*Carroll Marr, pastor, Southcliff Baptist Church, Fort Worth, Texas (located near the I-20 exit where the gunman likely drove to get to Wedgwood Baptist Church)*

Many notes came from Littleton, Colorado, and Columbine High School and were especially meaningful. The following five are examples:

"The students and staff of Columbine High School want to extend our deepest sympathy to your church and community. We understand the difficult times you are facing in light of this terrible tragedy. We are sending the Healing Bear that has been around the country. It started out in Oklahoma City and was then sent to Montoursville Area High School after they lost lives on flight 800. Montoursville sent us the Healing Bear in April after the tragedy at our school. We have cherished the bear as a symbol of hope and caring. We hope this Healing Bear brings some comfort. We hope that the violence will end, and you will not have to send the bear to another community."—*F. D., principal, Columbine High School*

"I have three children currently attending Columbine High School and I can tell you that I truly know what you are going through. It will be six months tomorrow for us. Remember everyone heals differently and most don't start for awhile."—*D. R.*

"Your loss has resurfaced the pain we in the Columbine community have experienced. He has directed us to bring the children to Him and this we will do regardless of the difficulties and obstacles the world imposes upon our work."—*K. W.*

"We pray for your community as we were greatly affected by the tragedy here in Littleton. We pray that God brings about revival as he has started to do here."—*W. & S. C.*

"My friends and I attend Columbine High School in Littleton, Colorado. We were watching TV and all got so quiet. It really hit home for us seeing the scenes of people aimlessly walking around, sobbing and looking for loved ones. Time heals, but not completely. While you will never forget the pain or your friends and family, you will have the opportunity to become stronger in your faith. We continue to pray and love you all."—*J. P.*

Following are eight of the notes from our friends and neighbors at the Altamesa Church of Christ who collected approximately two hundred messages and sent them in notebook form:

"We are neighbors. We are friends. We are family. We have been in prayer and will continue to pray for you. We want to serve you in the Name of Jesus. God has already blessed us with a sense of love for one another, a light in the darkest of hours. These prayers reflect that love, and the heart of this community as well. May God continue to bless us all as we partner to share His glory in southwest Fort Worth. And may He enable you to overcome. I know He will, and I know you will. On behalf of the Altamesa Church of Christ, and in the Peace of Jesus."—*Danny Sims, senior minister*

"Our prayers are with you. You are a big part of us. You are our most precious neighbors; our family in Christ. We love you."—*M. & D. A.*

"Our prayers and support are with you even though we are of a different denomination. It could have just as easily been our Wednesday night service. The Lord will bring to good somehow the fragments of this tragic event."—*C. P.*

"My heart was broken as I saw the streets I used to play on full of ambulances, bleeding people, and chaos. My prayers are with those who lost loved ones and friends."—*H. K.*

"Words are not enough to tell you of our love, so listen to our hearts!"—*R. S.*

"Blessed are those who mourn. I'm sorry you are so blessed this evening."—*E. D. K.*

"God's soldiers never die!"

"To the family of Sydney Browning, there is so much I wish I could tell her now. How very, very much I appreciated and admired her. I wish I didn't have to wait to tell her. A martyr's crown! How very beautiful it looks on her."—*J. L. S.*

Messages from the Nations of the World

"It is Saturday evening in France and our minds and hearts are in Fort Worth and around the world with other Wedgies. We have such a strong desire to be with you and to grieve with you and to love you in person."—*J. & L. L., France*

"We saw the sad news on the web several hours after it happened. From age one through ten I lived about two hundred yards from Wedgwood Baptist Church. Know our prayers are with you."—*S. & J. H., China*

"On Monday after the funerals I decided to watch a local TV program in the north of Lebanon—a closed city of over one million. I turned on the TV and, on the screen, there was the seminary chapel and the speaker speaking to the group. His whole message was aired to my city. Would you ever believe that this tragedy would spread through closed borders and into the hearts of my people? I am having many come to me to ask for an interpretation of these events."—*K. M., Lebanon*

"We've thought about you much during the past couple of days and for all the special people at Wedgwood. Sydney Browning was our girls choir director while we furloughed there."—*B. & T. H., Brazil*

"We were shocked to hear of the shooting in Fort Worth. Our prayers are with each of you. The kids in the singing group that night, Forty Days, are from our home church."—*H. & C. C., Taiwan*

"We are supposed to come home on furlough next year and it is funny to be a little worried about going home to your own country."—*R. & K. C., Japan*

"Know that the family here at the Macau Baptist Mission were and are praying for you. All of us were at home at the time because of the typhoon that hit Macau that day and prevented any of us going out. So we all immediately began praying."—*M. H., Macau*

"I can say that since hearing of the shooting and reading your web site and especially hearing your pastor speak, my ministry has taken on a new life. I have just spent the last two days before God bringing my life and ministry under His Lordship as a result of what has been and is happening at Wedgwood."—*B. L., Scotland*

"I'm a junior attending Seoul American High School. I will keep you and all those who need prayer in my prayers."—*P. S., South Korea*

"Just to let you know our prayers are with you and that I have done what I can as a webmaster for an International Anglican News Service to pass on your updates."—*S. T., England*

"Please bear with me. I am trying to translate this out of a Bible written in Norwegian. Solomon summed it all up by saying that 'after all I have witnessed and tried to understand God's will, all I know is what I began with, and that is God is God.'"—*E. H., Norway*

"Just a quick note to let you know that we have been praying for Wedgwood Baptist Church here in Ukraine."—*Ukraine Mission to the World, Ukraine*

"I lived in the Fort Worth area for a year and have several close friends there. My thoughts and prayers are with everybody affected by this tragedy."—*P. B., The Netherlands*

"I heard on BBC radio today of the shooting and was saddened. I'm from Texas and have friends in your neighborhood. I pray that He will shine through this especially as the media flood you with questions."—*A. T., Gaza*

"Our church prayed for you that you would have your church back for Sunday services. I am a newly baptized Christian."—*M. C., New Zealand*

"We hope and pray that as you literally are walking through the valley of the shadow of death, you will be able to see the Lord there with you."—*E. S., Sweden*

"We here in Russia rejoice with you, grieve with you, pray with you and grow with you."—*A., Russia*

"I am a fellow brother in Christ from Romania. Sorry I don't have money for the Internet access, and was unable to visit your web page. So I prayed for you."—*M. D., Romania*

"It is difficult to be physically separated from a church family that you feel a part of. Wedgwood will never be an obscure church lost in the 'W' streets ever again and the glory that God has received is phenomenal."—*D. A., Singapore*

"The love and prayers of the Baptist Christians in the southern Area of the Baptist Union of Great Britain are with you."—*M. N., Britain*

"I, the Chairman of Charismatic Crusades International—Pakistan, from myself and on behalf of the Pakistani Christian community convey our deepest concerns over the recent incident at your church."—*S. K., Pakistan*

"We in Ireland know a little of the grief which you must be going through and we want to identify with you in your time of sadness and pain."—*Donegal Baptist Fellowship in the Northwest of Ireland*

"We are an independent boarding school and we have just finished our morning worship. We prayed for you in your trauma, but are greatly encouraged that even in your grief you are able to see God as an awesome God. God's specialty is redemption and we pray that even out of these circumstances God would release blessings and power."—*T. H., Wales*

"Just to let you know we are praying for you, that the Lord will bring you great comfort and use this tragedy in a mighty way to bring glory to His name."—*J. H., Cayman Islands, former Wedgie, always a Wedgie*

"My husband and I are from Fort Worth and are now missionaries in Uruguay. It really hits us that something like this could happen in Fort Worth."—*N. Family, Uruguay*

"We were members of Wedgwood in 1985-1988 when we were attending Southwestern Seminary. News of the tragedy was printed in the Bangladesh newspaper. We were crushed. We are praying for the church."—*K. & H. G., Bangladesh*

Members of Wedgwood Baptist Church have been reminded of the value of family support. The deep gratitude we feel for the thousands of expressions of support cannot be expressed by words alone. So to those who sent such expressions, we say as one e-mail said to us, "listen to our hearts."

Appendix J

Songs in the Night

(Job 35:10)

God's people have often sought comfort and strength in music. The Wedgwood experience was no exception. Following is a sample of some of the songs that got us through the night.

Adonai

Amazing Grace

Awesome God

Blessed Assurance

El Shaddai

From the Rising of the Sun

Great Is Thy Faithfulness

Holy Ground

How Firm a Foundation

I Could Sing of Your Love Forever

Jesus, You're My Firm Foundation

Knowing You

A Mighty Fortress Is Our God

My Eternal King

My Jesus, I Love Thee

Open the Eyes of My Heart

Sanctuary

Shine on Us

Shout to the Lord

The Steadfast Love of the Lord

Stepping on the Clouds

Sweet Beulah Land

Sweet Mercies

Thank You

There Is a God

We Bow Down

You Are My All in All

Further Acknowledgments

Every attempt was made to acknowledge the efforts of those who have contributed to this book. The author and publisher express their regrets for any acknowledgment that has been inadvertently left out.

Portions of the stories offered here previously appeared in the Fort Worth *Star-Telegram,* Southwest High School's *Raiders Review,* and the Baptist Press.

"Only Heaven Knows" in chapter 3: Words by David W. Barnett, music by David W. Barnett and Juliana Barnett. Copyright, 1999. Authority Music. All Rights Reserved. Used by permission.

"Steps to Peace with God" in chapter 14 is reprinted by permission of the Billy Graham Evangelistic Association and World Wide Publications.

Appendix B was reprinted by permission from *The Christian Chronicle,* a Churches of Christ publication.

Appendix E is reprinted by permission of the author, Danny Sims.

Portions of Appendix F were previously included in the author's book *Before Revival Begins,* published by Scripta Publishers of Fort Worth and used here by permission.

Appendix G is reprinted by permission of the author, William Murchison.

Appendix H is used by permission of Wesley O. Black, organizer of the symposium.

The poem on page 372 in Appendix I is used by permission of Jene Lindamen and Lon Thomas.